W9-BZW-516

Mary O'Hara-Devereaux

Navigating the Badlands

Thriving in the Decade of Radical Transformation

JOSSEY-BASS
A Wiley Imprint
www.josseybass.com

Published by Jossey-Bass
A Wiley Imprint
989 Market Street, San Francisco, CA 94103-1741   www.josseybass.com

Jossey-Bass books and products are available through most bookstores. To contact
Jossey-Bass directly call our Customer Care Department within the U.S. at 800-956-7739,
outside the U.S. at 317-572-3986, or fax 317-572-4002.

Jossey-Bass also publishes its books in a variety of electronic formats. Some content that
appears in print may not be available in electronic books.

Library of Congress Cataloging-in-Publication Data

O'Hara-Devereaux, Mary.
  Navigating the badlands : thriving in the decade of radical transformation / by Mary
O'Hara-Devereaux.—1st ed.
     p. cm.
  Includes bibliographical references and index.
  ISBN 0-7879-7138-3 (alk. paper)
  1. Twenty-first century—Forecasts. 2. Social change—Forecasting. 3. Civilization,
Modern—1950—Forecasting. 4. Social institutions—Forecasting. 5. Information
society—Forecasting. 6. High technology—Social aspects—Forecasting. 7. Technological
innovations—Forecasting. 8. Technology and civilization—Forecasting. 9. Science—
Social aspects. 10. Globalization. I. Title.
  CB161.O29 2004
  303.49—dc22

                                                                          2004012066

Printed in the United States of America
FIRST EDITION
HB Printing   10 9 8 7 6 5 4 3 2 1

◁≈ Contents

I dedicate this book with love and gratitude to my great husband, Hughes Andrus, who supported me in every phase of this book—including many insights about how to navigate the Badlands—and to my great friend and China mentor, professor Chen Zhangliang, vice president of Peking University and president of China Agricultural University, who continues to inspire me with his vision for China's future, his amazing accomplishments, and his fabulous Chinese cooking.

Flash Forward . . .

The year is 2020. And you're one of the lucky ones—
one of the prosperous few who have successfully weathered the single
most challenging upheaval of the past thousand years.

Like the American pioneers of old, during the 1990s you were one
of many who plowed confidently ahead, traversing the relative calm
of the Industrial Great Plains, with their seemingly endless opportunities and wealth. You crossed into the new millennium full of confidence, weathering the recession of 2001 and adjusting to the stark
reality of 9/11. The world had changed but not as much as you
thought it would; you felt cautiously optimistic about getting back to
business as usual. But ten years ago, all that changed. The familiar territory of the Plains turned to global tumult and chaos as the world
plunged headlong into the economic and cultural Badlands: a landscape just as treacherous and unpredictable as that found in the Dakotas. No one believed it would last two full decades, but the past twenty
years were indeed characterized by continuous, unpredictable, and
often violent weather systems—a host of challenges and complexities
that arose without warning, that demanded entirely new ways of
thinking and radical strategies to keep your journey moving forward.

And yet you survived. Like the most resourceful, adaptable pioneers, you courageously trekked forward; you availed yourself of the tools, knowledge, and relationships necessary to make it through a rugged journey punctuated by abrupt shifts in the landscape, eroded by powerful forces, and driven by inexorable change. And here, now, as you pause to reflect, safely landed upon the Foothills of the Far Future—a future that beckons from the last range of the Badlands—you notice the fundamentally altered landscape around you.

The opinions of a global elite—highly skilled executives and champions of social change—dominate the evening news: government voices have receded. You still marvel at the surge of women's leadership at the end of the decade that brought a new, powerful, and effective voice for sustainable globalization. The balance of global power has shifted, and a new tension between social and economic growth has become visceral and very real. You are adjusting to the unanticipated flow of groundbreaking innovations from China, and China's rising global role. Your professional network, independent of any one firm but highly interdependent among its many members, spans geographies, disciplines, and generations.

If you're a Baby Boomer, you are thankful that the maturing Net Generation's insistence on a healthy work-life balance has touched even a workaholic like yourself. You are passionate about inventing your second middle age—thankful for the extra twenty-five years you have—a gift not to squander. You marvel at how useful connective technologies have become: peer-to-peer networks actually deliver, and independent, energy-efficient fuel cells have facilitated moving entire segments of people and organizations off the grid. You are thankful for the many cures for cancer, the circulating sensors in your body that provide early warnings of disease—as well as the breakthroughs in biotech that have significantly extended life expectancy (although living to 110 still seems a bit scary).

The sustained volatility of the stock market has given rise to multiple new metrics (new global accounting standards, new valuation processes for IPOs, new methods for perceiving and measuring value), and to a thorough globalization of the market. Organizational structures are now so diverse that talking about them is irrelevant. They are now driven by economies of scale as well as economies of structure, and their dispersed, myriad value webs are of chief importance. You are thankful that the clash of civilizations is still held at bay, even though the major cultural groups are more powerful than antiquated ideologies such as communism, socialism, or democracy.

As you look back on your journey, and how you thrived in the Badlands, you are suddenly aware of how much you have changed, personally. Weathering the myriad shocking changes around you has greatly influenced your outlook, opinions, and codes of conduct, as well as your professional, emotional, and spiritual life.

Armed with vital tools, strategies, knowledge, and an identity as a global citizen, you are now a wise, prosperous, driving force in a world forever changed.

CHAPTER ONE

Making Sense of the Big Picture

The Badlands is a metaphor that invites us to embark on a journey of discovery. It is the context in which the complex story of globalization is unfolding.

As we look ahead to the year 2020, the Foothills of the Far Future, we ask ourselves, how do we get from here to there? Navigating the Badlands is a metaphor for taking the journey through this challenging transition zone between the end of the Industrial Era and the full promise of the Information Age. The Badlands is the rugged stretch that bridges the past with the future, a time after massive structural shifts have rendered the old economy and its social foundations obsolete, and new values and structures are not yet firmly in place. In the Badlands we experience considerable pain and bewilderment as one way of life ends and we grapple with how to create the next.

THE JOURNEY

This book is about making the journey through today's Badlands, a journey that will last more than a decade. It delineates a set of inevitable pains that will assail individuals and organizations in this extraordinarily turbulent environment, as well as the new capabilities we must develop to navigate this unmapped territory successfully. All of us must cross this rugged transition zone, adapting courageously and creatively to the comprehensive economic and social structural shifts under way, or perish by the wayside. Although we will take this journey as individuals, as members of organizations, as community members, and as global citizens, the focus of this book is on our roles in organizations and the challenges they will face.

These challenges are not centered in the ebb and flow of the business cycle or the stock market. This is not to say these factors will not be part of the journey, but focusing on them at the expense of understanding and responding to the bigger forces at play will not produce a good long-term outcome. By using the data and insights in this book to reach a deeper understanding of the powerful driving forces that even now are transforming the entire context of business, you will gain the opportunity to control your future rather than be controlled by it. Our new global context demands that we innovate to create and grow tomorrow's industries and organizations. It further demands that we build new social institutions, such as a better health care system and a set of global organizations that can support our shared human goals, since business cannot thrive without a vibrant society and society cannot change if the economy is anemic.

Our dream should be the creation of a vibrant, equitable, and fully integrated global society underpinned by robust economic growth worldwide. To realize this dream we need better, more, and different kinds of leaders and organizations that will match the needs we will face in the new global reality. Today we have a mismatch.

My vision of the future derives from research that I directed at the behest of a diverse group of global business clients striving to make sense of a volatile business environment and eager to know how their organizations would have to change to survive and prosper. It also draws deeply from my own life experiences. I have worked in the villages of Africa, consulted with businesses and governments of the emerging economies of Asia and Latin America, and conducted strategic sessions with technology innovators of California's Silicon Valley.

My most recent research is being conducted through Global Foresight, the think tank and strategic consulting firm I founded in 2002. It builds on research I spearheaded as a director at the Institute for the Future, a spin-off from the RAND Corporation, where I was leader of the Emerging Technologies Outlook Program, as well as research in the Center for the Future of China, a nonprofit I founded in California and at Peking University in Beijing. The research that culminated in this book began in the late 1990s, when, despite the fast-growing economy, rising stock markets, and hype about the New Economy, it was increasingly apparent that the future was going to be very different from the past. As a forecaster and futurist I found it no simple matter to predict trends for the first decade of the new millennium, given the continuing surge of new technologies and the fast-expanding global economy, and with them the new driving forces that continue to shape the rugged landscape of the future into an ever more inscrutable environment. My research team included economists, technology experts, sociologists, political scientists, anthropologists, sociologists, and historians. Working across disciplines we struggled to weave our findings into a coherent pattern. But something was missing.

We were finally able to put pieces of the future together when we looked back at other periods in history notable for disruptive innovation. We examined eight such turbulent times, reaching back as far as 3500 B.C.E., when writing was invented, through our own time period, with all its breakthroughs in information, communication, and biology, ending with a forecast of the upcoming wave of disruptive technologies taking us through to 2020. This historical lens informed our insights, enabling us to make better sense of this forbidding future terrain.

Times of innovation are inherently messy, making it difficult to match cause to effect, but we ultimately developed the view that disruptive innovations are part of a bigger cycle whereby new technologies, the economy, and society churn together to create an evolutionary leap in human identity. No one knows for sure exactly how many such cycles of innovation have occurred; scholars and historians identify and count them differently. My colleagues and I settled on the belief that we are now some fifty years into a seventy-five-year historical cycle of disruptive innovation. In such cycles, surges in new technologies lead to structural shifts in the economy, which in turn hit people full force, driving rapid and monumental changes in both business and organizational life. Pushed off balance, the economy churns and spins faster than society can respond, and social institutions begin to fail. As the cycle progresses, social issues, technological inventions, and economic shifts are all caught up in the maelstrom; we can scarcely differentiate cause from effect. "Every few hundred years in

Western history there occurs a sharp transformation. Within a few short decades, society rearranges itself—its worldview; its basic values; its social and political structure; its arts; its key institutions. Fifty years later, there is a new world. And the people born then cannot even imagine the world in which their grandparents lived and into which their own parents were born. We are currently living through just such a transformation" (Drucker, 1993, p. 50).

The decisions we make during this transition period will shape the new era. At the end of this process our very sense of identity breaks apart, opening the way for the emergence of a new sense of self, appropriate to the new context. At this point social and economic drivers of change have come together again in a new, more stable pattern, bringing the cycle of innovation to a close—and another begins. If this is the case, then we as humans have been in the Badlands before many times, indeed since time immemorial, for its ravines have always been a predictable part of every historical cycle of disruptive innovation and the upset that attends it, as sketched in Figure 1.1.

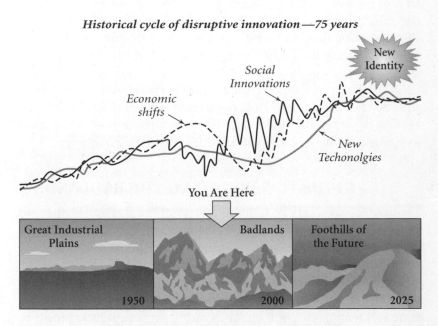

Figure 1.1.   The Badlands: Transition Zone.
Source: Global Foresight, 2004.

New technologies and their subsequent innovations don't directly cause social change; instead they create problems and dilemmas that drive society to seek new solutions from a diverse set of choices. This is the purpose of the journey through the Badlands. When cycles of disruptive innovations result in major structural shifts across all economic and social dimensions, as they are doing today, they create enormous transition costs as society struggles to move from one era to the next. How well today's leaders manage the transition through the churning marketplace and failing social institutions of the early twenty-first century depends for the first time on a global cast of characters. Their knowledge of their colleagues around the world is incomplete, their ability to craft solutions together is untested, the stakes for all parties are extraordinarily high: the good or bad choices they make will lay the foundation for the next era. It is within this macro context that business leaders and organizations will also take their journey.

I am an optimist and I passionately believe that we can build a great future that includes all of us—but not without making radical changes in how we work and live, focusing consciously and continually on doing the right thing globally. We have the resources, both human and material, to do this, but no external force or agent guarantees we will succeed. Participation is not optional. The new environment with its continual supply of disruptions will force us to make new choices. To accomplish our mission of shaping the next era, as many of us as possible need to make a hero's journey in quest of a new way of life, embracing the uncertainties along the way. Throughout history the hero's journeys have always been painful; this one will be no different.

GUIDE TO NAVIGATING THE BADLANDS

We have only just arrived in the entryway of the Badlands—the foot of the cliff at the left edge of the Badlands map—so we face at least a decade of continued volatility. I believe we are at the point of maximum turbulence in this cycle of disruptive innovation, where the churn between society, politics, and the economy causes sufficient stress and strain to finally break down the old systems. This will take time and managing it will be the defining process in this transition zone between eras that I call the Badlands. Transitions are always painful, and escape is only an illusion. To help you on your journey, I have organized the book around four themes that are as interlinked as they are distinct:

- *Globalization:* Understanding the big picture is not optional.
- *New Leadership Crucible:* The Badlands demands a hero's journey.
- *Organizational Metamorphosis:* Partial responses are fatal.
- *Social Choices:* Stepping up to the planetary plate and making the right social choices to create a global commons is essential.

I will cover all four of these themes, but my primary focus will settle on the middle two, our journey as leaders of organizations and the transformation organizations must achieve. The world needs great leaders and organizations to have a robust society and economy. Today I see a severe mismatch between what we have and what we need. It is my hope that this book can help bridge that gap. Crossing into the Badlands presents one of the most dangerous and disorienting phases of the journey through it. The Badlands arouses extreme emotions caused by individual and organizational pains that surface and resurface as we scan, scout, and steer our way around obstacles.

A Badlands pain arises when the shifting environment forces organizations and individuals to make strategic choices and changes in direction, structure, or relationships in order to progress. Pains are not death knells, but should be perceived as signs of what needs to change and change fast. Like the severe warning signs of serious illness, they require a speedy and aggressive response.

Pains in the Badlands are difficult to resolve. Often the viability of a solution won't be revealed until a choice has been made, acted upon, and the results have made themselves known. This experience is less like short-lived pain and more like severe chronic pain, in that it can, and likely will, recur throughout the journey. Organizations and leaders will need to engage in a constant dance of moving forward and backtracking, recalibrating and moving on. Ultimately the pain will fade away as new capabilities replace old competencies. These new capabilities are aimed at supporting the organizational metamorphosis that is most likely to result in an exemplary, profitable organization that will fit with the new context of the future that lies beyond the Badlands. Much of this book discusses a set of pains and new capabilities you will encounter on your journey:

Pain	New Required Capability	Discussed in ...
Leadership Insecurity	Leadership Readiness	Chapter Three
Competency Addiction	Systemic Innovation	Chapter Four
Network Angst	Support for Social Networks	Chapter Five
Strategy Tragedy	Growth Through Disruptive Innovation	Chapter Six
Talent Tantrum	Deep Engagement with People	Chapter Seven
Consumer Conundrum	Customizing Personalized Relationships	Chapter Eight
Value Vexation	Sustainable Globalization	Chapter Ten

As we confront the unavoidable need for individual and organizational metamorphosis, we must release patterns, mind-sets, and behaviors that have no place in the Badlands and beyond. Putting an end to what no longer works is the first phase of any transition, and it is sure to be painful. But with each release we take a step forward, preparing ourselves for the confusing middle phase of this transition where, perhaps for years, nothing will feel solid or provide much continuity. This is the second phase of all major transitions, in which we thrash about until we learn enough to begin anew. In this middle phase we must make huge social choices and experience their results, learning from our successes and failures. Then we must push on and make more choices. It is through making trade-offs in this environment of prolonged uncertainty and ambiguity that we will construct the new beginnings, the third phase of the transition and the foundation of the next era. This will be an ongoing process of successive approximation. It will take time and it will take guts.

Globalization: Understanding the Big Picture Is Not Optional

Understanding and keeping the big picture in mind is not optional in the Badlands. You have now entered a perilous phase of globalization where you can easily lose your way in a constantly morphing landscape. Think of the driving forces described in this book as the diverse weather systems of globalization that can suddenly appear, changing the landscape so much that you have to reorganize your expedition and reset your compass. Globalization is an emergent phenomenon; we will spend the next fifty years figuring out just what it is.

People tend to overestimate driving forces in the short run and underestimate their long-term impacts. These driving forces are shaping and reshaping not just the business environment but the entire global context in which we live and work. No one can accurately predict the future, even under stable conditions, but you *can* think about it systematically and make choices that help you steer toward opportunities and avoid threats. Those who don't are sure to face ugly surprises.

Globalization is not intrinsically good or bad; how it evolves depends on the choices we make. As an emergent phenomenon it is immature and highly uncertain. However, its driving forces are known, so you can anticipate their impacts and adapt early. It is particularly important to begin to see the new patterns these forces will weave by their interaction with each other. Business will feel the impact of all the driving forces, with each company and industry needing to map their specific impact and likely timing. Of utmost importance is the rapid aging of populations not just in the advanced economies but in the developing economies as well. Thanks to medical breakthroughs, many of us who are middle-aged today will live to be a hundred, extending middle age until eighty. This will have myriad impacts on the workplace, from increasing cross-generational workforces to defining new work arrangements. At the same time, the rapidly growing number of educated and sophisticated young people around the world, particularly in Asia, will facilitate the expansion of knowledge work, resulting in a redistribution of high-value jobs to emerging economies. Global transnational corporations will extend their geographic reach and will continuously adapt their structures and work arrangements to take advantage of resources in many places. Advanced economies like that of the United States will come under increasing pressure to reinvent themselves through widespread innovation, as much of the old economy moves offshore. There will be increased social shifts and challenging domestic politics as workers come to grips with having to reinvent themselves under pressure from massive job shifts, some of which will be caused by the relentless introduction of new technologies, rendering products and at times whole industries obsolete. Companies and workers alike will have much to contend with.

Individuals and organizations will have an increasingly tense relationship as the old social bargain between them completely dies out.

Work life for both will be stressful in the coming decade. Global competition will increase among a growing number of small and large players enabled by a networked economy that levels the playing field between advanced and emerging economies and makes it easier for both individuals and firms to engage in creating new wealth. The wealth gap between and within countries will increase in the absence of a new social agenda. The Information Age polarizes global populations; you need the right skills to play, and relatively few have them.

As women go to work around the world the traditional notion of a household breaks down. No social trend has as much impact as the change in women's roles. It changes the meaning of marriage, motherhood, and consumption, to name just a few effects. Business will want to take advantage of these highly skilled workers but will need new ways to attract and retain them. Increasingly, women will make more choices as consumers, pushing marketing and sales processes to match their values. Women will be most concerned about the failing social institutions and will play increasingly important roles politically to share the challenge of their reinvention. As the major family caretakers they will experience the human needs along the life cycle and the impact of our institutional mismatch with social needs.

Globalization means a new geopolitical context. Our governmental mind-sets, rules of engagement, and institutions are both too big and too small for the global problems wrought by a fast-moving global economy. How is a global epidemic managed and contained? Who has the right to wage war and in what fashion? How do we agree about protecting the environment? And to further complicate matters, power is being redistributed as countries like China and India surge forward economically. Of particular importance is China, which will grow to be such a major global power in all dimensions by the end of the Badlands that I've devoted a whole chapter to its culture and prospects. All these changes increase uncertainty and risk for business. Each of these drivers alone and in combination needs to be continuously monitored and factored into business decisions.

Leadership Crucible: Taking a Hero's Journey

Needless to say, this kind of environment will require leadership from as many people as possible. The second theme I weave through the book is *the importance of using the Badlands as a leadership crucible.* The Badlands provides leaders with an innovation imperative. Many observers of leadership posit that we are seriously deficient in the kinds of leaders we need, and I agree with them.

This global Badlands environment has the capacity for helping potential leaders around the world take advantage of these times and make a hero's journey, leaving behind old ways and learning through action what works not just for them but for everyone. As you take a hero's journey, new capabilities and leadership readiness will emerge from the trek itself, as you interact with the environment and other travelers. This leadership crucible forces us to face who we are, providing each of us with multiple defining moments. It provides unimagined opportunities together with harsh ordeals. As a hero you have to live your own life, not an imitation of another's life. The journey will evoke your character and test it; as you journey deeper into the Badlands you too will be reformed by its rigorous demands.

Heroes set off on a series of adventures beyond the ordinary in quest of something lost, or glory, or redemption. Your own hero's journey is the search for a new global identity for both yourself and your organization. The Information Revolution is already transforming both the economy and society, creating a future that will be very different from the past. Heroes must be extraordinarily courageous to leave the familiar world of the old era shaped by industrialization, over which they have some control, and venture out into a landscape full of new features, constantly evolving through the erosion of the old. Heroes must believe in themselves, trust in their web of relationships with others, and learn ultimately to engage only with organizations and individuals with whom they have shared purpose and values.

Only you can choose to proactively use this crucible to become the best leader possible. Leaders grow by jumping into the refining fire of a crucible and coming out changed, not by reading books, attending executive development courses, or getting an MBA degree. While those may be useful tools, leadership is a performing art that can only be learned through action. The Badlands crucible is different from the past in which many leaders honed their skills. It is a new place where we can unleash our dormant abilities, define and refine our character, and extract the wisdom of the future in pursuit of our goals. To date we know little about how leadership crucibles work for women, for young people, and for the diverse cultures that populate this planet. Yet these are the groups where most of tomorrow's leaders must come from. It is imperative that we create more opportunities in this environment for more leaders to emerge.

Vital to a successful journey is coming to grips with the fact that the Badlands possesses the power to transform you—or leave you behind if you don't adapt and can't get connected. It has the power to destroy people and businesses, making it seem a dangerous place, particularly as we see the tombstones of those who came before us and perished—the New Economy Suckers—who succumbed to the irrational exuberance and greed of the late 1990s. This brings us to our first predictable Badlands pain: *Leadership Insecurity,* with its deep feelings of fear and inadequacy. Not only will the new leaders who emerge in the Badlands not fall prey to these feelings, they will be capable of enormous adaptability and unbridled curiosity—critical characteristics to creating the new capability of *Leadership Readiness.* Those who embrace the new context and adapt by developing new competencies to match the shift in environment can thrive in the Badlands, not merely survive. But even then, many gifted leaders will fail, given the environment's demanding and relentless nature.

A successful journey requires principles of transformation to guide your way, as well as a new leadership paradigm to anchor them. At its heart is the importance of being a leader in multiple ways and accepting that leadership is neither a solo act nor a celebrity role. First and foremost you need to be able to lead yourself on the hero's journey and share leadership with others across generations and cultures, times and places.

I have distilled the following set of principles from my research with pioneers in the Badlands:

Principles of Transformation
- Scan, Scout, Steer
- Act with Integrity
- Seek Collisions
- Learn Rapidly
- Engage Cultures
- Innovate Radically
- Make Decisions Fast
- Execute with Discipline

These principles are all presented in more detail in Chapter Three, along with some of the stories of those pioneers. I also refer to them throughout the book as strategies to help resolve pains and create new capabilities. They support organizations and leaders in making a total metamorphosis during their trek. Because they aren't oversimplified, or in any way locked to a single corresponding pain, they apply widely and in overlay, making a rich and complex tapestry of solutions that is both critical to success and strategically applicable to every phase of the journey.

Organizational Metamorphosis: Partial Responses Are Fatal

The book's third major theme is *the inescapable demand that organizations not merely change but undergo a metamorphosis.* The results from my research indicate that organizations put off change until it is too painful not to move. This is why so many business organizations made only partial responses to the environment changes of the late 1990s. Fortunately, they were able to create wealth even with mediocre performance. They got caught up in management fads and half-heartedly participated in so-called change management programs that often only exacerbated their long-term problems and increased the tensions between firms and individuals.

Now the churn in the economy and in society is reaching its peak, and the rest of the structural shifts will swiftly take place, leaving only a tombstone to mark the resting place of those with partial responses. At the end of these massive structural shifts the mismatch between organizations and the needs of both the economy and society will become obvious. The innovation imperative of this turbulent transition can no longer be ignored or treated half-heartedly. My research shows that organizations and leaders demonstrate a dangerous reluctance to face a host of truths. Many have not faced up to the inevitable fact that they cannot rely on outmoded behaviors in a context that is utterly changed. They cannot continue to do business as usual if they truly want to survive and thrive. Pain is not only a barometer of truth but also a formidable gateway to growth, new understanding, and powerful, positive evolutionary change.

Being successful in the Badlands demands skills and mind-sets different from those that brought business success in the late Industrial Plains. It is harder to create and sustain profit in the Badlands, because performance peaks are harder to climb and easier to fall off given the pace of technological innovations that quickly render products and processes obsolete, and the global nature of competition. The Badlands is a laboratory for truly radical innovation, not just in technology but in business models that invent new industries and recombine existing ones.

Most of us are getting oriented to the features of this new landscape and assessing our readiness to go on. In our perennial quest for security, we humans tend toward repetition. While humans are blessed with the ability to make behaviors automatic, the dark side of this capacity is that mindless behaviors become difficult to extinguish. In this way, behaviors that were once successful (within the context of the Industrial Plains) may become dangerous traps and formidable barriers to success in the Badlands. Most of us will therefore begin our journey by defaulting to old behaviors and mind-sets that only delay moving on. We call this *Competency Addiction,* the second of eight predictable pains, one accompanied by feelings of *Smugness and Arrogance*—a deeply defensive response as leaders of old business competencies and products try to convince themselves and others that the old way is still the best way forward. Resolving this pain includes reconstructing who we are, and in the process, dissolving an identity embedded in the old ways of working and living.

Leadership Insecurity and *Competency Addiction* are almost always first encountered by organizations at the entry to the Badlands. The other pains hover over the landscape toward the center of the map like a black tornado ready to touch down and demand a response when the conditions are right. This is a nonlinear journey in a nonlinear environment, and it includes some issues beyond the scope of this book, such as the developing technology infrastructure and regulatory environment.

As noted earlier, every organization will encounter strategic junctions at various points along the journey that will cause it pain. These junctions are places where changes in the environment create issues that intersect with the organization causing its leaders to make strategic choices—changes in directions, structure, or relationships—to continue executing its mission. These changes can come in the form of new global competitors, disruptive innovations in the industry, obsolescence of a key technology central to a core business model, dramatic shifts in customer desires and purchasing habits, or loss of key talent, to name but a few. Although smart organizations that keep their eye on the big picture can anticipate these junctions, the fact that they exist and have to be responded to, early or late, preemptively or retro-actively, will cause pain.

Resolving the pains is distinct from creating the new capabilities that correspond to each one. Both processes must proceed simultaneously. Ultimately they serve as a powerful antidote to the reemergence of these old pains. Similar to the pains, the new capabilities are holo-graphic; working to develop one affects the development of the others.

Each capability enables the organization to innovate, engage, and integrate a web of relationships needed for long-term success. For no organization can thrive without a robust culture of systemic innova-tion, an engine of growth for disruptive innovation, and the capabil-ity to engage diverse people deeply anywhere and everywhere around the globe. Those who cannot design resilient networks, customize cus-tomer relationships, and renew purpose and create knowledge won't survive. It is through building these capabilities that the organization undergoes the metamorphosis needed for a viable future.

Armed with the truth about the journey—both its challenges and its gifts—individuals and organizations will pass through a number of maturing forms and stages, as the experience of the Badlands resem-bles nothing so much as a biological metamorphosis. Like all evolving organisms, these will be fragile and vulnerable at certain key stages of their maturation. Armed with the principles of transformation and in-creasing resiliency, we are most likely to survive and succeed.

Choosing Our Destiny: Making the Right Choices for the Global Commons

The fourth theme in the book is *the need to step up to the global plate and make the right social choices to create a global commons.* The commons are the shared agreements and institutions we craft for the well-being of all of us on the planet. If we fail to make globalization sustainable, the world will simply roll on, becoming more dangerous day by day. We must act with integrity on a global scale and make the right moral choices about economic and social development. We have the human and ma-terial resources to do so, but too few people understand globalization and how they fit into it, or could do so. The unavoidable truth is that the Information Revolution tends to polarize us as humans, to grow the gap between the haves and the have-nots. Without people consciously striv-ing to reverse it, the wealth gap will continue to grow.

Seduced as we were by the frenzy of wealth creation over the last ten years, we missed the full truth of the early stages of this present shift from one era to the next. This myopic economic view, common at this stage in the cycle, obscures growing social issues. As the whirlwind of globalization swirled about the planet, it has been both inclusive and exclusive. Localities and people who have the education and capacity to use information are valued and included. But many who do not possess the right skills have been excluded and marginalized as economically irrelevant. The business architects of the global economy are nothing if not pragmatic: they do whatever works, wherever it is most cost-effective, whenever it is most likely to create profits. The information economy is inherently predisposed toward polarization, creating growth in the numbers of people both at the top and at the bottom of society, causing social disparity. Those at the top are able to learn quickly and adapt to the changing global opportunities because of their advanced education. They can make great gains and continue to build on them, amassing more wealth. Those at the bottom are forgotten, mere bumps in the road.

In the long run globalization has the potential to lift everyone up, but in the short run it is highly dislocating. We need leaders who can help integrate currently marginalized economies and people into the prospering global economy. We need leaders who understand the importance of providing everyone a safety net, along with realistic long-term strategies to firmly connect them to a successful life in the future. This is a challenge given the great ambivalence around the world about safety nets. However, it is totally unrealistic to expect people who are marginalized by lack of education and access to the tools of economic growth to be able to lift themselves up on their own. We need innovations in our strategies to help them in the long term, but we also need safety nets.

Plug-and-play capability for the global knowledge economy is not readily available across vast swaths of the planet. One of the greatest challenges in the Badlands is to resolve these marginalized localities that occur everywhere, in every country and region, from the United States to Brazil, from Europe to the Middle East and to the rising Asia Pacific region. Despite the rise in income of some groups in the transition economies, the gap is increasing and for most the means to catch up is elusive. Not only is it the right thing to do to find those radical innovations that include more people, it is essential for sustainable growth and the continued wealth of the early winners. Growing and intense tangible expressions of social resistance can be heard, as those left out form defensive communities built around primary identities of religion, locality, ethnicity, or family. Examples of these are Al Qaeda, the religious right, urban youth gangs, drug networks, and militias, to name a few. Throughout human history defensive communities have been formed, for good or for ill, in response to great social and economic shifts, although never before have they been so visible nor globally interconnected around their point of view and so well organized to resist. Never before have so many people been involved at both ends of the economic spectrum. Numerous signs of friction can be felt as the gap grows between those who are included and those who are not, between those who have and those who have not. Should this continue much longer, there will be less appetite for global closeness on all sides.

As things stand now we have created an unstable and interdependent global economic system built on a foundation of a multiculturalism consisting of extreme differences. This is not necessarily a fatal trajectory; it could just as readily be a platform for future evolution. Harmony between economic and social systems must be created; otherwise, globalization will fail, denying billions of poor people an opportunity for much-needed development. Those who say that the failure of globalization would be a good thing do not present a compelling scenario of a better world.

Thus as we get a glimpse of the far foothills of the future beyond the Badlands we see that it is not predestined. Instead, it consists of two radically different scenarios: one is fragmented and dangerous, as the haves hope to escape the wrath of the have-nots; the other is an integrated global society where inclusiveness is on the march. The choice is ours, for the most part, but even with good decisions we should expect wild cards, those highly improbable events that could have a big impact. We need to learn from everywhere we can—and that includes a few lessons from history.

LESSONS FROM THE HISTORY OF DISRUPTIVE INNOVATIONS

I close this chapter by presenting some insights and lessons from historical cycles of innovation. These can serve as beacons in this murky landscape that we face. During our research, my colleagues and I probed deeply into several historical periods marked by disruptive innovations. We described the climate that contributed to making these possible, examined the new disruptive technologies and the clusters of technologies around them, and analyzed the churn between the economy and society and the social innovations that emerged. At the end of our research we synthesized a list of key lessons from this history and examined some of their implications for business during our own turbulent time.

TIMES AND CYCLES OF DISRUPTIVE INNOVATIONS: SELECTED TECHNOLOGIES

Bronze Age—(circa 3500 B.C.E.): writing, pottery

700 B.C.E.: Greek innovations: phonetic alphabet

100–999 A.D.: Period of Chinese innovations—classics on stone, elementary zoetrope, books printed

1400–1499: Renaissance—printing technologies

1650–1690: Penny press

1760–1830: First Industrial Revolution

1860: Vaccines

1870–1914: Second Industrial Revolution

1920–1945: Nuclear bomb

1950–2000: Information and communications

2000–2025: Biotechnology and other likely technology combinations across disciplines

Source: Global Foresight, 2004.

The following discussion is not meant to be exhaustive but rather to serve as food for thought, a means to extract lessons likely to be useful in the decade ahead. We can also derive some comfort from seeing that the human race has been in the Badlands before and thrived, although each cycle presents its own unique challenges. I encourage those of you with an inclination to delve deeper into this history to take advantage of the resources of the Internet or any good library.

"We are today on the rising slope of a third technological revolution. It is a rising slope, for we have passed from the plus-minus stage of invention and innovation into the crucial period of diffusion. The rates of diffusion will vary, depending upon the economic conditions and political stabilities of societies. Yet the phenomenon cannot be reversed, and its consequences may be even greater than the previous two technological revolutions that reshaped the West and now, with the spread of industrialization, other parts of the world as well" (Bell, 1989, p. 164).

Historical Lessons

- Change comes from the fringe as stasis grows at the center.
- Dynamic trading and human migration stimulates innovation.
- Social ferment feeds commercial innovation.
- Innovation requires optimal diversity.
- Interchangeable parts and standardization provide infrastructure for the next cycle.
- Mismatch of scale produces instability and breeds innovation or dysfunction.
- New self-concepts: "identity" derives from innovation.

Lesson One: Change Comes from the Fringe as Stasis and Corruption Grow at the Center

Innovation usually springs up at the edges of established centers of power and wealth, and is often created by people who seem less than central to the day. Often they are people from newly emerging economic classes and occupations, dissatisfied with current conditions and imagining ways to change them. By definition the centers of power tend not to be responsive to outsiders. Having created large, complex systems to sustain its power, the center responds to dissatisfaction and innovation from the fringe by ignoring or contesting them; tensions rise as new ideas take hold. Corruption of the powerful increases as they feel increasingly threatened.

There is no better historical example of this lesson than from the late Middle Ages and the Renaissance, when the Catholic Church was a monolithic force in control of knowledge and therefore of people's lives. Merchants and traders on the fringe of society absorbed new ideas on their travels and invented places people could gather to discuss ideas outside of churches. Soon there was a growing desire for knowledge among ordinary people. The Catholic Church tried to squelch both the ideas and innovators, calling them heretics and damning them as opposing God and Church beliefs. As the Church's power became increasingly undermined by trade and literacy, it became more corrupt in its quest to cling to power, a grip that was ultimately broken by the invention of printing technologies, making possible a surge of innovations from creating maps to books to the reorganization of knowledge into new fields such as architecture and engineering. What followed eventually developed into the Age of Enlightenment, in the century that saw the formation of the United States of America.

Today we can see all about us examples of tensions between innovators on the fringe and those at the center who hold fast to the status quo. Consider Linux developers and their open-source software, with its implicit threat to New Economy juggernauts like Microsoft, who try to monopolize markets by excluding others. Think about Move On, a sociopolitical movement organized on the World Wide Web and focused on transforming the American political process, and how it creates tension with the existing political process. Consider microenterprises in towns and villages all around the world funded by small loans to women (initially provided by the Grameen Bank), which are growing in importance to economic development and being called into question by such large institutions as the World Bank. Think about the tension between apartheid in South Africa and the popular power of Nelson Mandela. Look at the festering corruption at the center of powerful corporations such as Enron, Tyco, Arthur Andersen, Global Crossing, and WorldCom, who tried to quell the voices of heretics opposed to their corporate ways. Think about the Bank of China scandals in Beijing as the government pushes for major reform.

Lesson Two: Dynamic Trading Stimulates Innovation

As traders travel to sell their wares they collide with new ideas and people different from themselves and learn to adapt their products to fit their alternative ways of living. They also bring news of these dissimilarities back home, which stimulates more people to travel to expand their ways of living.

In the Bronze Age, from 3500 to 3100 B.C.E., hunting societies transformed into farming societies and trade began. This was the earliest time period we studied, a time when writing was invented, allowing people to transmit and store information beyond the reach of human memory for the first time. The first cities sprung up in today's Iraq, and an urban economy rooted in trade began. It began with innovations in crafts, including specialization and early forms of mass production. Sumerians invented the potter's wheel to manufacture vessels that were then traded over vast distances. This in turn demanded innovations in recording systems for tallying inventories, shipments of goods, and payments. Merchants needed to preserve records of their transactions to resolve disputes. Building on the innovation of writing, they created clay envelopes that could carry and store tokens of commerce and make for ready filing in libraries.

Today dynamic global trading is also stimulating a multitude of innovations through the distribution of high-tech industry, what I call the Global Silicon Network (GSN). Talented engineers migrate from India, China, Israel, and France, to name just a few countries, to California's Silicon Valley, where they learn technical and organizational innovations and return home to start similar science and business endeavors, creating whole new industries in their countries. In this way social innovation spreads as well. Through business travel, many educated women meet similar women in other countries, giving rise to global organizations such as the International Women's Forum that allow women to support each other globally to achieve common social goals and to advance the role of women in society.

Lesson Three: Social Ferment
Feeds Commercial Innovation

The context in which innovation takes place is absolutely crucial. Both disease and war give rise to innovation whereby additional clusters of innovations build one upon another. Louis Pasteur, a "fringe scientist," demonstrated the power of laboratory medicine by helping to end the threat of anthrax to cattle in the 1880s. He took his laboratory to the field and cultivated the anthrax microbe, then created the first vaccine. This was a small-scale experiment with a big ripple effect, creating a new theory of vaccines, launching the beginnings of the modern public health movement, and extending the practice of medicine to the farm and other commercial areas. Through this successful, and certainly disruptive, innovation, the scientific method became accepted and led to the use of statistics to chart the rise and fall of disease—one of the biggest stepping stones in the development of epidemiology since the invention of the microscope. This surge of innovations launched a new relationship between science and society that is pervasive in our lives today.

Social ferment has been a hallmark of our current cycle of innovation, beginning with the protest movement in the 1960s in the United States. The segregation of blacks and whites created intense social ferment that led to all sorts of social innovations from new social organizing principles and practices, from the Civil Rights Act of 1964 to voter registration drives. Activists used this new knowledge about organizing against corporations. One such effort was led by a fringe leader named Ralph Nader, who successfully sued General Motors for harassment in response to his negative book on the Corvair. This led to commercial innovations to create safer, higher-quality products. Saul Alinsky led a shareholder protest against Kodak. Recent similar movements like Move On's political efforts are examples of leveraging commercial innovation, in this case the Internet, to resolve social issues.

Lesson Four: Innovation Requires Optimal Diversity

Disruptive innovations are not engineered; they arise spontaneously, fueled by dynamic interactions between diverse people. They occur when people are motivated to think and act in new ways, and when there is a rich variety of ideas and perspectives. Preceding examples alluded to the importance of the diversity that occurs in dynamic trading, during social ferment, and among the heretics and mavericks on the fringe. One impressive story of the role of diversity in innovation was the production of the nuclear bomb in the early 1940s, during the historical cycle of innovation that preceded the one we're living in today.

Even though H. G. Wells forecast the possibility of a nuclear bomb in 1914, and scientist Leo Szilard is the legally recognized inventor of the atom bomb through the patent he filed in Britain on July 4, 1934, the bomb as we know it was developed by the Manhattan Project in the United States under the scientific leadership of Robert Oppenheimer. The diverse gathering of scientists that contributed to the

Manhattan Project might not have been possible were it not for Hitler's persecution of the Jews, driving much of Germany's intellectual elite to flee to the United States. In his maniacal drive to persecute a minority, Hitler also succeeded in slowing the pace of war technology in Germany.

A further contribution came from Vannevar Bush, the head of the U.S. Office of Scientific Research and Development, who provided the radical idea of putting together scientists and engineers. From the very outset Oppenheimer demanded a new approach to the work on the bomb: "We need a central laboratory devoted wholly to this purpose, where people could talk freely with each other, where theoretical ideas and experimental findings could affect each other, where the waste, frustration, and error of compartmentalized experimental studies could be eliminated" (Weiner and Smith, 1980, p. 50). Oppenheimer was able to create much of this climate of innovation, despite the frustrations imposed by the need for secrecy.

Building the atom bomb created an unprecedented experience of community among scientists and engineers, as the exigencies of wartime dissolved the normal boundaries between disciplines and organizations. This restructured scientific research community became a nexus of institutions and people that created a new innovative culture of science. This was the platform for the disruptive innovations of the cycle we are in today.

Lesson Five: Interchangeable Parts and Standards Provide the Infrastructure for the Next Cycle of Innovation

In the early phases of innovation different inventors often compete to get their standard adopted to gain bigger market share; social innovators compete for power. Once a given innovation has taken hold, the winning standards become the platform on which new innovations can emerge. Computer technologies that were created to track German aircraft and break Germany's secret codes became the standard for a series of simulation and gaming innovations that led to computer networks such as the ARPANET. These standards were widely adopted in turn, becoming the platform for this innovation cycle's communication and information technologies, which led to the Internet and the World Wide Web. There are many examples of this throughout history.

Eli Whitney's cotton gin in 1793 resulted in standardized forms and interchangeable parts for production of cotton, leading to increased production of a commodity that had been available only to the elite, bringing it within reach of ordinary people. The steam engine harnessed a vast new source of power, leading to new feedback mechanisms such as float valves, centrifugal governors, and pressure regulators that enhanced the ability of the steam engine to adapt to various needs and made the access to power available all the time. It became the platform for a number of innovations that characterized the First Industrial Revolution: new industries, urbanization, year-round production, and reliable transportation, to name just a few.

Lesson Six: Mismatch of Scale Between Organizations and Social Issues Produces Instability

Institutional and organizational structures evolve to solve the problems and meet the demands of the times. They need to be the right size for the problems and issues at hand. As innovations build upon innovations the economy changes and social issues shift, rendering a mismatch in scale between existing problems and institutions. This creates instability until sufficient organizational innovation takes place to begin to change the organizations *enough* so that they can begin to solve the new problems.

Each historic cycle has experienced these mismatches. The guilds that formed around specialized crafts in medieval times began to decline in the sixteenth century. Their conservatism, monopolistic practices, and selective entrance policies developed in response to creating high standards for quality and a rigorous training program for new members wanting to learn the trade. But as time went on they became centers of power that dominated town and city governments and became hostile to technical innovations that threatened their economic interests. They set extremely high standards for apprentices and journeymen, slowing industrial growth. But as demand for products grew and capital became more available, merchants set up different kinds of companies to compete with guilds, exploiting new production technologies to produce more goods for the growing middle class. The guilds broke down under this pace of new technologies and trade, their restrictive cultures unable to respond fast enough once their control was broken.

Today most organizations and institutions developed to solve the problems created by innovations of the Industrial Era. In fact, the modern corporation developed to support mass production and manufacturing. Organizational innovations ranging from Frederick Taylor's scientific management (which viewed both people and organizations as machines) to Henry Ford's mass production assembly line fit the needs of the times. They enabled scalability, standardization, and mass merchandizing. As the Information Era (which arose in the 1950s) matures, it requires new forms of organization based on innovation and globalization and knowledge work. It should be no surprise to see Industrial Era structures breaking down around us.

Lesson Seven: New Identities
Evolve from Innovation

The human sense of self also evolves as history unfolds and the context of life changes. As clusters of innovations are adopted they reshape the economy, the society, and daily life. Identity is a set of reference points, markers that individuals use to distinguish themselves from others. They include everything from your name to your role at work to your group memberships to your national and global identity. Reference points change during cycles of innovation. The reference points we have today are more diverse and numerous than at any point in history, and dramatically different from previous cycles of innovation. Identity no longer answers the question, Where have I been placed in the world? It is no longer defined by bordered places.

The sense of identity has changed dramatically over the last five hundred years. It has gone from a God-centric sense universe to a materialistic idea of who we are. Ordinary people have become more important too—it is not just the wealthy who have power. As Chandra Mukerji described it in 2000, in a lecture at UC San Diego, "Prior to these developments, a high degree of localism and determinacy measured your life. If you lived in a rural town and lived more or less directly off the land, as did most people in the Middle Ages, you had no reason to imagine who you were as a person or what community you belonged to. It was obvious. You were what your community knew you to be, and your community was made up of the people in your town." The rise of trade changed all this; the newly wealthy were merchants, not nobles. Due to their links with other parts of the world they could consider themselves in terms beyond their immediate neighbors. As Mukerji says, "They could become cosmopolitan consumers and members of imagined communities."

The Badlands of the Renaissance embodied the Reformation and Counter-Reformation and the reconfiguration of the religious and secular world. It was caught up in the chaos of painted images of God and Heaven being replaced by maps of trading routes, as the natural order was re-imagined not just as the domain of God but as a resource for business and commerce.

Today once again we are challenged to represent ourselves when so many of our local and global reference points are being dislocated by multiple short-term relationships in both a physical and an electronic landscape. What markers represent your truly authentic self? And in this increasingly complex world our sense of "we" becomes as critically important as our sense of "I." Knowing who "we" are—and how that group identity fits with "I"—is especially important in an economy where the creation of knowledge is achieved through the collaborative sharing and sense-making of small groups of people. For this to occur there must be deep trust.

IMPLICATIONS

If we can learn from the lessons of the past, they can help us stay oriented in a landscape with few clear paths through it. Here are a few implications these lessons provide for today's journey through the Badlands:

- We are at the point today where the economy is churning faster than society can respond to it. We need to focus on the new problems and issues this creates and not get lost in old ideas and processes that could prevent us from surviving this journey. We need new and better leadership to design new kinds of organizations at all levels to match the needs of tomorrow.

- The dramatic changes we need to make can come from listening to new voices. The tension between the fringe and the center provides fertile ground for innovation; embrace it, don't try to squelch it. Leaders in business, government, and nonprofits need to make contact with their fringe—the heretics and mavericks and young people who inhabit those marginalized places.

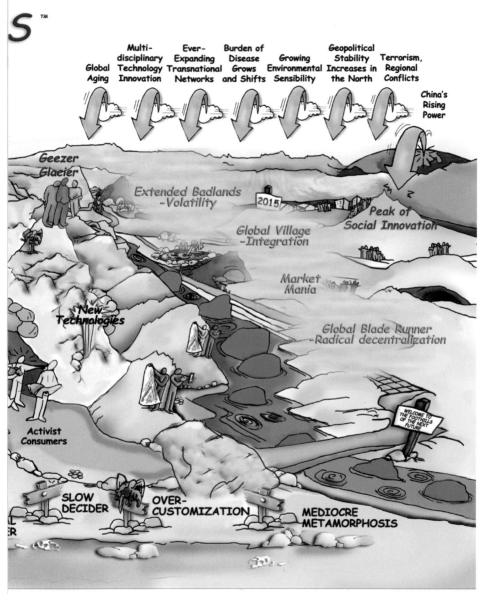

S ™

Global Aging

Multi-disciplinary Technology Innovation

Ever-Expanding Transnational Networks

Burden of Disease Grows and Shifts

Growing Environmental Sensibility

Geopolitical Stability Increases in the North

Terrorism, Regional Conflicts

China's Rising Power

Geezer Glacier

Extended Badlands -Volatility

2015

Peak of Social Innovation

Global Village -Integration

Market Mania

New Technologies

Global Blade Runner -Radical decentralization

Activist Consumers

WELCOME TO THE FOOTHILLS OF THE NEXT FUTURE

SLOW DECIDER

OVER-CUSTOMIZATION

MEDIOCRE METAMORPHOSIS

- Dynamic world trade that takes advantage of the technologies of connection provides an opportunity for the betterment of all people. It is our choice to seize it or not.

- Today's social ferment from the growing global networks is the breeding ground for radical innovations, for good and for ill. Social experimentation with new disruptive technologies will be a prominent feature of the next twenty years.

- Attempts to monopolize information and knowledge by powerful institutions will break down in today's societies, just as they did in the Renaissance.

- Innovation requires optimal diversity, which can come from many sources—geographic, cultural, interdisciplinary, and intergenerational, to name a few. Keep seeking collisions with the new and engage deeply in cultural learning to achieve the mix needed to create a vibrant global society and economy.

- We are in a cycle of disruptive innovation where new knowledge, not just technology, continues to explode across myriad disciplines, from physics to biology to energy, changing our fundamental knowledge base, which will result in a new identity.

PARTING THOUGHTS

The world has changed in the last fifty years as much as at any time in human history, if not more so. It will change as much again in the next twenty-five, as we come to the last phase of this seventy-five-year historical cycle of disruptive innovation. We have passed the point of no return; taking the rest of the journey is not optional. At the end of it, the future that we weave together will not resemble the past. As in the Renaissance, much of the transformation will be caused by the continuous creation not merely of new technologies, but of new knowledge. This extraordinary period will be similar to the explosion of knowledge and social reorganization that occurred during the Renaissance, and before that with the invention of writing in the Bronze Age.

As the twentieth century ended, we slipped into the Badlands phase of this cycle. With the loss of the easy wealth creation in the late 1990s we find ourselves less resistant to change. Now the transformational effects of the Information Revolution are taking hold. They will change the very way we do business and organize our work at the center of our lives. We truly have passed the point of no return. The phenomenon of the Information Revolution can't be reversed, and it will reshape not only the Western world but the entire world as well.

The fact that this journey is a global one adds to it both intensity and complexity, promising everyone an experience that will mark their lives like no other in history. How well today's society can manage the transition through market mechanisms and political forces will lay the scaffolding for the next era. The challenge is daunting, yet that is the task at hand. By the end of this long journey through the Badlands, your life will have changed in the most profound ways. Not only will your work and organizational life transform as you shift your commitment from local to national to planetary, your very identity will also change—your sense of who you are and what you mean on this earth. Welcome to the Badlands.

CHAPTER TWO

Weathering the Badlands
Global Drivers of Change

———

The next decade will be shaped by increasing globalization and the turbulence caused by its seven driving forces. Think
of them as weather systems that can generate tornadoes, flash floods,
glaring sunshine, gentle rains, or dense fog. (Some of the "tornadoes"
we've already experienced include 9/11, SARS, human genome mapping, preemptive war in Iraq, and corporate and accounting scandals
in more than a few major U.S. companies.) These driving forces will
generate change independently, but even more so in combination with
each other, and the resulting turmoil will be among the few certain-
ties in a decade filled with many imponderables. Together these drivers have already created the structural economic shift we now face,
ushering in a networked knowledge economy that is relentlessly becoming the dominant economic model, surpassing the previous industrial model.

The next three to five years will be uniquely treacherous as globalization adapts and expands in new ways. American business, which
has been a major force for globalization, will respond to the excesses
of the 1990s by making new investments cautiously and only slowly
adding jobs. Many transnational corporations (TNCs) will move

skilled jobs offshore to further cut costs and will expand operations closer to new markets. This will result in a recovery that will cause angst in the United States. Volatile global political conditions will persist, changing the business landscape in real time, complicating strategy.

Ultimately your readiness to thrive in the Badlands will come from your personal experience of traveling through it. You can, however, increase your readiness to step off on your journey by recognizing the importance of understanding the big picture and keeping it always in view.

This chapter does not try to provide an exhaustive analysis of globalization and its seven driving forces (a book in itself) but rather serves as a wake-up call, inviting readers to think seriously and systematically about the threats, as well as the opportunities, that these forces will precipitate within domestic businesses and throughout the wider global environment.

GLOBALIZATION: THE POINT OF NO RETURN

Recession and terrorist threats have dampened enthusiasm for global closeness. Doubts are stirring about globalization's benefits as the successes and problems it has created become more obvious. While some developing countries, notably China, India, and Mexico, are benefiting a great deal from the global economy, others have been left out. Countries with weak economies have been unable to create environments conducive to growth, and today gaps between rich and poor continue to widen. Persistent unemployment in the United States at the end of the recession in 2003 and the movement of jobs offshore to developing nations is causing growing concern within U.S. borders. Despite these shifting conditions and the reactions to them, I forecast that globalization will gather force, fueled by the powerful TNCs from the advanced economies and joined by a key group of developing countries that benefited from their participation in world trade in the 1990s. Trade will continue to drive global growth, and globalization will continue to transfer wealth through trade, the growth of transnational corporations, and the flow of global capital.

Although GDP will be outpaced by world trade, it will return to healthy levels in the United States and continue to be fueled by rapid growth in the Asia region, particularly China (Table 2.1). However, the context for globalization will remain very volatile. More than sixty years after its publication, Joseph Schumpeter's seminal work on the

	Regional GDP Growth in Percentage				
	1971–1980	1981–1990	1991–2000	2001–2010	2001	2002
United States	3.2	3.2	3.3	3.1	0.3	2.4
European Union	2.9	2.4	2.1	1.9	1.5	0.9
Japan	4.6	4.1	1.5	1.3	0.4	0.2
Developing Asia	5.4	7.0	7.3	7.4	5.8	6.4
China	6.7	6.3	11.1	8.7	7.5	8.0
Developing Western Hemisphere	6.0	1.6	2.8	2.2	0.7	0.1
Eastern Europe and Former Soviet Union	4.0	1.8	3.0	3.9	5.1	4.2
World Total	3.9	3.4	4.0	3.2	2.4	3.0

Table 2.1.   China and the Rest of Asia Fuel Global Growth.

Source: Global Foresight, International Monetary Fund.

processes of creative destruction, *Capitalism, Socialism, and Democracy* continues to describe the world around us. Schumpeter defined economic turbulence as a process of "creative destruction where the old gets replaced by the new through a relentless testing of new ideas." He said that this was the inherent nature of capitalism and that economic turmoil is to be embraced. The only way to survive is to invent new products and processes and organizational structures continuously. You can only anticipate volatility, not eliminate it. As free markets and capitalism diffuse globally so will the process of creative destruction, driving massive adaptations at every level.

Despite this volatility and all the pain it brings, globalization has many reasons to gather strength, including widespread support for it in many countries, as shown in Figure 2.1. Although globalization remains a divisive topic among groups ranging from social protestors to government policymakers, the general global public seems favorably disposed to it, despite their concerns.

Few people have a global identity yet or feel like citizens of the world, rather than of their nation or region or state. People do cite some improvements, most notably the availability of medicine and food. But primarily, most believe that things are getting worse—jobs

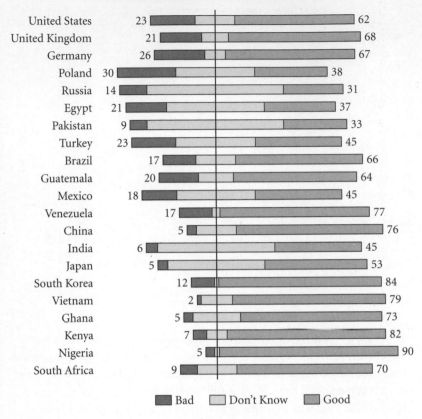

Effect of "Globalization" on Your Country

Figure 2.1.   Support for Globalization.
Source: Views of a Changing World, The Pew Research
Center for the People and the Press, June 2003.

paying less, working conditions failing to improve, gaps growing between rich and poor—but few blame their woes on globalization (Figure 2.2). These are all signs of the critical need to develop a new civil society that matches the needs and issues wrought from this fast growing global economy.

Yet despite this widespread support, people also do not want their way of life threatened in the process. Around the world, the tendency toward nationalism and cultural superiority remains strong, as illustrated by Figure 2.3.

The business reasons for pursuing globalization are compelling. Rising numbers of educated young people in the developing econo-

The Gap Between Rich and Poor Is Getting Worse

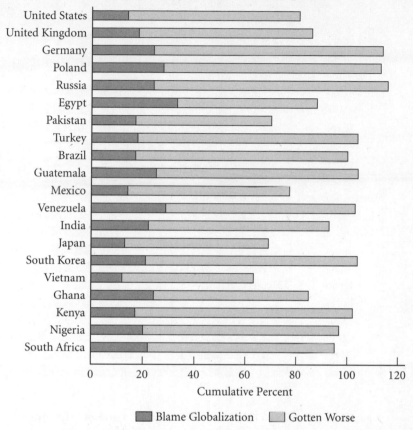

Blame Globalization   Gotten Worse

Figure 2.2.   Globalization Not Blamed for Social Ills.
Source: Views of a Changing World, The Pew Research
Center for the People and the Press, June 2003.

mies make it easy to create local businesses and link them to global
networks. As they grow they provide the infrastructure of global business, together with more growth in developing countries. In 2003 the
top hundred transnational corporations accounted for more than $5
trillion in sales and provided some 20 million jobs, 60 percent of
which were in developing countries. New TNCs are developing in
these emerging economies, generating additional sales and jobs.

Globalization still offers many advantages to large companies.
Economies of scale continue to be very important for some sectors,
particularly manufacturing. TNCs can also manufacture much more

Our Way of Life Needs to Be Protected Against Foreign Influence

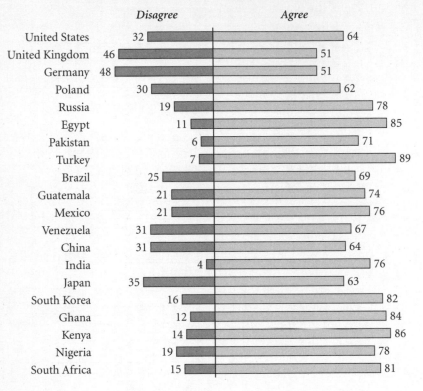

Figure 2.3.   Perceived Need to Protect Against Foreign Influence.
Source: Views of a Changing World, The Pew Research
Center for the People and the Press, June 2003.

cheaply in developing countries. By having multiple locations they can enhance their position for other business activities, from purchasing supplies to R&D. Furthermore, they can tailor their manufacturing to localities that match their specific needs for items like raw materials or tax incentives. As the level of education rises, so does the number of sophisticated consumers who enjoy the advantages of the cheaper prices of global goods and services and are comfortable buying foreign brands and comparison shopping.

These positive aspects of globalization should not deter us from looking at its downside. Despite the global economy's rapid growth over the last decade, we have little experience with its weaknesses;

some are not well known, and many have yet to emerge. Given its embryonic state, the global economy has shadow sides to contend with:

New anxieties caused by seemingly anonymous economic and technical forces. Although people are generally aware of globalization, no one really knows what it is and what all its consequences will be. New technologies are not well understood by the average person. This gives people a new sense of vulnerability and anxiety about having to make it in a world they don't truly understand and have little control over.

Codes of restraint are lacking. Very few global standards exist. This means that intellectual piracy and fraud are easy to commit. Potential exists for abuse of human resources as firms try to capitalize on their far-flung global resources by making workers available 24/7. And with no true global code of ethics and agreements, safety and environmental concerns also loom large.

Rogue individuals and groups acting out. Not only nation states and the military have access to weapons and technologies that can cause great harm. We now have individuals who already possess them or can acquire them. Their access to smaller and more powerful weapons with greater ranges is a cause for great concern.

Uneven flow of benefits from trade and capital. Global capital flows where it is most likely to pay off and leaves quickly if that doesn't pan out. This can cause havoc in financial markets and economies, as we witnessed during the Asian financial crisis that began in 1997.

Growing gaps between the wealthy and the poor. The Information Revolution accelerates the wealth gap because it spreads the global economy with an emphasis on places that provide the right conditions of skilled labor, capital, technology, and potential markets.

Ambivalence toward globalization is to be expected in this transition between eras. We will spend the next twenty-five years sorting out just what globalization is. By the end of this historic cycle of innovation, though, many citizens around the world will come to feel their own global identity and interconnections.

THE DRIVERS OF GLOBALIZATION

Seven factors act to induce and sustain globalization:

- The aging of the population
- The introduction of new enabling technologies
- The spread of transnational business networks

- The rise of education and sophistication worldwide
- The appearance of new geopolitical issues and boundaries
- The growing wealth gap
- The failure of institutions

Each of these driving forces is gaining momentum as the decade unfolds. Together they will sculpt a new global landscape over the next twenty years.

An Aging Global Population

Demographic changes can be seen for a long time coming, but they always cause formidable transformations, often amplified because they are ignored until it is too late. Much of the developed world has gone through a demographic transition over the last hundred years as countries made dramatic progress against infant and childhood mortality and infectious diseases. Fertility rates declined and mortality rates for all age groups improved considerably. This demographic will soon be replicated in the maturing less developed countries.

For centuries the elderly have been a growing percentage of the population. What is new and challenging is the pace of aging (Figure 2.4). Except for Japan, which aged very rapidly after World War II, the pace of aging (in this case the number of years required for the percentage of the population aged sixty-five and older to double, from 7 percent to 14 percent) in developed countries ranged approximately from forty years in Spain to over a hundred years in France. In contrast, many of the less-developed countries are aging much faster. China, for example, achieved these growth rates in twenty-seven years, Brazil in twenty-five years, and Tunisia in fifteen.

This accelerated pace of aging in developing countries means that most of the increase in aging populations globally is occurring in economies with relatively undeveloped social systems. This causes serious issues for countries such as China, which faces terrific strain on its pension system, for example.

THE FUTURE OF AGING IS FEMALE. In many countries, those over seventy-five years of age are the fastest-growing subgroup of the elderly. In 1996 more than 43 percent of the most elderly lived in four countries: the United States, China, India, and Japan. Around the world women

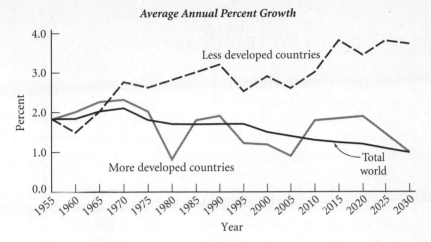

Average Annual Percent Growth

Figure 2.4. Growth of the Elderly Population.

are outliving men, which means that the female share of older populations rises with age. Not only are widows increasing in number but also the percentage of never-married women is rising, causing concern about the quality of their lives and their economic security. What is a "healthy" old age and who will be likely to achieve it? Although women who reach the age of sixty-five can expect to have a higher absolute number of disability-free days than men of the same age, since they live longer they become more vulnerable to disease.

The impact of aging, women's longevity, and a decline in dependency ratios on the global workforce will be huge, and it will be felt in the economies of both developed and developing nations. It will be a significant factor in the Badlands, particularly beyond 2010 when the percentage of people over the age of sixty begins to accelerate around the world.

KEY AGING IMPACTS IN THE BADLANDS. It is wise to remember one of the informal laws of population dynamics: If the problems of aging are already evident, then we have missed the optimum moment to resolve them by preventing them from occurring in the first place.

In developed economies, we will see the reversal of a declining retirement age as longevity and economic necessity drive older workers to remain in the workplace longer. This will happen most readily in the United States, but Europe and Japan, with their different

A GLOBAL CASE STUDY:
CHINA MOVES INTO FIRST PLACE IN AGING

By 2020, nearly 250,000,000 Chinese people, a group nearly the size of the entire population of the United States, will be over sixty. Their presence will be a driving force in the economy, the society, and the political system. By 2030 China will have the distinction of supporting more than 25 percent of the world's aged. Over the next five years China has a window of opportunity to make major strides in resolving the difficulties attendant on its aging. To meet the growing tidal wave of senior needs, China must be a pioneer in designing satisfactory programs in pension funds, health care, and housing support, and must roll these programs out across its vast population.

Historically, China's families bore the sole responsibility for support of their elderly. Now, however, several disparate forces are undermining the viability of this arrangement, even in rural areas. Among these forces are China's rapid shift to a one-child, two-parent, and four-grandparent family structure, its increase in nuclear families (households with just parents and children account for more than 50 percent of families in urban areas), and the trend of rural migration to the cities.

The Pension Conundrum: Shifting the Burden

Approved by the State Council in 1997, China's new unified pension system reform moves the country toward a three-pillar model, whereby the state, employers, and employees share pension contributions, thereby shifting the burden from the shoulders of enterprise. China is experimenting with alternative policies as well. State-owned enterprises (SOEs) have a spotty history of paying pensions and managing their funds well, not to mention that the current programs are all aimed at urban areas where only 30 percent of people live, not rural areas, where 94 percent of workers do not earn salaries and therefore lack any access to pensions. And whatever pension reform is set in place will be administered by provinces that possess widely varying abilities to oversee it. In addition, China has no national regulatory and legal framework, little infrastructure to support it, and a hierarchy of government officials who face a long learning process. Although solutions are not impossible, it looks like even with the best efforts only about half of urban retirees will be covered by a pension in twenty-five years, and such pensions as exist are unlikely to be sufficient to cover living expenses.

Some Indicators to Benchmark Progress

- Is there a sustainable population policy?
- Are there diverse special programs that target the vulnerable— primarily rural elders and women?
- Is pension coverage in urban areas proceeding at an accelerated pace?
- Are there more experiments with elder-friendly communities?

Source: Global Foresight, Center for the Future of China, *China Five-Year Forecast,* 2003.

social and cultural values, will struggle with solutions and worker acceptance.

The rapid aging rate in emerging economies such as China, Mexico, and Brazil will challenge their fledgling social systems' ability to provide health care, pensions, and housing.

Most countries will face a pension conundrum much like China's. Financing old-age programs will not be easy. Dependency ratios make most public retirement plans unsustainable—they will not have sufficient resources to cover an expanding older population. Governments will put pressure on business to help with solutions. Aging policies will be front stage around the world. Look for a decrease in mandatory retirement rules and mandated incentives to employ older workers.

A global health care crisis also looms. Of particular importance is the need for a better global public health system that can manage the cross-border flows of infectious diseases and mount a rapid response to new infections as they crop up. Public health competencies vary widely around the world. As we learned from the SARS epidemic in 2003, these global flows of viruses are bad for business as well as for public health.

A redefinition of what is "old age" and "middle age" is under way. People aged fifty to sixty today will live long lives, with many women living to a hundred and many men to age ninety. This fifty- to sixty-year-old cohort around the world will redefine its lifestyle in dramatic ways. Look for middle age to extend to seventy-five or eighty years of age, for the mandated retirement age to increase to over seventy (particularly for knowledge workers), and for old age to begin for many in their eighties.

New Enabling Technologies

The development of new technologies accelerates in the Badlands, fueled by the rapid adoption of technologies in daily life and the accelerated pace with which science is creating new knowledge across many fields. We are poised to experience revolutionary breakthroughs in many domains—biology, materials science, and energy—which will, in turn, lead to a plethora of new technologies. The first decade of the twenty-first century will be exciting for science, as new information tools allow scientists to work smarter and faster. Many advances will come from the creation of new knowledge at the intersection of different disciplines. Imagine wearing clothes made from bio-interactive materials that could respond to the external environment and change their characteristics to improve your comfort level. Such materials could, for example, become more porous in hot weather, increasing your ability to cool down. Think of applications of bio-interactive materials and biosensors inside the body in the prevention and treatment of disease. The intersection of biosensors and smart materials will revolutionize medical care. For example, miniaturized bio implants are likely to regulate certain drug levels from within.

Human history has always been shaped by tools. While we may have reached the end of some of the trajectories of information technologies, we are just beginning to experience their far-reaching impact. These transformations in daily life will occur often in the Badlands.

A BRIEF TWENTIETH-CENTURY RETROSPECTIVE. The twentieth century had four distinct scientific periods, times in which one science after another took the lead like a series of ever-larger waves (Figure 2.5). Chemistry, physics, and information technology were each preeminent for a time, and the century ended with the promise of a new scientific engine: biology.

Although they each had times of prominence, new science and technologies continue to flow from each field of study, interacting and enabling one another. Each science wrought huge impacts on the economy and society, but none was as transformative as the tidal wave of new information and communication technologies unleashed during the last thirty years. This era's capacity for knowledge creation

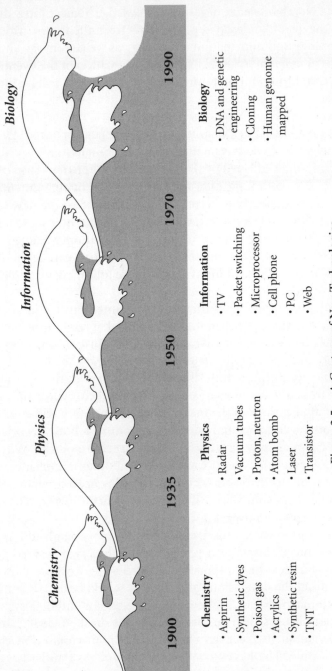

Chemistry
- Aspirin
- Synthetic dyes
- Poison gas
- Acrylics
- Synthetic resin
- TNT

Physics
- Radar
- Vacuum tubes
- Proton, neutron
- Atom bomb
- Laser
- Transistor

Information
- TV
- Packet switching
- Microprocessor
- Cell phone
- PC
- Web

Biology
- DNA and genetic engineering
- Cloning
- Human genome mapped

Figure 2.5.   A Century of New Technologies.
Source: Global Foresight, 2004.

made it one of the most powerful cycles of innovation since the Renaissance. New knowledge begat new knowledge. Expect more of the same in the next two decades, particularly from the intersections of biotechnology and information technology as well as energy and innovations in materials science. Expect a continuation of the twentieth-century trend to manipulate smaller and smaller things, including molecules.

EMERGING INFORMATION AND COMMUNICATION TECHNOLOGIES. Even if we had no dramatic new technological breakthroughs, our lives would still be profoundly affected by the diffusion of the current crop of information and communication technologies, and by refinements on those discoveries. Looking across the spectrum of all the new technologies, from wireless telecommunications to the Internet to smart tags, it is clear that the impacts to come will be exponentially greater than the impacts of the computer in the first thirty years of the Badlands. Look for continued innovations in the following technologies over the next decade:

Ubiquitous computing: We have always wanted our technology to disappear, and the big story in the Badlands is that computing will become invisible, woven inextricably into the fabric of our lives. Although not likely to be fully mature for twenty years, the technologies that enable ubiquitous computing will be evident in the near term, like peer-to-peer technologies, and will truly take off when they find their best applications in the marketplace. Computing will continue to move off our desktops and into our environment, both at work and at home. Chips already have become low-cost commodities. Wireless technologies accelerate the pace and scale of adoption. Appliances and machinery will notify repair vendors when they need servicing. Sensors circulating in your veins will determine when the next release of insulin is needed and trigger it.

Wireless: Just as wired capacity took off with more bandwidth in the early 1990s after a slow, fifteen-year adoption phase, wireless has done the same—but in a shorter time frame. Wireless networking allows us to integrate all the dimensions of daily life—work, home, recreation, and health management. It allows converged voice and data systems that can seamlessly switch protocols to find the most efficient channel at any given moment. It enables a huge increase in machine-to-machine communication. There is no convergence in wireless standards, however, and more are likely to proliferate, with lots of surprises. The recent takeoff of *Wi-Fi* (a wireless standard that uses a free, unlicensed spectrum and adopts the 802.11 standard) and the fast appearance of "hot spots" have taken the wind out of the huge investment in 3G, but other new standards are being invested in, particularly by large operators that could give Wi-Fi some serious long-term competition.

Wireless technologies will allow large organizations to build and operate lower-cost services than wired. Densely populated areas will use short-range wireless networks to provide convenience and low-cost communications. Ultimately, wireless will have a solution for the legacy problem of not always being able to connect existing wired lines and cable (the final-mile connection) both to business offices and the home.

Sensors: Finally, this old innovation is now small, smart, and communicative enough to become commercially viable. The primary use for sensors will be in wireless, in distributed computing environments, and in machine-to-machine communication. Sensors change the nature of the data that can be collected, analyzed, and disseminated by detecting images, moisture, sound, light, heat, and more. They will have enormous impacts on health and medicine, revolutionizing how monitoring is done. Sensors that take pictures and are embedded in all sorts of things will be another major application.

Voice: Voice technology is more efficient and practical than ever before. It is poised for much more innovation in the next decade, ultimately being delivered in packets small enough to be embedded in microdevices. Its major use early on will be in cost savings in dictation and transcription, voice-activated phone services, and other services based on the Web. Currently, systems are useful only for limited contexts and tasks that can be highly structured, such as voice-activated tracking systems. Voice recognition and Voice XML digital tagging permit telephone-based speech recognition; this is what allows a computer to interpret a caller's question and then search a database for an answer.

Voice technology works best in situations of limited vocabulary and domain. Its highest uses will be in specialized domains, such as call centers, where it is evolving to give callers a sense of a conversation with a real live human. The big breakthrough this decade is likely to be natural language recognition, the ability to understand human speech.

Biometrics: Reliably identifying people with their own peculiar biological characteristics such as retinal patterns, hand geometric patterns, and DNA will become commonplace in the next decade. The goal is to be able to authenticate people for who they are. The commercial uses are immense, from matching people to their airline boarding passes to letting shoppers make secure purchases with their credit cards. It is likely that biometrics could become the log-in method of choice once the costs come down. It will be quickly adopted by consumers because of the convenience and customization. With the vast expansion of information in our lives that we want to use anytime, anyplace, this technology provides privacy plus convenience. It will extend automation to more aspects of the individual user, obviating the need for more expensive human interfaces.

Biometrics tantalizes with obvious applications to security. This will be accepted by the public with some ambivalence because of privacy concerns about government invasiveness into our personal lives and potential threats to civil liberties. The aftermath of 9/11, however, finds many more people ready to give up some civil liberties for greater security. Biometrics also promises many applications in police and crime work. Thus far the most reliable technologies are finger and hand scanning. The perceived need for more accurate and reliable verification is key to widespread consumer adoption. Terrorism and security concerns will drive faster discovery of better methods in biometrics.

Peer-to-peer (P2P): This technology enables small-scale networks to function without the need for a server as an intermediary. It allows small groups to interconnect directly, bypassing central servers and large centralized computing systems. P2P based on open-source coding is a critical technology to ubiquitous computing. P2P will not diffuse quickly in large companies because of all the legacy client server networks and the challenges to hierarchy and control, but its benefits—like easily pulling together project teams across boundaries and rapid decision making—will continue to drive adoption.

P2P is part of the "out-frastructure" (technologies that allow people outside an organization's formal boundaries to connect easily) that empowers teams, social networks, suppliers, and other parties to collaborate efficiently. It makes rapid decision making and fast learning a cinch. Because it is narrowly focused, it avoids permissions, slow download times, and advertisements. It enhances the use of just-in-time data and discussion sharing, and it allows the use of intelligent agents (bots) across the network to search for files, prioritize tasks, and zap viruses. Although P2P is primarily used for managing information, in a wireless environment it has the potential to transform the humble PC into an extremely powerful distributed computer.

Displays: New technologies can allow just about anything to become a display. No longer will we be bound by a flat, rigid, heat-emitting screen. New display technologies will be portable, printable, flexible, and extremely lightweight. Combined with other technologies, new displays will give us labels that can talk to us, smart cards that deliver e-mail messages, and more. Essentially they will make information more interesting, more current, and more widely available. They will make all sorts of materials and devices more intelligent. They will give us information whenever and wherever we want it.

Obviously, this is a radical innovation that creates whole new industry segments and new products that, in turn, will change consumers' expectations about how and when they will receive information. These new display technologies will bring efficiencies to the supply chain and to customer relationships and transportation. The upside creates all sorts of opportunities for multi-tiered customer service; the downside is yet more information in an already information-heavy environment.

THE COMING BIO WAVE. Biological innovations will define much of the technological landscape throughout the Badlands over the next several decades. But look for these innovations to be developed and adopted more slowly than those in information technology. Biology is very complicated and not well understood by many people, whether inside or outside science, including most consumers and most business leaders. Biology also poses ethical considerations with regard to many new technologies that will slow and even stop some innovations from being used broadly, particularly in the realm of health care and food. The health care system in most countries is either highly bureaucratic or fragmented; both structures are impediments to adoption of new technologies.

Despite these factors, many new biotechnologies will come into use, particularly in the areas of diagnostics and monitoring. The intersection of information technology and biotech will drive medicine even further into its new role as an information-based service. In particular, look for these transformative health technologies:

New genetic technologies: In the next decade, expect gene therapy for breast, colon, and lung cancers; Parkinson's disease; and heart failure. Expect new diagnostics for early detection of infectious diseases and for therapy monitoring. Look to see stem cells being used to regenerate skin, cartilage, blood, pancreas, and muscle tissue.

Bio-informatics: This is a rapidly advancing field that lies at the intersection of systems biology, biotechnology, analytical computing, and large-scale computing. These tools allow study and manipulation of genes at the molecular level. Pharmaceuticals will be matched to people based on their genetic predisposition to respond well to a particular drug. Bioinformatics also will allow the development of DNA-based vaccines.

Bioinformatics promises many uses, from mining databases to linking therapies with outcomes to providing a platform for understanding biological research data. With the use of sensors it will revolutionize patient care, enabling "anytime, anywhere health care." It will support transformations in home care as well as provide physicians with an information-rich environment to make sense of clinical cases quicker, faster, better. Like information technology, it will take advantage of sophisticated sensors, wireless technologies, and Web services. These new medical technologies will come at a price and will drive up the cost of health care. Access to these new health technologies will often be limited to those with the means to pay for them out of pocket and with higher premiums.

EMERGING ENERGY TECHNOLOGIES. People and businesses will want more control and reliability from energy, considering how wired they have become. More and more consumers will produce their own energy and sell their excess capacity back to the grid. With the convergence of more efficient small-scale generating technologies such as fuel cells, solar, and wind microturbines, together with the deregulation of the industry and the rise of smarter, more sophisticated consumers, it is quite possible that whole countries will someday go off the power grid, with the capacity for distributed energy production.

These developments will create a new energy supply chain that will redefine competition and promote the entry of new entrepreneurs into the field. People and businesses will want more control and reliability for energy, considering how wired they have become.

GLOBAL PERSPECTIVE: UNEVEN DIFFUSION. The United States is the leading creator and adopter of new technologies and will keep that place for the foreseeable future, or at least over the next twenty years. American culture puts more trust in technologies than other cultures and supports the view that humans can control nature. Other cultures put more trust in nature, God, and fate. This makes for upcoming collisions between cultures around technology adoption and use. Also, infrastructure capacities vary widely around the world. With wireless it is now possible to think about leapfrogging industrial models to create a modern infrastructure—but which countries and regions can make that leap?

Most processes in emerging and developing economies follow an elite diffusion process, which seldom is inclusive of others downstream. Other options should be tried. A good way to increase the positive impact of new technologies in emerging economies is to facilitate participation in a global network. As more and more TNCs develop their far-flung networks for manufacturing, marketing, and supply, countries that are not playing can strategically target a portion of one of these networks and engage. They can then use that step as a platform for more engagement. And finally, countries can simply declare a technology to be critical to their growth.

KEY IMPACTS FROM NEW TECHNOLOGIES IN THE BADLANDS. The next ten to twenty years will continue to see more surges in the development of disruptive technologies along many key dimensions. They will contribute to the transformation of daily home and work life, but first they must find their viable commercial applications. This will take some time and contribute to the promises and pitfalls of technology in the Badlands.

Here are some of the most likely long-term impacts we can see clearly:

- Advances in small-scale power will accelerate the diffusion of wireless by extending the time devices are able to work without recharging. This will enable businesses to adopt them much faster because they can depend on them for core and critical business information and transactions needs.

- Advances in biometrics will diminish the need for human interfaces for additional common activities in daily living. There will be more and more secure automated systems that increase the convenience of users and save time.

- Different cities and regions can invest in new advances in wired and wireless technologies and gain competitive advantage in attracting more business. Those with prior investments in infrastructure by government and industry will build on this capacity and compete very well.

- Wireless technologies accelerate the expansion of machine-to-machine communication, allowing more monitoring of all kinds of systems at a distance. They will combine with sensors and smart materials to monitor changes allowing remote adjustments.

• P2P technologies enable high-performing social networks and hot groups to improve collaboration and innovation. The right people can easily connect with each other and the right information. This leads to more efficiency, productivity, and creativity.

• Voice technologies can streamline call centers and make them more convenient. They will decrease reliance on real-time human support, providing more access to consumers and more convenience. They also will increase support of remote workers and facilitate communication of vital business information any time, any place, in any language.

• Smaller and more personal computing devices will increase access to information, because they are cheaper and thus can be adopted by individuals and both small and medium-size enterprises.

• The adoption of information and communication technologies in health care will give rise to an activist health care consumer. The current asymmetry of information between medical providers and consumers will diminish, ultimately unleashing the consumer as a driver of change in this failing system.

• Breakthroughs in energy technologies will increase the use of alternative energy sources, breaking the stronghold of oil and its volatile politics.

• The Information Age and its new technologies tend to increase polarization between the haves and the have-nots. The world has a huge digital divide—a huge health divide—a huge education divide—a huge wealth divide that new technologies will only increase without a conscious effort to find new ways to make them accessible to poor people.

Transnational Business Networks: The New Power Brokers

Transnational corporations—TNCs—have been expanding their size and influence much faster than the overall growth of world population, the world GDP, and world trade. They have taken advantage of the surge of new information and communication technologies that occurred in the 1980s and 1990s to globalize their industries, reaching far and wide into localities that offer them business advantages.

TNCs are the economic engine of the growth of globalization and over the long term will accelerate the growth of world trade. Although the Badlands provides a much more rugged environment than the one in which TNCs grew so rapidly during the 1990s, nevertheless many of them will ultimately learn to steer through it successfully. Some of them won't survive the Badlands, but others from an increasingly diverse set of countries and regions will arise to take their place. The ultimate result will be the expansion of the vast global trading arrangements that I call the Global Silicon Network (GSN), with its worldwide framework of information and communication technologies, serving as a democratic infrastructure that allows both large and small players to engage in an infinite number of wealth-generating eco-webs. Comparative advantage comes from who you are connected to, not where you are.

The GSN will operate independently of any one country and will control a rapidly increasing share of the world's gross domestic product. In 2003 there were approximately 65,000 TNCs with some 850,000 foreign affiliates around the world. They employed about 54 million people (compared with just 24 million in 1990) and by 2010 will employ some 120 million workers. Increasingly they are creating more jobs in their developing country affiliates and sourcing higher-skilled labor from a variety of countries (Figure 2.6). They had sales

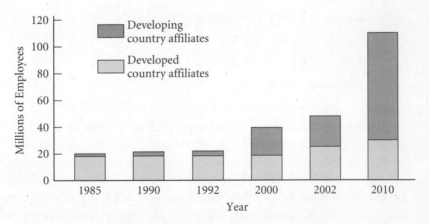

Figure 2.6.   Employment in Affiliates of Transnational Corporations.
Source: United Nations Conference on Trade
and Development, *World Investment Report 2003.*

of around $19 trillion in 2001—more than twice as high as world exports. They now account for one-tenth of world GDP and one-third of world exports. By ensuring an increasing supply of high-quality goods to the global marketplace at relatively low costs, TNCs have increased world trade 33 percent faster than the overall growth in world GDP. The hundred largest TNCs account for more than half the total sales and employment.

Thus far most TNCs have originated in the United States, United Kingdom, European Union, and Japan, but China and Australia are beginning to make their presence felt. By and large, it is developed-economy firms that have organized the global infrastructure for trade and investment, extracting and moving raw materials, manufacturing parts in one area of the world and assembling them in another, and ultimately moving products to myriad markets.

TNCs are rooted horizontally in multiple places, allowing them and their chosen locations to prosper. They have made critical investments in many emerging economies, from business and transportation infrastructure to education and training programs and facilities, as well as building supply chains and alliance webs with large, small, and medium-size enterprises. As a result of these strategies, five companies headquartered in developing countries made the top 100 TNC list in 2000 for the first time:

- Petronas (Venezuela)
- Hutchison Whampoa (Hong Kong, China)
- CEMEX (Mexico)
- Petroleos de Venezuela (Venezuela)
- LG Electronics (Korea)

During the recession years, the number fell to three in 2001 and two in 2002, but I expect it to rise to more than five over the next five years.

This phenomenon of increased economic growth from TNC investments and their interrelationships with small and medium-size firms will continue to stimulate needed economic growth in emerging economies, creating new, specialized regional roles for certain countries. China, for example, will probably become the world seat of manufacturing, while the Baltic region will deliver a range of specialized

The story of Costa Rica's growing export competitiveness in the 1985–2000 period is a good example of the impact of TNCs on global trade. In 1985, Costa Rica's exports totaled $1.1 billion. More than two-thirds of these were primary products, those that are simple to process. High-tech products, such as electronics and pharmaceuticals, amounted to little more than 1 percent of all exports in 1985. Costa Rica was highly dependent on the U.S. market: nearly two-thirds of all exports went to the United States.

By 2000, however, Costa Rica's exports reached $5.5 billion. Foreign direct investment grew from a 1985 level of $70 million to $409 million in 2000 as more and more TNCs chose Costa Rica as a regional manufacturing center. In fact, twenty TNC affiliates represented almost half of all of Costa Rica's exports. Intel was by far the largest investor, putting over $400 million into a new microprocessor assembly and testing facility that churned out 24 percent of all exports by 2000. Other key investors—each representing between 1 percent and 3 percent of total exports—included Dole Food, Del Monte Foods, Abbot Laboratories, and Sara Lee.

At the same time that exports were growing, the types of items exported reflected greater sophistication in Costa Rica's manufacturing industry. Exports made from Costa Rica's natural resources decreased by more than half, going from 73 percent of all exports down to 32 percent during the period. In 2000, high-tech products such as computer components accounted for 35 percent of Costa Rica's total exports.

During this fifteen-year period, Costa Rica also became less dependent on the United States as a market. In 1985, the United States represented 65 percent of Costa Rica's exports. After investments from other countries in the late 1980s and the 1990s, however, 2000 exports to the United States decreased to 24 percent of Costa Rica's total. At the same time, this percentage reflected a doubling of Costa Rica's U.S. market share.

Source: United Nations Conference on Trade and Development, *World Investment Report 2002.*

technological innovations, such as new wireless devices. Costa Rica, with its highly educated population, has become a thriving node in the GSN with increasingly diversified products and markets.

FAVORABLE CONDITIONS EXIST FOR TNC EXPANSION. TNCs' expansion has been fueled by the rapid liberalization of policy in many countries that support many different kinds of foreign direct investment (FDI) and nonequity arrangements. In 1991, thirty-five countries made changes to FDI regulations, while seventy-one did the same in 2001. Most of the changes, in excess of 90 percent, were aimed at improving the investment climate (Table 2.2).

The number of bilateral investment treaties mounts as developing countries scramble up the learning ladder to become more sophisticated evaluators of how to gain and manage TNC investments and relationships. Fueled by falling transportation and communication costs (enabled by rapid advances in these related new technologies), distance is no longer a major impediment to profit, and companies have seen the economies of integrating their dispersed operations. Efficiency plays an increasing role in attracting FDI as it contributes to export competitiveness. Ten years of the rapid expansion of TNCs have fueled more competition, driving firms to innovate by entering new markets, moving production offshore to save costs, and experimenting with new kinds of ownership and contractual relationships.

KEY TNC EXPANSION IMPACTS IN THE BADLANDS. Transnational corporations will continue their unending search for greater advantage in costs, resources, logistics, and markets. They will innovate pragmatically as they focus on enhancing their competitive advantage through optimal geographic and alliance configurations, favoring certain locations in the evolving Global Silicon Network.

Certain TNC trends will play out in the Badlands, producing plenty of churn and spitting out both winners and losers:

- The nodes (people and places) of the GSN will continue to expand, but those that are already included will have the most wealth growth and comparative advantage.
- Value chains will become more fragmented as they break into more specialized activities.

Item	1991	1992	1993	1994	1995	1996	1997	1998	1999	2000	2001	2002
Number of countries that introduced changes in their investment regimes	35	43	57	49	64	65	76	60	63	69	71	70
Number of regulatory changes	82	79	102	110	112	114	151	145	140	150	208	248
of which:												
More favorable to FDI[1]	80	79	101	108	106	98	135	136	131	147	194	236
Less favorable to FDI[2]	2	—	1	2	6	16	16	9	9	3	14	12

Table 2.2. National Regulations Favor Foreign Direct Investment.

Notes: [1] Including liberalizing changes or changes aimed at strengthening market functioning, as well as increased incentives.

[2] Including changes aimed at increasing control as well as reducing incentives.

Source: United Nations Conference on Trade and Development, *World Investment Report 2003*.

- The focus on innovation and knowledge-intensive components of the value chain—R&D, marketing, brand management, and management services—will increase.
- International production systems will become more intensely integrated on larger scales, both regionally and globally.
- Efficiency of the system—will receive the major emphasis, with less concern with precise ownership arrangements and more focus on coordination.
- Competition will be between whole production systems rather than individual factories or firms.
- Skilled workers high up the value chain will be found in emerging economies. This will affect the job structure of advanced economies, like the United States, which will be forced to innovate to create new and hybrid industries and more high-end jobs.

TNCs will also experience intense stress points along the way:

- *Increase in travel time and expenses:* Just as executives are responding to a global marketplace with a multitude of new locations, the environment will become more dangerous and costly to move around in.
- *Stress levels will increase for global workers:* Employee travel and concern about security will make life more difficult for the people involved, possibly having effects on their performance that affect their companies' bottom line.
- *Far-reaching effects of China's cornering the market for manufacturing:* From toys to technology, China will become the world's leading manufacturer; neighboring economies will have to face the long-term effects on their own manufacturing endeavors.
- *Greater difficulty for some countries to compete:* As systems get more sophisticated and assessment of the long-term potential for a global business site becomes better, companies can choose between high-risk and lower-risk sites with more confidence. This will make it more difficult for high-risk sites to be selected for investment.

The Rising Education and
Sophistication of the World's Populations

The educational level of people around the world has risen at a startling rate over the past two decades (Figure 2.7). This has helped drive the expansion of TNCs I just described.

As TNCs extend their reach into these educated regions, a new dynamic arises that further accelerates the increase in education. These regions see the potential for growth and the importance of skilled workers and respond by investing in more education and training. This groundswell has spawned a growing group of diverse, savvy, upwardly mobile workers and consumers—a global middle class—wherever the GSN extends its reach. This rising tide of knowledge workers in diverse

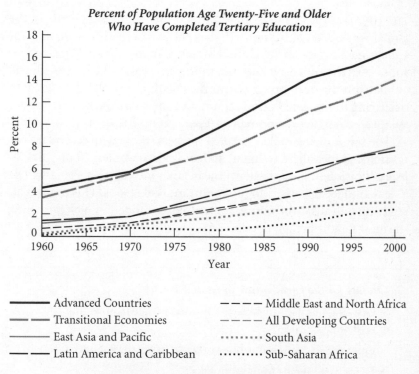

Figure 2.7. Rising Levels of Education.
Source: Robert J. Barro and Jong-Wha Lee, *International Data on Educational Attainment: Updates and Implications, 2000,* Center for International Development, Harvard University, 2000.

global locations will result in the creation of jobs all along the value chain for manufacturing, not just the lower-end jobs and cheap labor. This is the driver for the significant structural labor shift in the Badlands. It has created four trends that I describe next in more detail.

Four Trends in the Badlands

- Localization of global work
- Increasing flexibility of work
- Migration of knowledge workers
- Women go to work around the world

THE LOCALIZATION OF GLOBAL WORK. Of the 2.5 billion people in the global workforce, only about 15 percent live in the high-income advanced economies of the United States, Canada, Japan, Western Europe, Australia, and New Zealand. In the future most labor growth will come from the developing economies, with over half of the growth occurring in the Asia Pacific region and the share of the current developed economies dropping to 10 percent by 2025.

The fast-growing ranks of skilled workers (those with secondary education and specialized training) and knowledge workers (four-year college education or its equivalent) means that increasingly TNCs will be able to find local workers to fill important skilled jobs. This trend is already under way as the number of employees added by TNCs is rising the most rapidly in their developing economy affiliates. (See Figure 2.6.)

Climate for the Localization of Global Work

- Growing numbers of college-educated people in emerging economies
- Emergence of large consumer markets, particularly in Asia
- Labor cost savings from wage gaps
- Growing different regional advantages
- Global communication and information infrastructure

The interplay of TNCs and the regions in which they choose to create business is resulting in the development of a dynamic cluster economy that is a win-win solution for both the host region and the TNC. The regions win because their economies grow, creating a larger middle class, which in turn fuels more economic growth. Their people win because they find increasing work opportunities up the value chain. Those people in emerging economies who take advantage of the opportunities gain new knowledge and skills; they acquire more training and sophistication, which in turn continuously increase their value as workers. Greater numbers of them become competent and adaptable for further types of advanced work. Simultaneously TNCs win by building a local workforce full of cultural know-how that will allow the TNCs to speed the learning process with new middle-class consumers, making it possible to expand the types of services and products for the region through more savvy customization, marketing, and sales. And the region also wins by raising its competency, diversifying its economy over time, and broadening its ability to attract more TNCs. And so the cycle continues.

TNCs will move quickly to expand their skilled workforce in developing economies, exploring revenue-generating possibilities in new markets as well as realizing substantial cost savings in labor. Just how substantial is amazing; in 2003, Global Foresight, *BusinessWeek,* and Forrester Research Inc. estimated that a company could save $6000 a month by hiring a financial analyst or chip designer in India rather than in the United States, and more than $9000 for a technical support specialist.

This tendency will result in changes in the employment patterns in the advanced economies like the United States. This can be seen in the sluggish behavior of jobs throughout our nation after the 2001 recession (Figure 2.8). While a good deal of the slow recovery in jobs is the result of gains in productivity and growth through investment and exports, the country will see an increase in the number of jobs created in developing economies by U.S.-based TNCs. In the wake of the 2001 recession, TNCs will move to save costs by off-shoring higher-end jobs such as engineering and accounting given the rapid rise of advanced skill sets in many countries around the world such as China, India, Mexico, and the Philippines.

This pattern of jobs lagging after recession will be similar in other advanced economies and results from multiple shifts. The part due to offshoring of jobs is an expected result of the success of globalization.

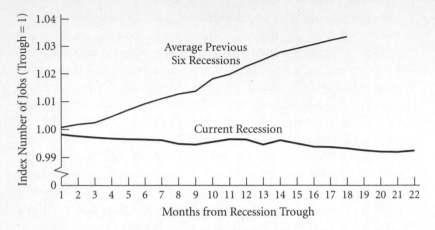

Figure 2.8.   Jobless Recovery.
Source: Bureau of Labor Statistics.

For the most part, unemployment of knowledge workers will be short-lived as they adjust to the shifts and ultimately find new jobs. But there is no guarantee that job shifts and flows will work out equitably. Some individuals whose jobs get offshored will not find replacements of equal pay and status. At the same time, many offshoring attempts will fail, resulting in the relocation of services and jobs back to the advanced economies. All this contributes to the volatility of the Badlands and the difficulty of creating new social bargains about work.

This presents a huge innovation challenge to the United States: to once again be the leader in restructuring its own economy at home by means of new and hybrid industries, new technologies, and advanced services for the global economy that in turn create the new high-end jobs. Although the next decade will feature persistent unemployment and underemployment, the U.S. economy will respond by adapting successfully to this increasingly globalized world. As an economy one of its core competencies is rapid job creation, which will serve it well in its economic transformation over the next decade.

INCREASING FLEXIBILITY OF WORK. The rapid rise of an information-based knowledge economy is breaking down the old social contract between employers and employees. In its place is a new arrangement that relies more heavily on fluid dynamics between companies and individual employees or subcontractors. The networked economy requires organizational structures that match it, dynamic interconnections to fuel growth and innovation rather than the hierarchy that supported the industrial economy. In response to market demands, management is decentralized, markets customized, work tasks decentralized. Work becomes real-time coordination through interactive networks of people who operate within organizations, across the boundaries between firms, or spanning entire continents. Workers focus on creativity and productivity in a world of work where quality is ubiquitous. The hallmark of the information economy is flexible work arrangements. This is a competition-induced, technology-enabled trend stimulated by the rapid flow of capital in a globally decentralized economy.

Climate for Increasing Flexibility of Work

- Demand from knowledge workers
- Demand from employers
- Rising number of women in workplace
- Rapid deployment of information and communication technologies
- New legal frameworks of support for alternative arrangements

---

Both the concept and practice of flexible work have existed globally for years as a tool created by large organizations to cut labor costs and manage staff more effectively. Flexible work, broadly speaking, refers to employment practices that differ from the traditional 9-to-5 job. In such arrangements, both workers and organizations gain flexibility in the time, place, contract, and tasks of work—for good or for ill. Indeed, most of today's flexible work practices fit into four categories: flexible time (flexible schedules, various hours), flexible place (working from home, telecommuting), flexible contract (independent contractor, temp-to-help work), and flexible tasks (multiskills, multitasking).

The lack of a new social contract between employers and employees and employers and independent knowledge workers often results in significant tension between organizations and workers at all levels. In the future these new agreements will be driven as much by the knowledge workers themselves as by the employers and contracting organizations, perhaps more so. Workers want and can demand a say in how, when, and where they work. New brokers and agencies will arise that will support and supply skilled workers on demand. The just-in-time worker will become a trusted option. Screening agencies will assess each worker's skill so as to efficiently match workers to specific situations. They will also show companies how to provide the right kind of technology infrastructure to support a flexible workforce and help bring them up to speed on how to facilitate effective flexible work. Companies will need to cultivate strategic relationships with these new brokers, to become their preferred customers. Often these brokers will provide workers with health and retirement benefits, education certification, and other opportunities. Individual workers will want to control their work life along as many dimensions as possible.

Employers and workers alike will experience much uncertainty and discomfort until these new arrangements are supported by a new social work contract, which may require working in the Badlands for a decade or more. But despite the uncertainty of how to accomplish it, flexible work arrangements will continue to expand.

GLOBAL PERSPECTIVE. The exact nature of flexible work will vary from country to country, depending on the social contract in each country—how social benefits such as health care, education, and pensions are provided.

United States: The United States will remain the global leader in new work arrangements. Although many countries have growing numbers of part-time workers, few have the innovations in flexible work arrangements seen in the United States. The American culture is one of trial and error as well as risk taking; its people are willing to try things out much more readily than other cultures. The nation's unionization rate is very low, and it has more flexible labor laws and regulations than those found in most other advanced economies.

Between 1985 and 1997 the percentage of full-time American workers with flexible work schedules doubled, from 12.9 percent to 27 percent; today some 30 percent of workers have flexible work arrangements. Some popular flexible work arrangements include flextime (working when and where it best suits the employer and employee), a compressed week (longer hours over fewer days), job sharing, and telecommuting. Soon, flexible work among knowledge workers in particular will no longer be considered alternative or nonstandard. It will be the norm. Such arrangements are increasingly being driven by knowledge workers, who prefer autonomy in delivering high-end services, not by the organizations who hire them.

Europe: While major flexible work forms, such as flextime, teleworking, and contracting, are offered by some European employers, they are far from prevalent. Part-time and temporary work remain the most practiced flexible work arrangements in Europe, while other relatively new flexible work options are just beginning to take hold.

As distinct from the American variety, European flex practices follow changes to the production rhythm of the networked economy, driven by customer and consumer demand as well as new information and communications technology. For example, the banking and insurance industries in Europe, facing cutthroat competition from new players and changing customer needs, extend service access hours and offer more sophisticated products and newer delivery channels than do their American counterparts. The structural change in this sector results in a rising incidence of flextime options for workers, such as flexible schedules and weekend work. As other sectors restructure in Europe, we can expect to see more of the same. A second driver will be the rapid increase in 24/7 customer service centers popping up across the Continent.

Japan: The highly rigid labor structure in Japan is under tremendous pressure to change but will do so slowly. Flexible work practices do exist in Japan, although incidence of the newest forms is marginal. The proportion of part-time workers is increasing and currently amounts to more than 25 percent of the labor force. But years of economic recession have created an employment doldrums and lack of innovation. As Japan solves its economic problems, flexible work patterns will probably evolve to fit the changes.

China: The employment prize now in China is to work for a multinational company full time, even though the goal is individual betterment and upward mobility. Interestingly, most flexible work arrangements occur within the state-owned enterprises (SOEs), among redundant workers and older workers who are not skilled; these arrangements are driven by the SOEs, not the workers. The Chinese are ultimately very entrepreneurial. As the conditions for internal entrepreneurship (within companies) improve, look for Chinese knowledge workers to innovate in all kinds of flexible work arrangements. Given the large technical and scientific workforce in China, these knowledge workers will be in huge demand both at home and abroad, creating a new dynamic between enterprises and workers.

Mexico and Latin America: Flexible work patterns have made only minor inroads among knowledge workers in Mexico and Latin America, regions that have a much stronger tradition of regular full-time employment. The knowledge economy within these countries is also growing at a slow pace, and competition for jobs at the high end is intense. Women play a less prominent role in the workforce than in other leading developing economies. These regions have not attracted as much FDI as, say, China has, and thus are not creating as many new jobs. Nor do they boast the large technical and scientific workforce of a China or an India. Ultimately, however, these regions will follow global trends in flexible work in response to the growth of the networked economy.

MIGRATION OF KNOWLEDGE WORKERS. The global marketplace for highly skilled workers will expand and become more integrated over the next ten years. These workers already account for a significant number of immigrants (twenty-five years and older) to OECD countries (Table 2.3).

Knowledge workers will more readily cross national borders, although various barriers such as the growth of global terrorism will persist. Most countries will reappraise their immigration policies, resulting in greater scrutiny and surveillance of some populations, particularly in the United States. Yet in the long run the need for skilled workers will overrule the security concerns of countries with advanced economies. But they must deal with a plethora of public policy, cultural, and social challenges if they are to achieve full, long-term economic benefits.

Climate for Global Flow of Skilled Immigrants

- Aging and shrinking workforces in advanced economies
- Better employment and living conditions in advanced economies
- Technical skills gaps and shortages in native populations in most countries
- Policies encouraging immigration of skilled workers
- Unemployment and underemployment across skill and education levels in developing economies

Country	Total Immigrants	Educational Level		
		Primary or Less	Secondary	Tertiary
East Asia				
China, PR	722,400	148,029	185,295	389,076
Indonesia	142,540	3,910	32,347	106,283
Philippines	356,134	27,605	70,079	258,451
Eastern Europe, Central Asia				
Turkey	1,913,782	263,078	534,429	1,116,275
Latin America, Caribbean				
Brazil	176,519	16,026	64,097	96,396
Middle East, North Africa				
Morocco	560,658	30,706	168,179	361,773
Tunisia	142,828	10,027	41,782	91,019
Egypt	20,373	733	3,796	15,844
South Asia				
Bangladesh	44,417	3,852	12,902	27,663
India	375,283	18,471	57,199	299,613
Pakistan	85,668	6,022	22,458	57,188
Sri Lanka	64,143	1,455	16,741	45,947
Total	4,721,944	539,396	1,263,951	2,918,597

Table 2.3.   Number of Immigrants to the OECD by Level of Educational Attainment, 2000.

Notes: No data available on number of immigrants from Albania, Armenia, Colombia, Croatia, Dominican Republic, El Salvador, Guatemala, Mexico, Nigeria, Peru, and Sudan. Immigrants defined as immigrant or foreign-born population by individual countries in the OECD, age twenty-five or over. Primary education or less corresponds to up to eight years of schooling; secondary to nine to twelve years of schooling, and tertiary to more than twelve years of schooling.

Source: Robert J. Barro and Jong-Wha Lee, *International Data on Educational Attainment: Updates and Implications, 2000,* Center for International Development, Harvard University, 2000; Organisation for Economic Co-operation and Development (OECD), *Trends in International Migration: Annual Report,* 2001.

International migration increased significantly during the last decade of the twentieth century. Those migrating did so both legally and illegally, and more than 50 percent wanted to reunify families. In two-thirds of advanced economies of the Organisation for Economic Co-operation and Development (OECD), foreigners—that is, noncitizens—accounted for more than 5 percent of the labor force. Although most immigration still brings in low-skilled labor, immigration policies are now bifurcating to reduce barriers and facilitate the flow of high-end talent. Many immigrants receive temporary employment permits; admission of permanent foreign workers is low, especially in Europe. However, the number of zones in which citizens of certain countries flow freely from their homeland to other countries is increasing: between New Zealand and Australia, between Britain and Ireland, among the Nordic countries, and more recently across the European Union. These passages, following the ebb and flow of business cycles, help keep labor markets flexible and relieve spot sector shortages.

People are migrating from a wider range of countries of origin to a wider range of destinations than ever before. This expansion to new countries and cultures will heighten cross-cultural issues. As global labor flows increase, policies and attitudes toward immigrants must change.

GLOBAL PERSPECTIVE. Despite the flow of millions of people across borders every year, most countries view immigrants and minority populations negatively. In fact Canada is the only country where a majority of the population report a positive attitude toward immigrants. Italy leads the list with 67 percent opposed. Out of forty-two countries surveyed by the Pew Global Attitudes Project, thirty-eight support tighter immigration regulations and controls. Americans are pretty evenly split on the subject and have the second-most favorable attitude toward immigrants of any of the advanced economies, with 43 percent opposed. Clearly, countries wishing to benefit from needed skill sets must improve potential immigrants' access to human services and must provide wider citizenship opportunities for both adults and children.

United States: Immigration greatly benefits U.S. economic growth, with estimates indicating that immigrants are responsible for adding $1 trillion to the country's annual GDP. The last fifteen years have seen a marked shift in immigrants' skill level and educational attainment. In just six years the number of foreign-born college graduates in the labor force has increased a whopping 43.8 percent. In 2000 some 26 percent of foreign-born workers were college graduates, on a par with the native-born employee population.

Undergoing a notable transformation, the American workforce is becoming the major center for the management, information resources, and professional services that drive global economic enterprises. The skill sets in demand for this expansion cannot be filled by natives alone. However, U.S. immigration policies, still guided by assumptions from the 1930s, are based on seeing foreigners as a threat to American job security and income and assume that family reunification is the main driver behind immigration; but that is changing. The realities of the new global labor force call for new approaches to immigration with more realistic assumptions, most especially an understanding that immigrants are a vital part of U.S. economic growth.

Europe: The immigration of skilled workers in Europe is also on the rise. Because of shortages and high demands, these new, more skilled immigrants demand greater social and economic benefits for themselves and their families than traditional unskilled immigrants received. Immigrants today also want to be more integrated into society; yet xenophobia in most OECD countries keeps immigrant populations isolated from the mainstream, which further feeds deep suspicions about foreigners. In effect, cultural attitudes have not kept pace with the demands for labor. Even when employment is high, proposals to use immigrants to satisfy needs for labor tends to inflame national passions.

Because most European countries are rapidly aging, immigrants offer host countries a much-needed youthful labor force, while simultaneously introducing greater labor flexibility. But before long-term economic gains may occur, these countries must address deep cultural and political issues.

Japan: Japan's deep aversion to immigrants and its recent economic doldrums prevent it from applying this global resource effectively. Nor will this change soon. Japan already has some of the strictest immigration laws in the world and the lowest immigration rate among the advanced economies. Its low number of calls for restricting immigrants is due to the existence of very restrictive laws now.

China: Like all emerging economies, China is experiencing a brain drain, particularly in the sciences. Many talented young Chinese who leave to study for advanced degrees in more developed economies stay to find work and ultimately try to remain. Still, China's growing knowledge and technology industries are filled with long-term opportunities. Look for brain circulation and bicoastal work flowing both ways across the Pacific as young Chinese become binational, making the best of both worlds.

On the other hand, China has been the recipient of a large share of the world's FDI, and with that come legions of expatriate workers from around the world. Few of them desire to emigrate to China, but China's strong desire for this investment has prompted the Asian giant to work fast and furious to make life more attractive to outsiders.

WOMEN GO TO WORK AROUND THE WORLD. Over the last half-century women have joined the formal workforce around the globe in growing numbers. They have increased their enrollment in education at both the secondary and tertiary level. Young women outnumber men among college graduates in many countries.

From a public policy standpoint, many governments realize that economic growth and low unemployment will depend on adding entrants to the workforce and the continued rise of small business. The last few decades have seen a consistent push to increase female higher education, and women are now performing better in school than men (Figure 2.9). Recently, new public policies ensure equal rights for women in the workforce and provide support for women starting their own businesses.

Many of the most educated and experienced women find greater satisfaction in working in small businesses and the public sector than they do in corporate life. Increasingly, they leave large corporations to create their own businesses or move into public service agencies. Many

---

Climate That Supports Women Entrepreneurs

- Increase in female higher education
- Public policy support for equal employment rights
- Government incentives for women to open new businesses to combat unemployment
- Increasing availability of start-up microfunds
- Retirement of older male managers, providing women with an incubator for leadership and management skills
- Rise in women's organizations that provide information and support
- Technology that facilitates communication with family anytime, anyplace

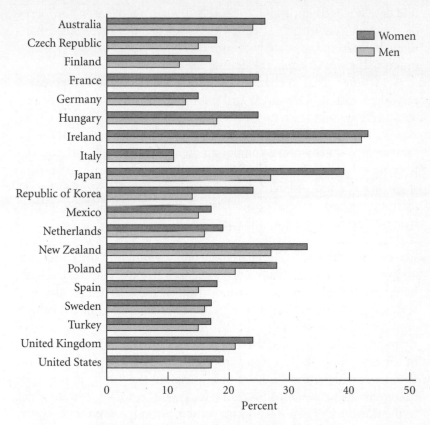

Figure 2.9.   Tertiary Graduation Rates, 2001.
Source: Organisation for Economic Co-operation and Development (OECD), 2003.

studies show that teenage girls and new college graduates find the environment of large companies unattractive. There is a sea change in the attitudes of young women toward work. They have seen enough to know that the harried superwomen of the Baby Boom generation didn't have it all. They place a high value on balance in their lives. Young women give flexibility a high priority and readily choose to stay out of the rat race.

Although widespread gender discrimination has restricted advancement up the ladder, women have made modest gains, achieving leadership and management positions in large and small companies alike. Increasing numbers of women have used that knowledge to become entrepreneurs, starting their own businesses in both advanced and developing countries, and especially in the United States. The role of women will gain further importance as older, predominately male managers retire in the advanced economies, and as the number of women entering the workforce in the developing world continues to grow.

Yet women need to change, too. As a group they have not created networks with other women and men that combine both work and social activities and that create access to future leaders. They also have not yet developed a leadership style for top management that can be emulated by other women coming up the ranks. They are just now beginning to support each other and to realize the importance of helping other women and actively providing role models for them. Nor are they as good as men at negotiating higher salaries and compensation packages. This is sure to change in the Badlands.

GLOBAL PERSPECTIVE. The changing role of women in the workforce and the rise of feminism are both long-term trends shaping the Badlands. Many regard them as the most radical social drivers of this historic cycle of innovation. These trends are still unfolding as women continue to struggle for equality. Around the world people are recognizing that life is more satisfying if women work and men share in household duties, but in many countries the belief that the husband should provide and the wife should focus on the family and household remains strong. Muslim countries are by far the most traditional in their attitudes toward working women, although even these countries are changing.

That said, younger women, particularly those from the Net Generation, are getting educated in larger and larger numbers in a multitude of countries. There will be more young female knowledge workers in 2010 than men.

United States: Women are often discouraged by the corporate glass ceiling and find better opportunities as entrepreneurs. Educational gains give women more control, and in turn more success in founding their own businesses. Women-owned businesses increased by 16 percent in the United States from 1992 to 1997, primarily in the service sectors, a fertile milieu for women to build leadership and managerial competency as well as create a work life that they directly control. What will give them an incentive to join the management ranks of large companies when the need to replace retiring male managers rises sharply?

Europe: European women have made less progress moving into management than their counterparts in the United States. They also have not been as aggressive in seeking to develop their own businesses. The number of women with higher education is smaller in Europe and less well distributed across disciplines.

Japan: The wage gap in Japan is widening, and most working women hold only temporary or part-time positions in large companies. This dismal situation has motivated Japanese women to experiment with entrepreneurship. Japanese women tend to start companies that offer services and products perceived as lacking in their daily lives. Women constituted more than 8 percent of entrepreneurs in 2000, up from 5 percent of entrepreneurs in 1995 and 2.4 percent in 1980. And the numbers continue to rise.

China: Chinese attitudes toward women at work vary widely across generations. Despite egalitarian slogans from the early days of Communism—such as "Women Hold Up Half the World"—China remains a male-dominated society. That said, most Chinese women work, although few hold high positions in business or government. China's younger generations, though, are much more egalitarian, if only for utilitarian reasons. Young Chinese families need two incomes in order to prosper. Large numbers of young women are enrolled in college, and they are ambitious to achieve their goals. As China's young women become more sophisticated and educated, expect them to be a major force in the workplace.

The Middle East: By and large the Middle East is very conservative about women working in general, especially when it comes to their working in the same places as men. Deep cultural definitions of gender roles and legal structures make it more difficult for women to develop their full potential in this region. Again look to young women to make bigger gains as globalization and connections with other women leaders around the world give them new ideas and support for pushing ahead; through much of the Muslim world, a majority of women already report favoring the possibility of outside work—and many men agree with them (Table 2.4).

Mexico and Latin America: Few women occupy high corporate positions anywhere in Latin America. Machismo still reigns in the corporate setting. More women leaders have found jobs in the nonprofit sector, where many feel they can do the most good for their countries. More and more women are pursuing and achieving higher education, but there is less social acceptance for women running businesses. Progress will be slow in Latin America.

South Africa: Politics and business are still dominated by men in Africa, and South Africa is no different. But African women are strong

Women Should Be Permitted to Work Outside the Home

	Men %	Women %	Difference
Bangladesh	36	57	+21
Lebanon	58	75	+17
Pakistan	24	41	+17
Uzbekistan	64	77	+13
Uganda	30	43	+13
Turkey	60	72	+12
Ghana	32	40	+12
Ivory Coast	66	74	+8
Senegal	60	68	+8
Nigeria	32	38	+6
Mali	51	56	+5
Indonesia	20	24	+4
Jordan	13	16	+3
Tanzania	47	47	0

Table 2.4.   Muslim Women Ready to Work.

Source: Views of a Changing World, The Pew Research Center for the People and the Press, June 2003.

community leaders and have made strides in the development of microenterprises. Look for continued leadership in microcommunity enterprises but slow progress in the world of business. Again, as more young South African women gain education, they will slowly break down barriers.

Key Impacts from the Rise of an Educated and Sophisticated Global Population in the Badlands

- Skilled labor and a growing cadre of young, well-educated knowledge workers around the world will facilitate the accelerated growth of the networked economy in major developing countries such as China, India, Mexico, Brazil, and Turkey, as well as in Russia and some Eastern European states.
- By 2010 China will produce more actual numbers of scientists and engineers as college graduates than the United States. India's numbers are not far behind. This will lead to more offshoring of high-end jobs to both India and China. Offshoring of jobs will continue at an accelerated pace as skills become available in the new emerging markets where TNCs want to grab market share.

- Women will continue to make strides in attaining top management positions and pay equity in the advanced economies. The accelerator will be the difficulty in filling the pipeline with traditional male types as well as a critical mass of women in management who will facilitate the recruitment of others. Progress will be slower in the emerging economies.

- The United States will continue to set the trends; U.S. companies will adopt new practices and new technologies first and fast, with a much slower uptake by other countries.

- Fewer expatriates will work globally as both education and sophistication increase in the global workforce around the world. More and more groups of skilled workers will offer their services as a high-performance team.

- Rather than one new social contract for work between workers and employers, we will see *many*. In the United States companies will experiment with different models, ultimately sorting out those that work from those that don't. Other countries will adopt the experiments that work out best.

- Tensions between workers and organizations will rise, and independent knowledge workers will drive the formation of decentralized and boundaryless organizations.

- Look for the continued increase in global middle-class consumer numbers around the world.

- Despite concerns about terrorism, migration of skilled workers will continue.

New Geopolitical Issues and Boundaries

Over the last fifty years geopolitics has been dominated by the major Western democracies in North America and Europe and has been governed by broad agreements among them, fashioned in response to the rise of Nazism, two devastating world wars, and the subsequent cold war with the Soviet Union. The democracies embraced mutual protection pacts, supported the stability of domestic market economies, and pressed for open international exchange. Some of the transnational organizations they created to support such efforts included the Bank for International Settlement, the North Atlantic Treaty Organization, the International Monetary Fund, the World Trade Organization, and the United Nations. Through these agreements they have prospered and, despite some squabbling over certain key issues (such as competition and the social safety net), they agree on the basic tenets of liberal democracy.

September 11, 2001, stands as a symbolic marker of the end of the old geopolitics and the beginning of the new. During the cold war a whole slew of powerful new weapons were created as a response to the threat of nuclear war, but the transnational terrorism of today demands a different response. Should terrorists gain access to nuclear bombs or other weapons of mass destruction and use them, the result would be devastating. And unfortunately, our outmoded command-and-control military apparatus and mind-sets are simply not geared for meeting this challenge. The tactics required by the Information Revolution apply to the military and security forces as well as to business organizations. We need a self-organizing defense network, not a hierarchal Homeland Security Department. We need to develop a new attitude about defense similar to that of the homesteaders of the nineteenth century, when everyone had a stake in personal and family security.

Terrorism is creating a new global power beyond the Western democracies because fighting it on a global scale successfully requires the active participation of the diverse rising powers such as China and India and Russia. Their collaboration gives them more power and opportunities to participate in a wider variety of decisions. An unintended consequence of terrorism is that it is helping people in countries at all stages of development realize the extent of globalization and the likelihood that it is not a reversible phenomenon.

But transnational terrorism is only one of the rising issues of the new geopolitics. Others include global disagreements on the efficacy of globalization, on the benefits (and pitfalls) of international trade, and on how to close the growing wealth gap among peoples. It is globalization of economies and societies, not a world war, that is reconfiguring power and creating a new world order. Making the choices that build a proper foundation for this new geopolitical reality is the critical work today's global leaders face in the rugged transition zone of the Badlands.

In the process of taking on this work we will experience several other divisive issues, coupled with healthy and sometimes bitter debates. These issues include war, as witnessed by the U.N. Security Council debate about the Iraq War. America's preemptive war in Iraq and its messy aftermath has unsettled world politics and driven a wedge between old global friends such as the United States, Germany, and France. This has led to a heated discussion about how to deal with the United States as the sole superpower and has led to an increase in a negative opinion about the United States around the world. While wars are probably inevitable in a world of stark economic disparities, if they occurred they would look very different from those fought in the past. They would probably be regional and on a much smaller scale, waged not by nations but by groups of terrorists. What does winning wars such as these really look like?

Formation of a global civil society lags far behind the global economy, resulting in the growth of a host of big social issues. For example, concern is growing about the potential for further global epidemics such as SARS. The world's public health infrastructure has not kept pace with the ability of viruses to travel across borders. Education is lagging behind the needs of a knowledge economy, and immigration laws differ widely.

Other major divisive issues must be resolved in the emerging new geopolitics, including access to oil and other natural resources, environmental protection, and immigration, not to mention the importance of closing the wealth gap. Two engines of the former political system, paternalism and nation states, are going into irreversible decline, displaced by the Information Revolution and growth of a networked society. All these geopolitical issues will sustain volatility in the Badlands.

Key Impacts of the New Geopolitics in the Badlands

- Terrorism and the threat of terrorism will continue, as will local wars in trouble spots around the world. The gap between the haves and have-nots is too wide to avoid violence and war.

- The global economy will move faster than politics and regulations. Issues of mismatch between problems and current institutions will increase. This is to be expected in a historical cycle of innovation at this stage. Global agreements will have to be created to address certain problems, such as the Global AIDS Project, or setting standards for business and technology. These global agreements will accelerate the pace of globalization as well as the restructuring of governments and large social institutions.

- The wealth gap will continue to grow and be more visible. This will make the political environment more volatile.

- There will be an increase in social networks of all kinds—for good and for ill. This has the potential to create a new civil society in many different places globally.

- New powers will arise by 2020. They will also go through a number of growing pains, but China and Asia will both gain clout.

- The likelihood that wild cards (high-impact, low-probability events) will occur is higher than normal. Consider the impact of a major epidemic that kills millions of people or of a major act of bioterrorism.

The Growing Wealth Gap

The long-standing wealth gap persists despite the growing integration of developing countries into the global economy. The developing countries of the Asia Pacific region have the most income growth, particularly in China, Korea, and India. These gains, however, are growing more slowly than the gap between richer and poorer countries, as shown in Figure 2.10.

Income growth tends to be regionalized within countries as well, as in China, which has a marked gap between its coastal and inland provinces. Within countries, disparities are growing between higher and lower income households across all strata in both the developing

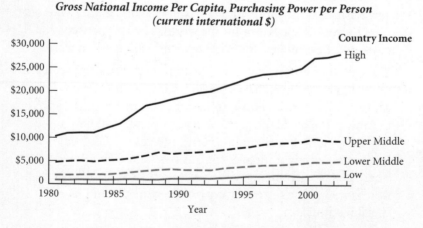

Figure 2.10.   Regional Wealth Gaps Persist.
Source: World Bank, *World Development Indicators Online,* 2003.

and the developed economies. As noted earlier, people are likely to hold their local and national governments accountable for their problems and tend to have a positive view of globalization's impact on their countries, although in some countries a significant number of people still have no opinion about globalization, including Russia, Pakistan, Bulgaria, and (surprisingly) Japan. This suggests that people are still fluid in their attitudes.

BLACK HOLE OF MARGINALIZATION. The information economy has a strong tendency to polarize the wealthy and the poor even further. To be included in the game means that you already have a strong base of education and sophistication—the skills in language, math, computers, and social interactions that sustain work in a multicultural business environment. Places where people already have the right skills tend to grow and build on themselves, and people elsewhere cannot play because they lack the skills and resources. More problematic is the fact that they can't attain them easily. Thus those countries that are excluded are like stars that fall into black holes in the universe: They will have a terribly hard time getting out. With the advent of the knowledge economy, people who have been marginalized in the industrialized economy become further marginalized. Roughly two billion people are at risk of permanent marginalization. They cannot escape the gravitational pull of poverty without help in closing the education gap—a very long-term investment indeed.

GROWING AMBIVALENCE ABOUT HELPING. Unfortunately, not a scrap of evidence suggests that this tendency to polarize both ends of the spectrum will reverse itself. At the same time that marginalized people are becoming further isolated, ambivalence is growing in many countries about offering help. Although people generally support the theory that government should see to it that no one is in need, the strength of support for government to actually act to care for the poor is slipping in most countries (Table 2.5).

Increasing numbers of people in many countries believe that it is the individual's fault, not society's, if someone is not successful (Figure 2.11). Taken together, these two trends do not bode well for finding ways to include society's marginalized groups.

KEY IMPACTS OF THE WEALTH GAP IN THE BADLANDS. The social trends and changes under way in this cycle of innovation, including the growing wealth gap, are not irreversible, but interventions are required to

Differing Views of Social Safety Net (Percent Completely Agree)

	Government Should Guarantee No One in Need			Government Has Responsibility to Care for Poor		
	1991 %	2002 %	Change %	1991 %	2002 %	Change %
Russia	33	74	+41	70	70	0
Ukraine	37	76	+39	69	57	−12
Czech Republic	35	58	+23	67	57	−10
Slovak Republic	51	70	+19	62	51	−11
France	51	62	+11	62	50	−12
Germany (Total)	47	57	+10	50	45	−5
Former West Germany	41	52	+11	45	43	−2
Former East Germany	67	77	+10	64	51	−13
Italy	64	71	+7	66	48	−18
Bulgaria	60	67	+7	81	67	−14
United Kingdom	59	62	+3	62	59	−3
United States	36	34	−2	23	29	+6
Poland	73	64	−9	56	59	+3

Table 2.5.   Low Support for Safety Net.

Source: Views of a Changing World, The Pew Research Center for the People and the Press, June 2003.

change their direction. Coming to grips with the wealth gap is the biggest social choice we will face. Thus far we are not doing enough about it. Although we do have programs aimed at specific issues affecting these marginalized groups, the problem is so systemic that piecemeal approaches will not reverse it. Few signs currently indicate that the requisite large-scale effort will be made, but we are still early in our journey through the Badlands.

Until we do make different systemic choices, the increasing wealth gaps within and between countries will continue. This is my forecast for at least the next ten years, and here are some of the likely consequences:

Increased business risk: The widening gap between the world's haves and have-nots will increase risk to business across most regions of the world. On a macro scale it is likely to spawn an increase in terrorism, within countries and internationally. Although firms can avoid dangerous countries altogether, they won't be able to avoid the wealth gaps

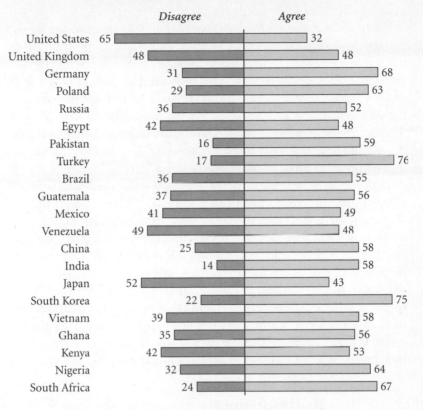

Figure 2.11.   Impact of Outside Factors.
Source: Views of a Changing World, The Pew Research
Center for the People and the Press, June 2003.

within countries. Nor will they be able to avoid preparing for global terrorism, given the climate of persistent threats. This will damage bottom lines, hit by increased expenditures for risk assessment and enhanced security as well as rising insurance costs.

Global criminal networks: Historically, wealth gaps have resulted in the growth of criminal networks, both large and small. If people cannot participate in the formal economy, they will turn to crime to earn money. An example of this is the revival of opium farms in post-Taliban Afghanistan. Al Qaeda is certainly the most visible global criminal network. The rise of kidnapping rings aimed at foreign business leaders in a number of countries such as Mexico is another example. These trends will add to the security concerns of global business as well as pose social challenges of some concern.

More social networks for the good: Not all responses to the wealth gap will be threats. Some of the popular ambivalence about the safety net is a concern that perhaps governments are not the best organizations to address social issues. With increased connectivity it will be easier for private individuals and organizations to form global social networks to address specific issues, like the recent Global AIDS Project. As more of these citizen-initiated efforts are launched, they could become quite powerful, both globally and locally, reaching a critical mass that could affect large populations. There are some signs that the increased wealth now at the disposal of private individuals and new private foundations could be put to good use. If these two groups are interconnected, their effectiveness could make a difference.

More regional responses: The GSN is an interconnected regional economic system that could spawn social innovations. The wealthier and empowered regions, for example, the nodes of the GSN, could begin to take on social issues on a regional basis and ultimately could work across regions to address the problems that poorer communities face, such as inferior education. This will not happen quickly, but the potential is there. Regardless of the pace at which such responses appear, look for more innovation at the regional rather than the national level.

Failing Institutions

We are poised at a moment in this historical cycle of innovation when we see social institutions failing and flailing all around us. Understanding this to be a predictable part of these historical cycles of innovation still leaves us to cope with many critical societal institutions at their weakest. As mentioned earlier, there is a mismatch between the scale of our problems and the ability of institutions to manage them, as with SARS. We are at the beginning of a cycle of innovation when we must begin to reinvent our social institutions, for better and not for worse. National governments are too small to solve the huge issues of globalization—either locally or globally—and the new solutions will probably be created in forums quite different from anything that exists today. Many institutions, from government to philanthropic organizations to agencies of education and health care, are ill suited to the evolving social issues created by the global networked economy and society. The existing means of financing key social services such as education and health care are simply not sustainable. Schumpeter believes that the process of creative destruction is inherently damaging to social institutions. He is very pessimistic that they can thrive and adapt well.

I disagree with him that it is a foregone conclusion that social institutions will not be able to innovate to match the realities of the networked free market economy. Although it is a huge challenge, I see no reason to believe that the leaders of this era are not up to their historic task. But in the meantime conditions will be very uncomfortable.

Here are some of the institutions that are in decline and in need of radical innovation in this Badlands transition zone between eras. They will continue being undercut by the ongoing creative destruction of the economy.

GOVERNMENTS. People around the world feel that governments are not run efficiently and are not very effective. Even though they tend to believe that their government has the interests of the people at heart, people generally express a mistrust of individual politicians and a tremendous disenchantment with political corruption. Even the United Nations, an early prototype of a future global governing body, is perceived as getting weaker.

BUSINESS LEADERSHIP. It is common knowledge that business leaders, especially in large companies, are not trusted and admired. This decline in confidence began years ago and has continued at an accelerated pace since the year 2000. Some of this decline was caused by a mismatch between the expectations people have of corporate leaders and the contemporary reality of running large, complex global corporations. Some of the lack of confidence is deserved, given continuing leadership scandals and excessive compensation packages that seem to keep soaring even when profits go down and job losses increase. It is not surprising that people have more confidence and trust in leaders of smaller companies than of larger ones. The increased difficulty of running large companies in a volatile global economy is reflected in the number of performance-based departures of CEOs over the last ten years (Figure 2.12).

MILITARY LEADERSHIP. People would like to see problems solved in nonmilitary ways and are increasingly wary of the way military campaigns are waged. They denounce ethnic cleansing, retaliatory raids

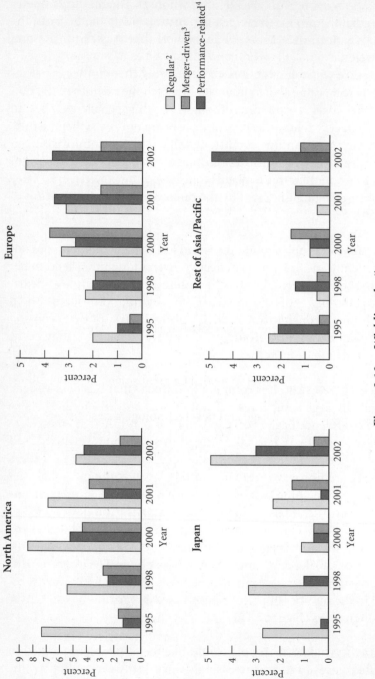

CEO succession rate, percent of sample[1]

Figure 2.12.   Wielding the Axe.

Notes: [1] Sample of 2,500 of the world's largest companies by market capitalization. [2] Planned retirements, a CEO's acceptance of a better position elsewhere, health-related departures, and death in office. [3] Departures initiated at board level, by poor financial and managerial performance or "personal reasons." [4] Where a CEO's job is eliminated following an acquisition.

Source: Booz–Allen Hamilton; *The Economist*, October 25, 2003. Used by permission.

on neighbors in response to suicide bombings, "clean" and techno-logically managed air strikes in Iraq, not to mention the ongoing regional wars between factions in a number of countries. The diffusion of television around the world and instant news has made war in all forms visible to people everywhere, providing them with a new opportunity to witness and react to war in ways never possible before.

EDUCATION LEADERSHIP. Although more people around the world are achieving secondary and college education, the availability of good schools and good teachers is tremendously uneven. The public education infrastructure in most countries is underfunded and has not kept up with needed investments in new technologies. Particularly at risk are those countries and regions that are not currently linked into the GSN.

HEALTH CARE LEADERSHIP. We are on the verge of a global health care crisis. Many countries lack a sustainable delivery system, and there is no global standard for public health to prevent and manage global epidemics, which are inevitable in a global world. The United States has one of the most expensive and fragmented health delivery systems, one that leaves millions of Americans without access to health care. And quality is declining everywhere. The great social democracies of Europe are finding it difficult to sustain their national health care systems as their populations age and new technologies raise costs. China let its health care system decline with the move to a market economy in the 1980s. People around the world are concerned about health care. Even while they are thankful for some new access to miracle drugs, most feel that their health care is getting worse.

Key Impacts of Failing Social Institutions in the Badlands

- None of these failings will be quickly or easily reversed and all will probably get worse before they get better. The innovation imperative in the social sector looms much larger than in the economic sector, and it's much harder to tackle.

- First and foremost, the Badlands must be a crucible for the kind of diverse leadership needed to reinvent civil society. Chapter Three takes up the challenge of leadership and the new paradigm that is needed.

- Global and local societies will be faced with big social choices, especially with regard to allocating resources to close the wealth gap and build new civil societies. The world has enough resources—financial and human—to solve issues and create new institutions that match the new environment, but the situation calls for radical reorganization and reallocation.

- We will have to come to grips with the need for safety nets for those who have not been included in the GSN to date—that includes the majority of the world's population. There is no way that individuals can close the gap between what they know and what they need on their own. We need to reinvent our social safety nets and couple them with other incentives to develop quickly.

- We run the risk of putting an excessive amount of resources into defending ourselves against some of globalization's effects—developing security and strengthening military programs. We must think differently about these problems and come up with innovative solutions that bring diverse groups together in dialogue and prevent destructive clashes of cultures and terrorism.

- We are likely to have more dysfunctional politics around the world. The current global institutions aren't up to managing our global political problems, and there is a mismatch between national governments and global problems.

PARTING THOUGHTS

Nobody really knows exactly what globalization is—or will become; nevertheless, it is the defining issue of this transition zone that I call the Badlands. Most of the first half of the twenty-first century will be spent figuring out what globalization is as we engage with it. It is very much an emergent phenomenon. The greatest uncertainty of the Badlands is what form of globalization will ultimately emerge. The globalization of the economy is well under way, but a global civil society lags far behind. In this sense the progress of globalization is quite narrow to date. Given the overwhelming positive attitudes toward globalization, it is unlikely that a backlash will develop against it powerful enough to slow it down significantly, barring a wild-card event like a significant increase in terrorism, a pan-global depression, or some hideous global epidemic.

For globalization to succeed, we must ultimately create a global civil society supported by supranational organizations. If global economic innovation is not accompanied by social and political innovation, then globalization will fail. By *failing* I mean that we will live in a fragmented, dangerous globalized world rather than an integrated, inclusive one. But these innovations depend on a robust global economy, not an anemic one. In all aspects of globalization, innovation replaces tradition. Political and social transformations will occur at a slower pace than the economic innovations we are daily experiencing. This is both the danger *and* the opportunity of the Badlands. Structural social and cultural changes are slow and messy. This has always been true historically and will be true during this new cycle of innovation.

In the rest of this book I delve into the predictable pains and new capabilities that leaders and organizations need to resolve and create in order to move forward. The next topic is leadership and how to use the Badlands as a crucible for the hero's journey we all will need to take.

CHAPTER THREE

Lead the Journey of Your Lifetime

We have been in the Badlands before and thrived, although each cycle presents its own unique challenges.

L eaders in the Badlands face many diverse and urgent challenges. Both history and the sheer amount of new science and technology in this historical cycle of innovation suggest that the next twenty-five years will see transformation on a global scale. How can you lead in such an unknowable environment? This new context calls for a different kind of leadership readiness. To borrow a phrase from Linux developer Eric Raymond, an organization's entry into the Badlands is "like moving from the cathedral to the bazaar."

In a cathedral roles and rituals are established, and your best opportunities come from playing by the rules. A bazaar, however, is a marketplace where anyone can play, and roles and rules are very flexible. Information flows in multiple directions and the best intelligence is embedded in social networks. Your best opportunities come from your connections and your capacity to learn quickly, seizing the moment over and over and over again. In the shift from the cathedral to the bazaar, hierarchy loses its supremacy as the definer of leadership. In much the same way the far-flung interconnectivity of the global economy, with its overlapping networks and flow of people and knowledge, will relentlessly change the reference points of leadership and identity for the next decade.

Nowhere is this more true than in companies like Motorola, whose board has been dominated by family for years. For a long time this was a successful formula. Family connections were the main reference points for leadership. But then Motorola faced growing difficulties and needed more diversity to compete in a global marketplace The recent resignation of CEO Christopher Galvin after struggling unsuccessfully to revitalize the company ended more than thirty years of family leadership.

Context is critically important to successful leadership; when the context changes dramatically, so must leadership. Many of today's leaders honed their leadership skills in the relatively stable economic

---

PAIN #1: LEADERSHIP INSECURITY—FEAR AND INADEQUACY

Since once-successful habits and intuition no longer apply in this turbulent environment, leaders throughout the organization are afflicted by profound feelings of fear and inadequacy. They find that their trusted inner circle, a homogeneous group, doesn't seem to be providing insights and strategies that fit the Badlands context. Things feel out of control.

New Capability: Leadership Readiness

Readiness is the capacity to respond extraordinarily well to whatever you encounter in your environment, no matter how harsh or how distracting it is, learning from it quickly, taking bold action and being ready for the next challenge already coming into view. Readiness requires courageously using the Badlands as a crucible for rapid learning of new competencies to match the challenges in this uncertain environment. Leadership is a performing art; if you are not acting, you are not learning. Readiness includes building habits of both collaboration and innovation. It calls for creating trust and intimacy with many different kinds of people that results in radical innovation. And—just as important—it includes Self-Leadership, personal development, and the expansion of identity.

environment of the late Industrial Plains; there they found they could rely on their intuition to respond to leadership challenges. They wielded a good deal of control over the environment, given their considerable knowledge of its hierarchal structure, organizational culture, and overall workings. But now they are traveling outside their comfort zone in a context that offers only uncertainty. And they sense that their old ways of leading won't work.

Each day today's business leaders encounter multiple, diverse decision-making canyons flowing fast with paradoxical information that demands a rapid read and reaction. It's easy to understand how leaders gazing into this rugged terrain from the edge of the Industrial Plains may experience feelings similar to those of Lewis and Clark as they encountered the Badlands of the Dakotas centuries before. Awe and a deep sense of inadequacy wrestle with excitement at the prospect of cutting a trail through this formidable landscape to the riches that lie on the other side. From the high plains, you can see a long way across the peaks of the awesome land ahead. But never mistake a clear view for a short trip. The landscape is slashed by deadly chasms and spiked with impassable crags, often hidden behind smooth, innocent-looking plateaus. Fierce weather systems can appear suddenly and exact a big toll if you don't respond fast and effectively. Just knowing that despite prior success you may lack the readiness to respond effectively lies at the root of the first Badlands pain, Leadership Insecurity, with its deep feelings of fear and inadequacy.

New Identities: The sense of self evolves as history unfolds and the context of life changes.

Imagine the feelings of Joan Vincenz, director of operations and planning for Delta Air Lines. After the terrorist acts of 9/11 shocked the nation and her industry, she took a key leadership role by encouraging flight attendants to keep flying and to stick with Delta, despite cutbacks, all the while maintaining a sharp focus on the airline's business goals. Despite the severe personal challenge caused by feelings of fear, insecurity, and inadequacy arising out of the completely new terrain she found herself in, Vincenz mustered the qualities of a born leader. During the difficult aftermath of 9/11 she showed compassion and inclusiveness, as well as the kind of hardiness the Badlands demands. She worked around the clock, making herself available to staff at all times, ensuring that every Delta flight attendant and crew member had the opportunity to discuss their concerns. Delta quickly began to hold face-to-face meetings, as well as audio conferences for employees around the world who could call in to Atlanta several times a day for updates. They installed more than two thousand phone lines to support management staying in touch with their people, particularly their flight crews.

Vincenz was the key person to provide the updates and answer questions during these calls. She spoke forthrightly of Delta's problems and the company's commitment to work closely with its employees to weather the situation. Her leadership paid off for both her employees and her company. Together they created a framework and a process for maintaining effective relationships that helped Delta struggle through that terrible time.

While Vincenz used the Badlands as a leadership crucible to forge new skills and refine the old, many leaders will fail to do so. Some will falter because of a mismatch between their leadership skills and their new environment. Some have already succumbed to excesses in the wealth-making frenzy of the late 1990s, while others have gone down merely due to bad luck. Whatever the reason, the last few years have seen an unprecedented exodus of CEOs. About 40 percent of Fortune 100 companies have replaced their CEOs since 1995, a trend that extends beyond the top companies, and across many industries. Lucent, Coca-Cola, and Campbell Soup changed CEOs in less than three years; Gillette, Procter & Gamble, Maytag, and Xerox replaced theirs in less than two. Half the companies listed in *BusinessWeek*'s top 50 companies in 2002 were toppled from the list a year later. They included such veterans as Capital One Financial, Citigroup, Calpine, Electronic Data Systems, Fannie Mae, Freddie Mac, Home Depot, Philip Morris, Tenet Healthcare, and Tyco International. In these extraordinary times, it is clear that the profile of past leaders is not a good fit with the rigors of the Badlands. But who will be the leaders of the future, and how can they create a readiness to lead? What skills and strengths must they possess, and what fears must they overcome?

LEADERSHIP READINESS

Readiness comes from setting off on the journey and learning as you go. Through the alchemy of this experience you will create, define, and redefine your character, but you must embrace the journey as a teacher

> Celebrity CEOs did not take a hero's journey. They are relics of the past era.

even though you know it will leave you behind if you don't or can't adapt. Two actions are essential: committing to a hero's journey and adopting new principles for the transformation ahead.

Self-Leadership: Taking a Hero's Journey

More than ever before, leadership depends on self-motivation and personal choice. This is not to say that organizations will not define their own values and leadership roles, but leadership will become increasingly distributed throughout entities and self-initiated rather than dictated by a formal role and title. This means that the ability of many different people to lead becomes critical to the organization. The days of depending on celebrity CEOs are over; leadership depends on everyone. Organizations will rely on people to lead themselves and decide jointly with them if they are a good fit with the leadership culture in the volatile Badlands. In this challenging environment mismatched leadership styles are a drag on everyone, as well as on the bottom line. For this match to be assessed swiftly, both parties need to make their values and styles fully visible. In essence, both need to make their leadership brand visible so that they can easily see their chances of forging a productive and harmonious relationship, and can part ways readily and without acrimony where prospects are not good.

What kind of leader will you become? How will you use the Badlands as a crucible for your undiscovered leadership capabilities? These are critical questions every leader needs to ask as we enter the rough terrain that lies ahead. First and foremost, Self-Leadership means that you must be willing to expose your own vulnerability to those around you. This is true of all heroes' journeys. Your capacity to lead is not centered on skills alone, it is more about attitudes and mind-sets that let you see in new ways and learn and inspire others to move on despite the uncertainty of the forbidding terrain of organizational or market changes. This means leaders must confront and manage their own stress and fears about letting go of old ideas and outworn roles, and seek collisions by learning to connect to new and different kinds of people who can help them change and grow.

It is important for all leaders to smoke the monsters out of their closets, all their fears and inadequacies, early in the trek.

All leaders have their own unique set of values, traits, and skills that will become obstacles or assets, depending on the environment. The findings from my research with pioneering leaders are presented in Table 3.1, juxtaposed with some the big challenges of the decade ahead.

Challenges	Personal Characteristics	Competencies
Disruptive innovation	Creative and imaginative	Contrarism, big-picture thinking, foresight
Ambiguity and uncertainty	Courageous	Managing complexity, contextual thinking
People's fears and self-doubts	Compassionate and trustworthy	Sense-making and emotional literacy-bonding with others, creating meaning; trust building
Rugged fitness peaks and high-risk big opportunities	Ambitious, adaptive, and collaborative	Managing diverse risky portfolios of opportunity, systematic long-term thinking
Volatile, anemic, vexing economy	Resolutely persistent	Creating results-oriented culture of discipline
Failures	Humble and resilient	Creating climates for innovation
Corruption	Ethical	Truth-telling in all circumstances
Regulatory riddles, policy problems	Widely influential	Cross-boundary networker

Table 3.1.   Challenges, Characteristics, Competencies.
Source: Global Foresight, 2004.

New Competencies Move to the Foreground

Today once again we are challenged to represent ourselves when so many of our local and global reference points are being dislocated by multiple short-term relationships in both a physical and electronic landscape.

A hero's journey requires embracing uncertainty with the courage of a warrior and the curiosity of a child, letting dormant abilities arise as needed. You want to be a leader who can deal with disruptive innovation, a constant feature that comes in many forms, including new technologies and competitive models. You will need to anticipate them and create them, not merely react to them. Instead of seeing the familiar view you must regularly engage in contrarian, big-picture thinking. You will need new reserves of creativity and imagination to resolve challenges in unique ways, and to invent ways of living and working and even birthing new industries. Vincenz is continuing her hero's journey at Delta through innovations in flight service geared to save $40 million dollars without sacrificing benefits deemed most desirable by the crew. After a thorough, inclusive process she was able to imagine a radically new way that served both sets of interests, preserving the crew's first priorities around time off and eliminating programs that were not of high value to the crew but saved Delta money.

Leaders will find strategy and foresight much more complex in the Badlands because of the need to manage complexity with great skill, understand patterns that emerge from multiple variables, and then act on that understanding. The key is to invest in an emergent strategy when it becomes clear it could be the winner. For example, the CEO of Galanz Corporation in China did just that—observing that Chinese apartments were too small for Western-style appliances, he invested quickly and innovated a small microwave, thereby cornering a huge market before other more recognized brands could get in.

Leaders in the Badlands will need to be able to summon compassion and include their work companions on the journey, not intimidate or marginalize them. Your journey will involve enough pain and suffering without adding to it. You will need to be personally trustworthy, as well as have the capability to build and preserve trust in others. Leaders who become successful will have shown a finely honed competency of emotional literacy, the capacity to understand and accept feelings in themselves and others; this allows them to engage in sense-making, to explain what is going on in a way that provides deep meaning and creates coherence out of the complexity and shifts. Vincenz could not have come up with a win-win new flight inservice plan had she not worked collaboratively with Delta's flight attendants. She worked diligently for more than two years after 9/11, engaging deeply with them, developing true empathy that allowed her to gain their trust and help her reinvent inflight services much more smoothly.

Navigating successfully through the Badlands calls for leaders to reorient themselves continuously, for they are in a transition zone between eras and can no longer be guided by old landmarks and principles. They will feel unsure about the markers of new meaning until they establish reliable guideposts in the radically changed society, economy, and culture that lie ahead. Vincenz says it was like turning a jigsaw puzzle upside down and having to put it together with no picture.

The landscape of the Badlands is marked by rugged peaks that provide both high risk and high gain. That means that above all you must be adaptable and ambitious. You must possess foresight and must practice systematic, long-term thinking to evaluate which opportunities to steer toward. Not all of your goals will be a good match for the competencies and skills of the organization.

Effective Self-Leadership means having the flexibility to manage a diverse portfolio of opportunities that provide a payoff, despite the risks. Few business leaders have been as successful at managing diverse portfolios over time as Steve Jobs has been with Apple. He has an uncanny knack for looking across highly competitive landscapes and experimenting with new business models, his latest successful gamble being iTunes, a Web site that allows music listeners to download from a large selection of music for 99 cents per song.

Leaders like Steve Jobs produce business results despite a vexing and volatile economy that lurches between anemia and growth, often without clear drivers for such shifts. These results can be created only through dogged persistence, and by creating a results-oriented culture of discipline. Some leaders will fail and fall by the wayside. Other leaders who did not develop a healthy capacity to respond to failures or challenges will be severely compromised. What kind of leader you become depends on how you respond to the terrific heat of this leadership crucible. For some seasoned leaders like Leo Mullen, former CEO of Delta, the best reaction was to step aside. Although successful at leading Delta through some harrowing times, he knew that the new task of renegotiating a contract with Delta's pilots was one he could not accomplish for the company. The rich pension and compensation package he had crafted for himself and other senior leaders put him at a severe disadvantage when it came time to ask the pilots to cut their pay.

The leaders who thrive must be humble as well as resilient, willing to fail in interesting ways, extract wisdom from the experience, and then move on. They must be able to create a climate that encourages risk taking and even an occasional heart-stopping failure. Vincenz still talks of the tremendous fear and sense of inadequacy she and other leaders felt when all their planes and crews were on the ground on 9/11, no one knew where they all were, and there was no protocol for easily determining their fate.

One of the lessons we have learned from the history of innovation is that corruption is common as one era comes to an end and a new one is born. This Badlands journey will be no different from those of previous times. Thankfully, corruption at the peak of wealth creation soon collapses under its own weight. A strict code of ethics, acted out every day, is the only way to avoid a collapse like that of Enron. As it has in previous eras, such a code will lead to long-term success in the Badlands. In a world of few familiar constants, this is one. As an individual and as a leader you must avoid the corrosion of character we saw so much of at the end of the great Industrial Plains. You must be able to build in yourself and others the habit of truth-telling in all circumstances. This is the only path to trust.

Sensing a mismatch between the rules and the new order of business, leaders will be caught in the dilemmas of their own Competency Addiction and the comfortable old ways of working. They will struggle to navigate their businesses through regulation riddles and policy problems. As new standards will be needed, certain leaders will step forward and be widely influential with their counterparts and competitors to achieve changes for a better climate for success in the global networked economy. To do this you must possess good skills as a networker who can set your organization's direction, see it in the context of outside drivers, and be able to influence conditions for yourself and for others across boundaries.

Leaders with these characteristics and competencies can successfully navigate the Badlands. Letting the Badlands support you in developing these precious qualities entails actively applying a specific set of principles.

THE EIGHT PRINCIPLES OF TRANSFORMATION

The historic journey to the next era will be unique for each leader and organization, but the following eight principles of transformation serve as general guidelines that can provide a better chance to survive, thrive, and ultimately achieve transformation in the Badlands. It is through applying these principles that leadership characteristics and competencies will emerge and jell. They can help leaders put an end to behaviors, strategies, and attitudes that no longer work, and to forge new beginnings. These principles support organizations and leaders in making a *total metamorphosis* during their trek through the Badlands. The alternative, a *partial* response to this challenging landscape, will only end in collapse.

Because these principles aren't linked to any single pain, they apply widely, making for a rich and complex web of solutions that are strategically applicable to every phase of the journey. To repeat the list from Chapter One:

Principles of Transformation

- Scan, Scout, Steer
- Act with Integrity
- Seek Collisions
- Learn Rapidly
- Engage Cultures
- Innovate Radically
- Make Decisions Fast
- Execute with Discipline

Scan, Scout, Steer

Weather systems in the rough Badlands terrain can often obstruct long-range visibility. At the same time global drivers will be constantly eroding and sculpting the land, putting leaders, individuals, and organizations at high risk for suffering major environmental impacts.

Leaders must remain flexible and adaptable, scouting for opportunities while nimbly steering around sudden pitfalls both for themselves and their organizations. They must scan, scout, steer, not just for their organizations but for themselves in their quest for growth.

The primary purpose of scanning and scouting for the organization is to gain accurate near-term and midterm foresight that keeps strategies properly attuned and ensures that you—and not your competitors—find the next big opportunity. In the heady days of the late 1990s, so many opportunities to create wealth arose that foresight and even strategy became hugely undervalued. It almost seemed as though anyone could turn over a spadeful of earth and strike gold. In the Badlands, though, having a continuous flow of information leading to visibility will be paramount to creating and fine-tuning strategies along the way.

Constantly keeping the big picture in view while scanning for shifts is not optional in the Badlands. During times of economic stability this focus can be less crucial because things are changing more slowly and are therefore more predictable. But in times of high uncertainty like the present, huge shifts can occur rapidly, posing a serious threat to the core strategies of an organization.

Bill Hambrecht, founder and CEO of investment firm W.R. Hambrecht, is an exemplary leader who applies many of the principles of transformation, including scan, scout, and steer. Hambrecht scouted the long-term future of IPO investing and determined that the prevailing system, whereby investment bankers controlled IPO shares for select customers, was not in the interest of creating new viable companies and industries of the future. He founded W.R. Hambrecht as a laboratory for developing new means of sustainable investment, including an online auction for IPOs, open to the public, which lets the market determine the opening share price. Despite launching his company right before the dot-com bust, he brought it through the ravages of the stock market bubble and continues to steer it forward, as the rest of the industry watches with keen interest.

Scanning for big shifts is not limited to global business. In 2001 few foundations and nonprofits were ready for the severe impact of the falling stock market on their endowments. Some, like the Hewlett Foundation, were not diversified and lost more than 50 percent of their principal, resulting in a major reduction in grant making, which in turn affected many organizations that had depended on them for years. But Patti Chang, president of the San Francisco Women's Foundation, began to Scan, Scout, Steer toward a merger with the Los Angeles Women's Foundation right before 2000. Patti Chang wanted to have more impact on bigger women's issues and felt if the two small foundations merged they would have more clout. Because of Patti's strong donor relations she was not worried about the impending economic downturn; in fact, her funding has continued to grow throughout this decade. Los Angeles turned her down in 1999, but Patti waited patiently—suspecting that the group would be more motivated as they hit financial hard times, and she was right. In 2002 the LA Women's Foundation had lost nearly two-thirds of its funding and its leaders were eager to merge, and within a few months the merger was completed. The two groups couldn't be more positive—they share the same mission and values and are taking on new issues neither could have done alone. They both see more clearly since the merger the tremendous opportunities to successfully address women's issues with women's leadership in the Badlands. (Navigating the Badlands effectively is not just about getting around external obstacles. It is often about steering around obstacles that organizations themselves wittingly or unwittingly construct.) Once she had focused on her best option, merging with the Los Angeles Women's Foundation, she had to move fast while the window of opportunity was open, steering through the major concerns put forward by officers in both foundations. Chang was successful. In August 2003 the California Women's Foundation replaced the other two entities.

Scouting that provides early warning of a major shift is critical because few organizations can survive major transformations. New core competencies and capabilities are difficult to develop quickly. But scouting can help target new areas in which to develop competencies, even before a specific opportunity emerges. Good scouting explores the industry horizon and identifies zones of likely opportunities. Although preemptive competency building has risks attached, it is far less risky than the ever-present Badlands danger of obsolescence.

Many companies lack leaders who are good scouts, and they relegate the scouting function to a strategy group isolated from the rest of the company. Although this old-paradigm scouting function is still useful, it is nowhere near sufficient to provide the business intelligence needed today. Even though some companies have leaders engaged in formal scanning and scouting processes for each of their specific business operations, still more innovation is needed. Often traditional scouts don't wander outside their old, familiar territories. Because

global competition is one of the big drivers of volatility in the Badlands, it is vital that scouts possess diverse cultural competencies, not
merely domain expertise. Smart companies will strategically improve
all leaders' readiness to identify both opportunities and risks, and will
enable them to act quickly on emerging opportunities by providing
the necessary resources and authority.

Act with Integrity

Leading in uncertain conditions demands great belief in yourself, as
well as strength of character. Integrity lies at the heart of every hero's
journey through the Badlands, just as it has in every historic epic.
Odysseus was a great strategist, but his tactics would have been use-
less if they had not been built on a foundation of character. It was his
force of character that brought him safely back to the shores of Ithaca,
to home and hearth.

Integrity is much more than honesty. It includes coherence, connectedness, wholeness, and vitality. It is the capacity to remain integrated
under the pull of entropy, uncertainty, and disorder—omnipresent conditions in the Badlands. Living your integrity is important, and you will
feel the difference when you do. Integrity it is not an abstract quality. It
is the core of Self-Leadership.

Bibbero Systems is a very successful fifty-year-old, privately held
medical records company that serves doctors and dentists across the
United States. The company's CEO, Mike Buckley, realized that electronic medical records would become more dominant in the marketplace, but the timing of that development wasn't clear since health care
has been slow to adopt information technology, and is still a cottage
industry with many small players. Buckley knew that electronic medical records would grow dramatically, changing his competitive environment in a way that made him uneasy about staying in the business.
The best personal financial choice would be to sell the company now
if he wanted to avoid the consequences of the change. But Buckley had
built a great management team and a group of employees who stayed
with him for many years, and after some soul-searching, he realized
that the company's highest value to him is its team, its culture, and its
customers. He decided to continue investing in the business and take
the time needed to seek new leadership more attuned to the values
and goals he had for Bibbero Systems, a leader who would be interested in a second-curve business such as electronic medical records.

Buckley made the decision to lead his company through this transition even if he makes less profit on the ultimate sale. He has found a way to maintain coherence and vitality by keeping his business, though either choice would have been a decision made with integrity.

For every Mike Buckley who acts with integrity, there is another leader who glosses over the realities of this harsh environment and succumbs to character corrosion, a common pitfall in the Badlands. Even highly successful people can decide to obscure the truth or cover up their problems to maintain stock value. When Global Crossing sought bankruptcy protection in early 2002 with a debt of $12.4 billion, investigators and creditors were shocked. Four years earlier its chairman, Gary Winnick, had taken the company public at a valuation of $38 billion, and it grew swiftly to an astonishing $47 billion. Global seemed unstoppable: in early 2001, despite the tech bust, the company announced that it had exceeded its revenue target for the first quarter. This time, however, Global sales had, in fact, been lagging, and a later investigation revealed that it had artificially inflated its revenues. By swapping cash with other carriers and booking the trades as sales, Global Crossing had artificially boosted its revenues for the first half of 2001 by $720 million, but unknowing investors continued to buy stock in the company at the same time that Winnick was selling his.

By the time it was no longer possible to dress up the income statement and Global Crossing declared bankruptcy, Winnick had cashed in over $700 million in stock. (By comparison, Enron's Kenneth Lay sold $108 million of stock.) Despite this enormous sum, the Justice Department announced in late 2002 it did not have sufficient evidence to indict Winnick on criminal charges, although he retired from Global several days later. In a parting gesture, Winnick announced that he would establish a $25 million escrow account to compensate employees whose 401(K) retirement accounts had vanished in the bankruptcy. The lawyer representing Global's employees said that their loss was at least ten times that amount.

Things are changing in the United States, thanks to the Sarbanes-Oxley Act of 2003 and the development of a culture in which stockholders are increasingly active on their own behalf. And there are signs of a shift elsewhere in the globe as well, but once again change is marked by turbulence. China is trying to stop widespread corruption by clamping down on high-level officials. In the few years since China's accession to the World Trade Organization, the country's central bank has been the subject of several corruption investigations. In 2002, the former head of the Bank of China was jailed for an illegal $23 million loan he made to his wife. Around the same time, bank officials revealed that more than $480 million had been embezzled by branch managers between 1992 and 2001. A new chief executive, Liu Jinbao, was named. Highly regarded, with leadership positions in the Hong Kong Monetary Authority, Hong Kong Exchanges and Clearing Ltd., and the Hong Kong Chinese Enterprises Association, Liu shocked the financial world when he was detained in 2003 for a corrupt loan he made to a Shanghai property tycoon.

What makes these incidents all the more egregious is that during this time, the Bank of China was preparing to list shares in its Hong Kong branch and purported to be cleaning up house. Bank chair Liu Mingkang, appointed in 1999, helped bring to light scandalous facts about the bank. A strong advocate for addressing nonperforming loans throughout the country's banking system, he released figures indicating that almost 30 percent of the bank's loans were nonperforming. Between 2001 and 2002, Liu Mingkang succeeded in reducing this figure by almost five percentage points.

When the Chinese government created the country's first banking regulatory commission, it tapped Liu Mingkang to chair it. Since taking the job in March 2003, and by exerting an amazing amount of courageous Self-Leadership, he has outlined a set of goals for banking reform to fight entropy and corruption, reducing the number of nonperforming loans among China's four state-owned banks. He is bringing vitality and a new coherence to China's banking system.

Seek Collisions

Once catapulted into the Badlands, most companies will lack both the right people and the diversity of people needed for continuous innovation. The practice of not just avoiding but seeking collisions will help them create the optimal diversity they need. Most leaders don't know what they don't know. Collisions will help them figure it out. To collide is to crash or smash into something, to have an accident in which something gets bent or changed or you have an "aha!" moment. Leaders need to choose pathways that will provide surprising encounters with outsiders, who can often see possibilities invisible to insiders. They will want to bring some of these diverse voices inside the company, whether through an alliance, a short-term contract with specific deliverables, or a direct hire. These collisions will be a vital part of building a richer, more robust intelligence web. Much innovation can be fed by simply talking with new people, then listening deeply.

It is essential that leaders expand their peripheral vision to learn to see beyond their usual line of vision. I call leaders scouting on the edge of their comfort-seeking "outposters." Intel's Fellows are one model of outposter success to learn from. The Fellows are all senior employees with deep expertise. They are free to explore new areas but must work outside Intel to ensure that they are accessing emerging knowledge from leading experts with something new to contribute. They are itinerants, free to roam the globe and act on what they find. Their collective goal is to continuously weave a widespread web of intelligence that will yield innovations that will keep Intel ahead of its competitors. They realize that their success depends on reciprocity. In a sense, they are traders as well as miners. To gain insights from the collisions they make they must have something to offer, whether it be knowledge, financial support, or new connections. That means they must have lots of know-how, communication and networking skills, intuitive ability, and intellectual curiosity. Another critical success factor is a good reputation.

These outposters also need to avoid developing too many ideas and associating with people of too little quality. It doesn't do much good for them to bring back the Yellow Pages. The real challenge is remaining totally open to all possibilities while using good filters for quality. Outposters must know how to keep people in the intelligence web until their contributions can be harvested. They must have an instinct for which ideas and people can eventually bear fruit.

Intel Fellows meet regularly to share intelligence, and in this way they actively position the company at the intersection of multiple pathways. This strategy yields rich and surprising new options, and also provides an easy return to home base if one of the choices winds up falling short. Risks and failures are an integral part of colliding. The only pitfalls are failing to recognize a wrong turn or failing to learn from it. Outposters have no second thoughts about leaving behind what doesn't pan out quickly.

An extremely important field in which to seek collisions is one's own customer base. Deeply understanding the customer will help leaders stay close to the often dormant and unconventional convergences between their business potential and their customers' pains.

UPS was not always customer-focused, but as part of its quest to renew itself leaders began to make visits to customers just to learn about them. As they listened to computer manufacturers they heard a common pain voiced about managing their parts inventories. UPS leveraged this knowledge to create a nationwide network of stock houses and manage them efficiently, eventually providing same-day air delivery service on Sonic Air, a company it had acquired.

Drinking at dangerous waterholes is another form of seeking collisions that targets competitors. Getting close to and perhaps even collaborating with actual or potential predators can be a useful collision. Haier Group, one of China's most globally ambitious and successful companies, has learned to collide productively with competitors like Sanyo of Japan. Gaining access to good distribution channels in China is difficult and important. Haier has a mature logistics system that it allows competitors like Sanyo to use, and in the process Haier learns how to better strengthen its logistics system as well as innovate in its core small-appliance business.

Learn Rapidly

You can't *lead* if you can't *learn*—and power in the Badlands comes from learning over and over and over again. Many leaders find it difficult to learn in unstructured, uncertain environments. Under these conditions, leaders often describe feeling fearful and closed down. This Leadership Insecurity is a huge obstacle in the Badlands. It takes courage to learn in a fast-paced, chaotic environment where the stakes are high. Leaders must find ways to move beyond fear and find a calm place that allows them to embody both shared leadership and Self-Leadership.

Trial and error constitutes a critical pathway for accelerated learning. Success means engaging in many experiments, knowing there will be many failures. The trick is to fail in interesting ways so that you learn as much as you possibly can about yourself and your strategy.

IDEO, a very successful product design company, has a religious zeal about learning rapidly through the IDEO principle of "enlightened trial and error." CEO David Kelley strongly believes that operating in this manner always outperforms even following the meticulous, flawless planning of the smartest people. IDEO provides significant rewards for both successful and failed risk takers. Its complex designs can't be leading-edge without shared leadership, and its executives learned early on that shared leadership can't be put into place without assuring workers they'll be given the resources they need to develop their ideas, as well as a chance to benefit from the success they bring the company. Rewards can come in the form of bonuses, or sabbaticals, or the opportunity to pursue another innovation. Everyone in the company has a deeply held value that every failure should be turned into a learning opportunity—not just for the group or leader who failed but for others on the extended team, for the rest of the company, and often even for the client.

Another company that strives for fast learning is eBay. The company learned a big, costly lesson when it changed the checkout procedure for completing auction transactions in favor of Billpoint, eBay's payment-processing service. It turned out that eBay's best customers, its thousands of frequent sellers, were passionately attached to PayPal, then an independent company. In response to an outraged eBay trading community, the company quickly made the new checkout process optional. They bought PayPal a year later for $1.5 billion, several hundreds of million dollars more than if they had bought it when the issue first came up. Big mistake. Lesson learned, at a cost.

Fast learning is a critical pathway for Self-Leadership. It comes from leaders' observing themselves in the continuous flow of critical Badlands situations. Each experience provides rich opportunities to learn things about themselves, both positive and negative. In eBay's expensive lesson, U.S. chief Jeff Jordan spearheaded the new transaction process pitting Billpoint against PayPal. This is an example of the many self-learning adventures that have built both Jordan's humility and his courage, adventures that have taught him to engage in new strategies, learn from his mistakes, and rapidly move on. But not *too* rapidly. You can't learn if you don't reflect.

Each leader must build a strong, lifelong habit of learning. In the Badlands we will find a continuous flow of lessons available, and part of the hero's journey is to take those lessons whenever and wherever we find them. They will build in us the habit of extracting wisdom from challenging experiences, a superior adaptive capacity needed to complete a successful journey. Many leaders confuse access to knowledge and information with learning. The knowing/doing gap stands as a prominent landscape feature in the early phase of our journey. It is only through acting on knowledge that leaders become intelligent. There is no time in the Badlands to sit around and devise the perfect strategy.

A free flow of information is also crucial to learning. Management practices must facilitate both sharing and generating knowledge. Together with a culture that encourages risk taking, we have the ingredients for Innovate Radically, another transformation principle.

Engage Cultures

Doing business across cultures adds another element of volatility, but the good news is that leadership qualities suitable for traversing the Badlands will also help leaders navigate the rough weather systems generated by multiculturalism. Authenticity, courage, resilience, adaptability, and persistence—all these will help leaders engage productively with one another. Other useful qualities that we haven't stressed include a sense of humor, discernment, and self-confidence. Robust self-confidence is critical to the process of cultural learning, since even the most seasoned global leader can feel a sense of failure as global relationships struggle to work. The very act of engaging in cultural learning results in anxiety as part of a natural process. Many potential global leaders ultimately fail because they are not able to learn enough about other cultures to be effective in situations when leadership is shared. In this increasingly global business world the goal must be maximum inclusion of all cultures within a global web of alliances.

The story of Carlos Ghosn's successful change program for Nissan is a good example of how a self-confident, skilled global leader can learn deeply about a new culture and meet success. In 1999, Renault and Nissan formed a strategic partnership to grow the companies' global market share and competitiveness. Nissan also gained a desperately needed investment, as the company's debt totaled $22 billion. Ghosn, then Renault's executive vice president of advanced research and development, manufacturing, and purchasing, was asked to become COO of Nissan. Ghosn had successfully turned around Renault after its failed merger with Volvo and, earlier in his career, had turned around Michelin's South America business. Now his challenge was to do the same for Nissan.

In addition to Nissan's debt, Ghosn faced a cultural challenge. He joined Nissan as the first non-Japanese COO in the company's history. Born to French and Brazilian parents of Lebanese heritage, Ghosn was educated in France and spoke five languages. Although he had worked on three continents, he lacked experience in Asia and knew little about Japanese culture and business. In its arrangement with Nissan, Renault agreed to remain sensitive to Nissan's culture, and Ghosn succeeded in following this promise while dramatically improving Nissan's financial position. He began his work by learning deeply about the Japanese company, initiating discussions with hundreds of managers and building their trust. In fact, he was the first manager to meet every employee in person; through his actions, he articulated a model of shared leadership at Nissan.

Ghosn observed how Japanese cultural norms of consensus and cooperation influenced processes at Nissan. Prior to decision-making meetings with their superiors, groups met to discuss issues and agree upon a common position. By forming these coalitions, or *nemawashi,* the functional groups protected each individual: no one person took the blame if upper management did not approve of the employees' recommendations. The practice of consensus building, however, created long and costly delays for the company.

Only after an intense engagement with the Nissan culture did Ghosn begin reform of the company, demonstrating from the outset respect for the Japanese cultural priority of consensus building. He began by enlisting the help of Nissan's employees by engaging in brainstorming sessions with managers. Ghosn observed that, due to the importance of ensuring personal career growth and avoiding blame, managers rarely considered alternatives outside their specific functional group. After company-wide brainstorming, Ghosn created ten cross-functional teams, which applied the cultural norm of cooperation while giving managers a new, broader perspective.

Ghosn strengthened the teams' authority and decision-making ability by ensuring that they had access to all company information. From their recommendations, Ghosn developed the Nissan Revival Plan (NRP). The NRP emphasized new product development, improvement of the Nissan brand image, research and development, and cost cutting.

Global competition demands that traditional companies change, and this reform inevitably reveals strain between cultures. The Japanese media criticized Ghosn for reducing jobs to streamline operations and called him a *gaijin,* or foreigner. He showed strength of character and resilience by staying the course and implementing the plan that the cross-functional teams had helped create. Nissan not only achieved the NRP, but did so one year ahead of schedule. After losing money for seven of the past eight years, the company turned a profit within twelve months of Ghosn's arrival.

Engaging other cultures fully will be essential to making savvy decisions about when to customize products or services and how to segment markets in different countries. If you don't have true knowledge based on experience, you will create a framework that only fits the culture in your mind—not the one that can be found in the real world all around you, wherever it is you live and work. China's consumers provide a market almost every global company wants to tap, yet it is hard to decipher. One basic challenge is the Chinese bifurcation between purchases perceived as utilitarian and those that contribute to "face value." Companies like Coca-Cola have faced continuing challenges to get Chinese consumers to purchase their products rather than competing Chinese brands for daily use. The Chinese saw high face value in having Coke available for special occasions but not necessarily for everyday use. At its heart, China is a utilitarian consumer society, and decisions are based on pragmatic considerations of value, price, and function more than brand.

Innovate Radically

Historically, radical innovation most often comes from the fringe. Seek out heretics and mavericks to ensure you optimize your opportunities for radical innovation. Beware of your leaders of old competencies, who will work hard to divert resources from vital new endeavors in order to maintain their power.

SEEK HERETICS

Historically, radical innovation most often comes from the fringe. Seek out heretics and mavericks to ensure you optimize your opportunities for radical innovation. Beware of your leaders of old competencies, who will work hard to divert resources from vital new endeavors in order to maintain their power.

In the Badlands it is far less dangerous to experiment with radical innovations in a core business than it is not to. Innovations, especially radical ones, are the milestones of the Badlands, where the process of creative destruction is fast and furious. Radical innovations build the scaffolding for the business models of the future. The result of the structural economic shift and its vast interconnectivity is white space, which will lead to many new industries, hybrid industries, and new types of organizations in the next ten to twenty years.

To keep up with the emerging business environment of the future, some portion of your innovation portfolio must be radical. Radical innovation comes in many forms—it changes customer expectations, invents new industries, reinvents industry economics, and redefines competitive advantage. The CEO of China's Galanz did just that by creating the miniature microwave and redefining competitive advantage in his huge market.

Even big and long-established companies can radically innovate. The story of United Parcel Service's Service Parts Logistics business offers a good example of how a mature, even elderly company can grow into the future with a radical innovation. UPS is a ninety-five-year-old business with some 370,000 employees, producing more than $30 billion in annual revenue. Its Service Parts Logistics business builds on the company's core distribution and small package delivery competency and its new strategy (since 1999) of enabling global commerce, a shift from the previous strategy (in the early 1990s) of achieving worldwide leadership in package distribution. This new business is a successful repositioning of UPS as a global supply chain management company. It began with repairing returned cell phones and other equipment, in which UPS handled all the logistics. After just a few years it had revenues in the hundreds of millions, and now revenues exceed $1 billion.

Applying the principle of Innovate Radically means making strategic information and targeted business results accessible and visible to all. You can't get synchrony in business development and innovation if the strategy and information are not easily accessible to everyone. Creating a free flow of strategic information is part of cultural change, as is making sure that both the technology infrastructure and the "outfrastructure" (the interface between the company and its external resource network) facilitate easy connectivity and interactivity.

Radical innovations should not be confined only to the business model. They can also involve a breakthrough in organizational structure. Semco, a Brazilian manufacturer of industrial equipment, introduced radical innovation to its organization as a way to drive more innovation.

When he took over Semco from his father, Ricardo Semler replaced the company's hierarchical management with an arrangement that supported shared decision making. He abolished all titles and eliminated secretarial positions. Employees set their own salaries and chose their own managers. Over a fifteen-year period, Semler reduced the number of company management levels from twelve to three. To replace the old pyramid, Semler created a lattice in which small groups of employees had full responsibility for specific areas of production. Semler made each group accountable for its own budget and implemented a profit-sharing program to increase a sense of employee ownership of the company. Employees broadened their skill sets through collaboration. They became comfortable assuming greater levels of responsibility and implemented changes to increase efficiency. Worker productivity increased, quality improved, and defects decreased to less than 1 percent of total production.

Semler gave employees even greater autonomy in order to spur more radical innovation. He encouraged the formation of "satellites," groups of employees who work on projects of their choosing and are compensated based on their results. These satellites are completely autonomous from the company but have access to Semco's resources. Today, about two-thirds of Semco's new products come from satellite companies.

Semler's commitment to shared decision making supported radical innovation that helped Semco grow significantly. Even in the challenging environment of Brazil's volatile economy—with four currency devaluations, mass unemployment, inflation, and a virtual halt of all industrial production during the period of Semler's radical changes—the company grew revenues from $35 million in 1990 to $100 million in 1996.

Make no mistake: building the capacity for radical innovation is very tough work. However, radical innovations don't have to be huge, they just have to be different.

Make Decisions Fast

While volatile conditions within the Badlands make decision making difficult, it is critical to make decisions that accelerate action as quickly as possible. Leaders must nurture an action-oriented stance throughout their whole company. For some leaders the fear of risk and making the wrong decision may be a paralyzing force, but in the Badlands it is better to act, evolve, and move on than to sit idle in the harsh sun. When good leaders make mistakes, which they will, they fix them fast and keep moving. A wealth of research in both business behavior and psychology clearly points out that attitudes *follow* behavior, not the other way around. To create a culture of action, push ahead and act on decisions on the spot. This is, of course, easier said than done. Most companies encounter a number of legacy problems with decision making, not least of which is talking more than acting. Talk should mobilize action, not substitute for it.

One way to facilitate rapid decision making is to persistently and intelligently simplify complexity, thus clearing the way for action. In the Badlands, simple and direct goals allow people to make forward progress. Appreciating the value of common sense and using language that is simple, direct, and clear act as lubricants for action. Of necessity, discussions are complex when people are trying to figure something out, but leaders often neglect to take the next step of simplifying the results of those discussions so that people are mobilized. In fact, it is all too common for people to think that those who articulate in the language of complexity have the right answer and are smarter. This myth needs to be constantly debunked, for it will always slow action. Simple terminology coupled with clear goals builds trust and launches action. Decision making needs to be distributed to those who are closest to both the issues and the action, regardless of their ability to perform in a meeting.

Leaders can enhance their decision-making capacity by maintaining a free flow of information and access. Among the benefits of free-flowing information, which can be supported by solid information systems and electronic tools such as e-mail and videoconferencing that interconnect everyone, is that it breaks down bureaucracy. In some companies people hoard information, equating it with power and prestige. To make things worse, in large companies with layers of bureaucracy and complex structures, rules tend to replace thinking.

Samsung has learned the art of rapid decision making and in doing so spectacularly reinvented itself in just a few years. In 1997, following Korea's financial crisis, Samsung had a debt of $10.8 billion and net margins of just 0.4 percent. Its products were considered inferior in quality to those of its competitors. Now, however, those competitors are paying close attention to Samsung's moves.

A large part of Samsung's turnaround can be credited to its emphasis on action. According to Samsung managers who have worked at its big competitors, Samsung has far fewer layers of bureaucracy, and getting a decision to create and launch a new product is fast. Speed at seizing new opportunities is generously rewarded throughout the company.

Samsung's aggressive restructuring has played a major role in the company's ability to compete at the top. It takes Samsung an average of five months to go from new product concept to rollout, compared to fourteen months just a few years ago. After Samsung formed an agreement with Germany's T-Mobile in April 2002 to market a wireless camera-phone, eighty designers from Samsung immediately went to work and produced a prototype within four months. By November of that same year, Samsung was mass-producing the phones.

To avoid the commoditization that often characterizes hardware businesses, Samsung continuously churns out new products to meet customers' changing needs. For example, the company planned to introduce ninety-five new products in the United States in 2003. Included in that number are twenty models of cell phones. Compare that to the twelve that Motorola scheduled for the year. Samsung also upgrades its product line every nine months, compared to the twelve- to eighteen-month schedules of its competitors.

Since its low point in 1997, Samsung Electronics has reduced its debt to $1.4 billion and increased net margins to 12 percent. It has the biggest market share of telephone handsets (10.5 percent) and is the most widely held emerging market stock. And in 2002, when many tech companies were struggling, Samsung's earnings were $5.9 billion on $33.8 billion in sales.

The goal in a complex and uncertain environment is to keep as many good options open as possible, which sometimes means postponing any choices that might limit opportunities down the road. Ellen Friedman, vice president of the Tides Foundation and director of the Community Clinics Initiative Program (a $90 million program to build the capacity of frontline health care centers), made a quick strategic shift in the middle of a granting cycle. She became concerned that the grants she was awarding might benefit only the individual health center receiving the funds rather than serve the strategic purpose of statewide interconnectivity. Despite her concern that she would disappoint those waiting for the funds, she decided to break awards up into incremental components that would meet both strategic *and* local goals. Changing the rules for grants in midstream is considered a big no-no in the philanthropic world, but Friedman took that risk. Her decision to keep her options open yielded a result that served everyone well.

After they make the tough decisions, strong leaders build the habit of debriefing. When possible, they identify learning points that may have been overlooked in the heat of the decision and its fallout. This process can begin by having colleagues imagine and discuss quickly what might happen if the action is successful, or if it fails. Once the action is completed, those involved can note what they learned—both the expected and unexpected. In this way they set the expectation that these lessons will be applied immediately to decisions going forward.

Execute with Discipline

Many companies have lived through the crippling cycle of great ideas married to poor execution. This behavior was not fatal in the slower, more stable environment of the Industrial Plains but is invariably lethal in the Badlands. Survival here requires that organizations create cultures that can execute masterfully with focus and aplomb. The Badlands is paradoxical in that to emerge from it alive requires both the discipline for great implementation and a climate that leads to radical innovation. With sales exceeding $15 billion, McDonald's is the leader in the fast-food industry. The company has struggled to keep growing in a mature market, however, and it hit rocky terrain in the fourth quarter of 2002, posting the first loss in its history. McDonald's and other hamburger chains are seeing an evolution in the current environment, the big picture. Consumers are getting more sophisticated in their eating habits and increasingly choosing fast casual restaurants that advertise fresh and healthful ingredients—and deserting the hamburger chains. McDonald's has started to address the changing needs of its customers by introducing a line of premium salads served with actor Paul Newman's dressings, adding new seasonings to its burgers, and changing its recipe for cooking buns.

The company has also recognized the market's saturation and has slowed its expansion plans. It has started to focus on increasing efficiency at existing locations rather than on opening new ones: in 2003, McDonald's opened up 360 restaurants, compared to more than 1,000 in 2002. In the words of former CEO James Cantalupo, the company needs to be "better, not just bigger." As a result, McDonald's has seen an increase in same-store sales and it plans to continue targeting higher store efficiency.

Technology is also playing a role in the new McDonald's strategy. In the United States, the company has formed partnerships with telecom providers to offer wireless Internet services in a number of its locations. It hopes to draw in tech-savvy customers who want Internet access while they grab a quick meal.

McDonald's has had to retool its strategy overseas as well. In Japan, for example, where the company has operated for thirty years, core customers have traditionally been families with small children. Due to a steady change in demographics, however, that group of customers is dwindling in size. Now young professional women have become the target for the New Tastes Menu, which includes a smoked beef sandwich with onions and tomatoes and a French ratatouille burger. The menu changes every six weeks, to keep in step with these fickle consumers.

The outcome of McDonald's long-term plans is yet to be seen, but signs have certainly been promising. In early 2003, the company saw its stock price soar 58 percent.

At the entry to the Badlands, leaders will find gaps between what they want to achieve and what their organizations are able to deliver. It is not uncommon for companies to insufficiently apprehend what they know how to do, which leads to assumptions about their ability to achieve new strategies without building new competencies. Just how transferable are your core competencies to each new opportunity? How well matched are they to the likely paths of evolution your industry might take? What are the unique and most valuable benefits that you deliver to customers? Closing competency gaps can solve a great many execution problems.

For Sweden-based H&M, a successful retailer that offers affordably priced versions of designer fashions, competency gap assessment played a critical role. In the fashion world, where styles change regularly, successful retailers must keep in step with the changing needs of their customers. In the words of one H&M manager, the company's goal is to "treat fashion as if it were perishable produce." The key to keeping fashion fresh is reducing lead time—how long it takes for a piece to go from the design board to the retail floor. H&M's solution was to develop competency in manufacturing outsourcing. Today, the company works with more than nine hundred suppliers in Asia and Europe. While H&M has long-term relationships with these companies, it is not tied to any single one. Instead, H&M planners are free to choose to work with any of the suppliers in their network to satisfy the requirements for a particular product, such as price, coping with import restrictions, or cutting transport time to its 844 locations.

Twenty-one company-owned production offices team up with suppliers to expedite the H&M manufacturing process. The production crew sends information to its suppliers about fabric types, so that the factory can prepare for manufacturing even before final design decisions are made. Workers from the production offices also conduct quality testing themselves—instead of sending samples to another, often more distant location—which further saves time.

As a result, the company has one of the shortest lead times in the industry. For its trendiest pieces, H&M can deliver on a two-week lead time. Compare that to The Gap's nine-month cycle! Overall, H&M has cut turnaround by 15–20 percent over the past three years. The company is also continually improving its buying process to make order decisions as late as possible so that the company can minimize its risk on any short-lived fashions. With three thousand of its more than twenty-five thousand employees in logistics, H&M is also honing its inventory management systems to whittle lead time down even further.

In addition to keeping the big picture in mind, like McDonald's, and developing new competencies, like H&M, a third step way to improve execution is to make jobs more meaningful. Many execution failures are due to job assignments that are too fragmented or too boring, with not enough authority delegated to function with any degree of independence. Edward Lawler's research-based concept of enriched jobs is very important to high-performance knowledge workers in the Badlands. People want meaningful jobs they can be responsible for as a whole. This places a burden on both the individual and the organization to recognize and arrange good matches between workers and their assignments. Individuals are just as responsible for ensuring their own role in creating disciplined execution as are organizations. Individuals should not take on jobs for which they are not suited—it hurts not only them but the organization as well.

Enhance execution by coaching people—the *right* people—to work only from their strengths. Unfortunately, most workers and leaders are keenly aware of weaknesses and less tuned in to strengths. That means that good leaders in the Badlands need the courage to reorganize people in a way that applies their strengths and passions. Leaders are often isolated from people on the front lines and get information filtered through layers of management. The trick is to become aware of what's happening in the trenches without micromanaging, which often slows execution.

A fourth factor in disciplined execution is determining if the work to be done is best suited to an individual or a team. High-performance teams are hard to create and sustain. Because it can take many months to create one, it is important to determine at the outset if a team is the best arrangement. The coordinated work of highly skilled individuals working more or less on their own has a prime role in a turbulent environment. Such groups work swiftly, and speed is of the essence in the Badlands. But some problems do require full team interaction. Once you get a high-performance team in which the individuals like working together, always try to find ways to redeploy them to other tasks as a unit. This kind of team is rare.

And last, demand contingency thinking from yourself and others. Things will change in surprising ways, and the ability to engage quickly in alternatives allows everyone to steer around the dangerous shifts in terrain and keep moving toward the goal in sight.

SUMMARY INSIGHTS

The pain of Leadership Insecurity with its feelings of fear and inadequacy will be experienced by leaders at all levels in the organization. It is natural to want to avoid making this trek, but there is no alternative. The Badlands is the new global context; all of us have to make the journey. In the process, leaders will come to grips with the need for true and thorough transformation of themselves and their organizations, because they won't survive if they don't.

- Leadership Readiness, the new capability, demands the courage to take a hero's journey using the Badlands as a leadership crucible. Here a new kind of intuition for this global environment will emerge, and successful leaders will build new habits of collaboration and innovation. We know from the lessons of historical cycles of innovation that the experience of this journey will lead to the emergence of a new identity.

- Every leader will experience fear and a sense of personal inadequacy. Spend some up-front time learning about yours. Smoke the monsters out of your closet early. This means having the courage to change on deep, personal levels, and exposing your vulnerability is a tremendous asset in doing so. The principles of transformation should be applied to the individual as well as the organization.

- The old reference points of leadership and identity are gone. People must all must lead themselves and chart their own paths, regardless of their position in any one organization. Leadership fit must be continually assessed and all involved should move on if it isn't optimal.

- Only those leaders who don't anticipate the future will be surprised by it. What are the threats, real or imagined, lurking ahead for you? What are the risks that most concern you? Hold sessions with heretics and trusted colleagues and practice resolving the events they imagine before you meet them in the rough landscape ahead. If you scan and scout the horizon you should be able to steer successfully through it.

- The Badlands is a complex environment that will prove fatal to simplistic thinkers and those seduced by glib slogans. The trick is to be able to think and manage complexity, break it down into its component parts, and communicate direction and action steps in clear, simple terms.

- Avoid the pitfall of getting blindsided by denying the existence of what you don't know. *Seek Collisions* at all times to fill in this black hole of ignorance.

- *Acting with Integrity* demands that leaders create meaning continuously and be vigilant about ethics. The changes currently under way in the economy and the social institutions of our global society are deeply disturbing. They challenge our assumptions about who we are, what we do, and the value we offer, which can be profoundly disorienting. Meaning lives in the hearts and minds of people, not in memos or strategic plans or organizational charts. In times of uncertainty, people need to know the higher purpose of an organization, not just its mission statement. People need unifying themes in order to build trust that can set them on common ground and provide new coherence and connectedness.

- Top leadership must respond to the *Innovate Radically* imperative of this environment. Power will ultimately come from mastering disruptive innovations in the marketplace. Leaders must ensure that a climate of systemic innovation develops and must invest in those innovations most likely to create the new wealth that will sustain the organization in the future.

- Although you need to be nimble, fostering rapid decisions and effective execution, relax—pace your progress. This is a long journey, one that will last a full decade or more. It will take time to build up the Leadership Readiness capabilities you need in order to transform yourself and your organization. There is no silver bullet, no rescuing miracle; escape is merely an illusion.

CHAPTER FOUR

Don't Get Lost
in Familiar Territory

Shortly after experiencing our first organizational pain, Leadership Insecurity, we run headlong into the second pain, Competency Addiction—the default use of old mind-sets and behaviors that just don't work in the Badlands. This pain presents itself when a company suddenly experiences unexpected pressures, either from without—such as a new technology, a change in customer preferences, or a new competitor that threatens vital business operations—or from within, such as a young hotshot VP pursuing a radical innovation that could replace the existing core business in a way that threatens the organization's powerful business leadership. In instances like these, an organization plagued with Competency Addiction will respond to the feeling of being threatened by focusing more intently on the old ways and moving to stamp out new ideas.

Take, for example, Sony, which has battled Competency Addiction more than once in the past decade and is yet again experiencing this pain. The consumer electronics giant has long been one of Japan's most successful companies, known for its strong tradition and its culture of innovation and discipline. Sony's list of successful products and revolutionary gadgets is a testament to the company's focus on innovation. From the launch of the Trinitron color TV in 1968 to the products of the 1980s and 1990s such as the Sony Walkman, portable CD players, and handycam digital camcorder, Sony has consistently performed on the cutting edge. On the surface it looks like Sony has it all. But underneath the values of discipline and innovation lies a culture that over the years has become arrogant, demanding, and rigid in its views.

PAIN #2: COMPETENCY ADDICTION— ARROGANCE AND SMUGNESS

Competency Addiction is the mindless, automatic repetition of legacy mind-sets and behaviors when they no longer produce the desired business results and indeed harm the long-term health of the organization. Competency Addiction is an intrinsic survival characteristic of the human species, but when it occurs in organizations and is driven by powerful leaders it becomes dangerous. It is particularly problematic when the behavior is driven by self-interest, simply because company leaders have much to lose if they get replaced. Arrogance and smugness often accompany this scenario, especially as leaders feel increasingly anxious that the old ploys might not work and fear the consequences. They prefer staying lost in the familiar territory of old ways of doing business rather than risk everything on the alternative.

New Capability: Systemic Innovation

The Badlands demands that companies give up their Competency Addictions and build a climate of Systemic Innovation. Whereas hierarchal structures and cultures tend to hold Competency Addiction in place, most innovation has been siloed in special, isolated groups such as skunk works or advanced technology groups. Innovation requires that both the conditions and the urge to develop new ideas be actively supported from top to bottom in the organization, as well as inside and out. Top leadership must set the conditions for innovation and actively support its growth until it is embedded widely enough to reseed itself. The leadership challenge here is to increase the flexibility and resiliency that innovation requires without eliminating the useful rigid structures that support innovation's full development.

Just ask Ken Kutaragi, currently president and CEO of Sony Computer Entertainment and the father of Sony's PlayStation. He didn't start out in this role. He came to Sony as a young creative engineer and ran head-on into a culture that was closed to his bright ideas and visions. In the mid-1990s he was forced to collaborate with the game company Nintendo in secret to develop the initial ideas for what would be PlayStation. Only one other person (his immediate supervisor in R&D) knew about his research project. The collaboration would have been killed if Sony senior executives had known about it; after all, Nintendo was just a game company, and Sony was the giant of electronics.

When the project became public, Sony senior executives were furious that a project with a rival company had been granted approval. For Kutaragi this turned into a grueling uphill battle. At one point he threatened to leave Sony if he couldn't work on the video game project. It took incredible persistence and a powerful vision of the idea's potential to overcome the internal obstacles and develop what turned out to be one of Sony's most successful new products ever. PlayStation became one of the world's top-selling game machines. PlayStation 2, the second generation, is breaking all kinds of sales records. In the first thirty months after its introduction, Sony sold 40 million units, more than twice as many as the original PlayStation in the same time frame.

> *Change comes from the fringe:*
> *Historical lesson of innovation.*

Fast forward to 2003. Sony revenues and profits in the consumer electronics segment have plunged, and the list of hit products is getting smaller and smaller. Ironically, PlayStation profits have helped Sony stay afloat. CEO Nobuyuki Idei has been struggling for the past several years to change the pattern of loss by restructuring the company and by cutting jobs. Some say that no amount of restructuring will help. The problem lies deep in the company's culture and its value system; the core electronics business is dominated by engineers with high resistance to change. In other words, it looks like a serious case of Competency Addiction.

Idei demonstrates an understanding that he is up against a serious threat to Sony's survival. To combat this threat he has Ken Kutaragi's team overseeing the development of the next big thing, a super micro-processor. Idei has also introduced rebel engineers from the outside into Sony's core product teams to send a message that things must change. Maybe he's hoping to find the next Ken Kutaragi.

Competency Addiction can also affect an entire industry. The American health care system, for instance, is riddled with legacy mind-sets and behaviors that have become gridlocked to such a degree that little significant innovation can take place. Slow decision making around any change is pervasive. And all the while, people's access to decent quality care declines while costs escalate relentlessly. For decades this industry has grappled with the same issues and has let talk substitute for action. Health care is littered with silos of special interests and patches of fiercely protected fenced-in turf: each has its own set of addictions. For example, most health care services and reimbursements are organized around a single patient visit, long known to be an inefficient way to care for many illnesses and low on cost-to-value. Yet faced with deeply entrenched patterns of power and hierarchies of services, few health care organizations are experimenting with new ways to deliver services. Further exacerbating the industry's problems is a tendency to tinker with process rather than actively seek solutions through much-needed innovation. Risk avoidance is all too common. Health care itself continues to be sidelined by old attitudes and practices with little hope of near-term change.

UNDERSTANDING COMPETENCY ADDICTION AND ITS IMPACTS

Mindless behaviors are part of our adaptive success as a species. We survive from day to day by repeating behaviors over and over again in all dimensions of our lives. This process has been well documented by a number of researchers. The human brain is set up to repeat behaviors, particularly if they are successful, but also when it doesn't receive specific feedback that they *weren't* successful. Unfortunately, these mindless behaviors tend to continue even when they result in poor performance. Yet we humans are as capable of changing our thoughts and behaviors as repeating them, although not without conscious effort. We tend to let memory substitute for thinking until we get pushed by ourselves or others to change gears and engage in active thinking and problem solving.

Jeffrey Pfeffer and Robert Sutton of Stanford University have provided rich insights and countless stories in how this very human characteristic harms organizations. In their books *The Knowing-Doing Gap* and *Weird Ideas That Work,* they describe how companies try to spark more innovation by using methods that actually stifle it. And they show how managers persist in the belief that they can reinvent themselves by simply repeating the practices that made them successful in the past. But organizations that do the same things over and over again cannot expect to create something new. For many, this is a hard-learned lesson, as we saw in the case of the Sony corporation.

Knowing-Doing Gap

- Knowing comes from doing.

- Fear leads to inaction.

- No action without mistakes.

- Internal competition undermines performance.

- Don't substitute memory for thinking.

  Simple measures, good judgment.

Source: Global Foresight, 2004; Pfeffer and Sutton, 2000.

Wal-Mart ran into the pitfalls of mindlessly repeating successful practices with its warehouse business, Sam's Club. Sam's Club is getting beaten out by Costco. Costco is only one-fifth the size of Wal-Mart, yet it is the clear leader in the warehouse business. Sam's Club has 71 percent more U.S. stores than Costco, yet for fiscal year 2003 Costco had 5 percent more sales. The average Costco generates nearly twice the revenue of a Sam's Club ($112 million to $63 million). Why the huge disparity? Costco innovates and Sam's Club imitates. Sam's Club merely applies the successful Wal-Mart discount model to bulk products. However, this business has turned out to require a lot more than just being able to offer the biggest jar of generic peanut butter at the lowest price. Costco approached the warehouse market much more strategically by gaining a better understanding of its target market—a sophisticated urban consumer looking for low prices on luxury items. This is about the high end meeting the low end.

As a result of innovative thinking and planning, Costco has created a unique and successful niche. Not only do you find the bulk basics of toilet paper, vitamins, and office supplies at Costco, you will also find that the chain is the biggest seller of fine wines in the United States, and in 2002 sold sixty thousand carats of diamonds! By contrast, Sam's Club didn't strategically plan for or adapt to this new breed of urban consumer. Sam's Club was blinded by its managers' addiction to their discounting competency and their narrow view of the big-box customer.

Many companies persist in using obsolete methods and ideas because of the powerful people who defend them, in contrast to the relatively low status of innovators. Certainly Ken Kutaragi at Sony must have felt very powerless and isolated when his project and secret collaboration with Nintendo came to the attention of Sony's senior management. Fortunately, despite being viewed as a heretic by the powers of Sony, Kutaragi persisted and quietly continued to build support for his vision. Companies face double jeopardy because leadership hierarchies and corporate cultures tend to support the status quo as a default position, and that naturally colludes with the human proclivity toward Competency Addiction, creating a formidable barrier to innovation.

My own research builds on Pfeffer and Sutton's excellent work on Competency Addiction, which is so ubiquitous in the threatening conditions of the Badlands. The relentless demand for innovation is far more important than the masterful execution of the day-to-day routine work to survival and success in the Badlands. Organizations face an extraordinary challenge when they decide to break down their addiction to their competencies and try to replace it with a culture that supports innovation from top to bottom.

The more successful an organization has been, the bigger the challenge it faces in breaking down old patterns. At IBM this is certainly the case. Big Blue is steeped in traditional ways of doing things. In recent years the corporation's very senior twelve-person strategic planning committee was disbanded, reflecting IBM CEO Samuel Palmisano's move away from the long-held view that strategy comes from senior management. Instead, he instituted a decentralized model with multidisciplinary teams charged with the responsibility for coming up with new ideas and strategies. This dramatic break from tradition has allowed IBM to create a completely new vision of itself, along with a wealth of possibilities for future success.

People with advanced competencies inevitably see their performance drop when they attempt new ventures. This frustrating experience can easily lead them to fall back on old behaviors that make them feel successful once again. This has been called, variously, the "success trap" and the "competence trap." Starbucks is a company that will need to guard against the success trap as it attempts to parlay its dramatic national accomplishments into success in the international marketplace. The Starbucks Experience (providing a destination for sophisticated coffee drinkers that passionately focuses on chic ambience and high-quality coffee) that has been such a hit in the United States may not translate so readily outside the country. In Japan, for instance, Starbucks reported that its profit for the first half of 2003 plummeted 58 percent.

The company admits to being slow to respond to some of the changes related to the slump in the Japanese economy. In addition, start-up costs and new ways of partnering through joint ventures and licensing agreements pose their own challenges. In some cultures, the Starbucks Experience may not be what people want when it comes to coffee. It's clearly time for Starbucks to approach things sensitively in these markets and not assume that its U.S. success formula can just plug in everywhere else.

In its competition in the cholesterol-lowering drug market with Pfizer, pharmaceutical company Merck paid dearly for clinging to old habits. Merck lost market share to Pfizer by failing to recognize that decision-making criteria for doctors were changing: potency and price were playing a more important role than study results, at least for cholesterol-lowering drugs. Merck continued to churn out clinical reports instead of focusing on the product and creating a dosage at a price that doctors felt comfortable prescribing to their patients.

So how does Competency Addiction differ from run-of-the-mill mindless behavior in organizations? Competency Addiction, for one thing, mimics other human addictions: it builds up unconsciously, is devilishly hard to break, and if vigilance lapses it can reoccur at any time. Left unmanaged it can become fatal. Furthermore, just dancing around major Competency Addictions will not work. Given the surge in new technologies, global competitors, demanding activist consumers, and new and hybrid industries, innovation is the name of the game. Competency Addiction looms as a huge barrier to the organizational readiness needed to achieve success in the new environment. At the beginning of the Badlands it is easy for companies to stay lost in the familiar territory of old successes.

RESOLVING COMPETENCY ADDICTION

Most of today's organizations, large or small, young or old, are unprepared for the Badlands journey. How *do* you get ready for a journey of such historic proportions? Begin by taking your first step without delay. Readiness comes from facing and dealing with the challenges in the landscape and then resolving any organizational pains, like Competency Addiction, that may arise. Tough times compel organizations to make choices and trade-offs to resolve the pain so that they can progress.

When Steve Jobs rejoined Apple in 1997, he had to face the company's addiction to making premium-brand niche products. Apple commanded less than 4 percent of the world's PC market. It had lots of cool stuff to sell but was spread very thin. In his first year at Apple's helm, Jobs eliminated all of the company's existing lines of computers. The company had invested more than six years and $500 million to develop these products, but Jobs made a choice to end the pain of their lagging sales and focus on core product lines, and thereby move Apple forward. Central to Jobs's strategy was the introduction of the iMac, Apple's "Everyman" desktop computer. Advertisements for the iMac emphasized its ease of use and plug-and-play qualities. Housed in a translucent, candy-colored plastic casing, the sleek iMac even made its way into modern art exhibits. With a price point of $1,299, the iMac was Apple's first dip into the lower end of the consumer market. Throughout Apple's history, sales had come mostly through replacement purchases made by the company's small but fiercely loyal fan base. The iMac, however, changed that trend: according to one study, 32 percent of iMac purchasers were new computer users, and another 13 percent were replacing their IBM-compatible machines. Competency Addiction can't easily take hold or stay rooted within a climate of Systemic Innovation.

Confront Your Competency Addictions on Entering the Badlands

Engaging early in the following action steps will increase your chances for resolving problematic Competency Addiction, clearing the way for you to build the rest of the behaviors you need for long-term success. Start out by internally scanning and scouting for Competency Addiction. Apply the principle *Act with Integrity* to determine the role it is likely to play as an obstacle to a successful journey by blocking innovation. At the same time, assess the current state of vitality and resiliency of your organization, a key indicator of organizational readiness. To make these assessments, you need to listen to outside voices as well as your own instincts and research.

A key indicator of organizational readiness is the number, visibility, and influence of heretics on the inside. With any luck, you still have a few; many leave companies that appear to them to have little capacity for innovation. This almost happened to Dell Computer. A survey taken in 2001—following the company's first-ever layoffs—revealed that half of Dell's employees would quit if they had the chance. Interviews with Dell's internal heretics showed that many employees found management impersonal and autocratic. Despite their own discomfort, CEO Michael Dell and President Kevin Rollins decided to engage in a dialogue with their disgruntled employees. Dell and Rollins gave self-critiques to a room of twenty of their top managers and showed a videotape of the meeting to every manager in the company. They invited employees to submit critiques anonymously. To address the issues that employees had identified, the pair used desktop props to remind themselves of the changes they were trying to make in their management styles. The practice of seeking out heretics is now institutionalized at Dell: once a quarter, employees complete a "Tell Dell" survey to communicate their thoughts about the company's strategy and management.

Heretics are extremely helpful because they are keen observers of the organization. They know the organization's competitive weaknesses and where its big obstacles to progress are. They spend most of their time on the fringes of the organizations, making forays into the heart of the beast and scanning the external environment. A key lesson from the history of cycles of innovation is that change usually comes from the fringe, not the center. All too often, top leaders have lost connection with their organization's heretics and innovators. These people tend to be perceived as troublemakers. Leadership in the Badlands means spending time with people who make you uncomfortable.

Map the Structure of the Organization's Social Networks

Most organizations and their leaders focus on the traditional hierarchal organization chart, although everyone knows that key people are interconnected in informal networks of influence that are invisible to most people, like the one illustrated in Figure 4.1. Leaders need to understand the human forces that keep Competency Addiction in place.

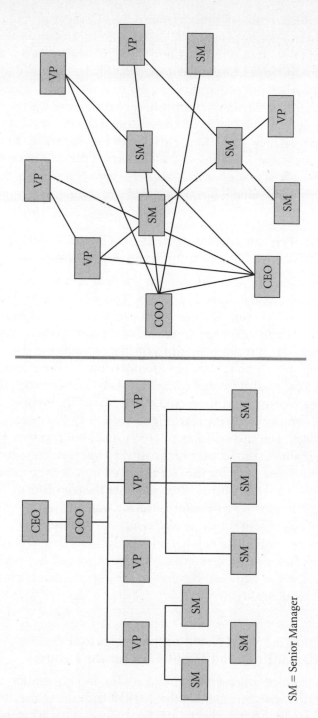

SM = Senior Manager

Figure 4.1.   Hierarchy Versus Social Networks.
Source: Global Foresight, 2004.

Social networks enable or prevent innovation. Competency Addictions get held in place by people in key roles who control flows of information and resources, directing them through their networks into fading core competencies. Over time these people have structured their personal networks in ways that make it easy to divert resources away from new ideas that threaten their position. Making these positions and interconnections visible reveals how these relationships work to reinforce Competency Addiction. This allows top leadership to put strategies in place that will systematically interrupt flows of resources that are not beneficial to the health of the organization. Left alone, these misaligned networks remain formidable barriers to forward progress.

Analyze the Intersection of the Global Drivers and Your Competency Addiction

During this assessment you can identify the power of your organization's Competency Addiction to impede progress. This will help you choose which issues to focus on quickly and which ones you can safely ignore.

Nextel did a terrific job of keeping ahead of the game. When market research indicated that young people identified it as a company for their parents, Nextel quickly bought up hip telecom company Boost Mobile. It approached the market for that company totally differently by offering cell phone service in surf shops and at extreme sports events.

Toyota is another company learning to keep its Competency Addiction in check. The Japanese concern has prided itself on being the most efficient auto manufacturer in the world. However, the value of its vehicles hasn't made up for the fact that even fans of the company find its designs staid and boring. Realizing that the company's Competency Addiction to low-cost manufacturing was stifling its creativity, Toyota's management turned to its design process. Design divisions now work more closely with engineering changes to infuse new ideas into the manufacturing process and to develop new models—such as the Scion, targeted at Gen Y car buyers—that meet consumer demand for style as well as quality.

Imagine What New Competencies and Capabilities You Might Need for the Future

Most successful companies are organized as silos of specialization performing the tried-and-true routines that led to their success; what innovation they indulge in is incremental and tied to their core competencies.

My research shows that despite the bust, the recession, and the subsequent slow-growth period of the 1990s, many companies are still relying on old competencies that are much more specialized than they realize, since they were developed in a different context from the Badlands. To further complicate things, most companies think not in terms of competencies but in terms of organizational structures, products, services, and roles. Few organizations have made the switch to thinking of themselves as a portfolio of competencies, capabilities, and people networks. Few have systematically thought about those competencies, how they support what they produce, and the way the company does business.

UPS has done an excellent job of creating new capabilities and competencies. The profile of this company is one of conservative tradition: UPS is nearly a hundred years old, and it has a tightly controlled and focused culture aimed at efficiency. Sounds like a perfect setup for serious Competency Addiction. But at UPS top management believes it has been given a special opportunity to lead this company, and it is motivated by a strong desire to continue to improve. One of its most successful initiatives was to decentralize the UPS approach to strategic planning, much the way IBM has done. In the early 1990s UPS was looking at declining growth and profits. It didn't wait for a crisis. In a proactive move, a multidisciplinary team of next-generation managers was formed for the sole purpose of thinking of new and different ways to do things. This group, the Information Technology Strategy Committee (ITSC), met twice a month and pulled in employees from around the company. Sales, marketing, cargo, and airline employees were engaged in conversations about new ways of doing things. Outside consultants and customers were also invited to participate. Rich dialogue and many small experiments allowed UPS to see the world differently. The group authorized development of software for large shippers, improved the material-handling process with new technologies, and started using the Web for tracking information and internal

---

UPS applied these Principles of Transformation:

- Learn Rapidly
- Seek Collisions
- Make Decisions Fast
- Execute with Discipline

use. This group even started a corporate venture fund to get a jump on evaluating how emerging technologies could play a role at UPS. The outcome of this strategic planning process was a dramatic shift in how UPS viewed its business and its mission. UPS has moved from being an on-time package delivery company to a global supply chain company.

Cardinal Health, a medical, surgical, and pharmaceutical distributor, has also expanded its core capabilities and competencies to help its customers be more efficient. Cardinal Health uses technology to offer just-in-time solutions to hospitals and medical centers in inventory procurement and management. As hospital supplies are used, Cardinal Health's system records this data, and the next day supplies can be replenished. Cardinal Health also offers a suite of products designed for very specific clinical settings. The company's products and services continue to grow because of its expanded vision of what its dynamic with customers should look like. Cardinal Health is not just a supplier but also an integrator and a collaborator. As the environment in the Badlands shifts, organizations will need to migrate those competencies to fit the rugged terrain, as well as create entirely new ones.

Define Your Innovation Gap

Once you have achieved a deeper understanding of your competencies and addictions, your next step is to determine your innovation gap—the difference between the speed with which innovation occurs in the marketplace and your organization's ability to create innovation and respond to marketplace demands. The rhetoric of innovation, so ubiquitous leading up to the Badlands, often failed to yield sufficient results: words substituted for action, helping the company fall into the knowing-doing gap. Through most of the 1990s this didn't matter, since organizations were able to make progress and create profits without much innovation. The unintended consequence of this flow of words in place of action was the residue of cynicism and resistance to innovation that it left in many organizations, which makes the innovation gap much harder to close today. In many ways, innovation is treated as a diversion from what people see as their real work—that is, ensuring profits from current business lines.

My recent research on innovation indicates a persistent innovation gap. Most of the companies I studied—73 percent of them, to be precise—reported that they were functioning in a highly unstable environment in which markets, competitors, new technologies, and consumer preferences could change rapidly and unpredictably. But only 30 percent reported that they had put effective innovation processes in place. Most reported they still adopt innovation cautiously, and then only after its benefits are crystal clear. Most still invest resources to support incremental innovation in core businesses.

My research indicates that most companies need to do considerable basic work to improve the internal climate for innovation. In the early stage, companies fail to provide sufficient support for developing new ideas and tracking what happens as a result. At the middle stage of innovation, their development processes are insufficient to permit them to transfer their best ideas to business units capable of taking them further. In the late stages, rewards lag for innovative knowledge workers and for sustaining innovation over the long haul. Less than a third of companies reported that they have much tolerance for failure. Although this appears to be bad news, in fact these results are much better than those I reported from an earlier study completed at the Institute for the Future in 2001.

A second barrier to closing the innovation gap is that many organizations don't actually know what an innovative organization looks and feels like. Nor have they thought through which specific challenges they wish to address through innovation. Each organizational structure provides its own strengths and weaknesses when it comes to innovation and adapting to the Badlands' innovation imperative. No one type of organization will thrive. In fact, most organizations will become complex arrangements of different elements, from hierarchy to multiple alliances to self-generating eco-webs. Self-generating eco-webs consist of people (within organizations or business units) who mobilize quickly to take advantage of an early business opportunity or to pursue an innovative idea that they are very passionate about. Eco-webs can be spun within any organizational type that has a sufficient Systemic Innovation capacity to include shared leadership. The webs thrive as long as conditions are right, and break up when the opportunity has been realized.

In Table 4.1 I look at some of the major organizational types and their ability to respond to the innovation imperative of this new era. Use the table to jump-start a strategic conversation about your innovation gap issues, and to help you think through your organization's innovation strengths and weaknesses.

Each organizational type has different innovation gap issues. For example, while extended enterprises have lots of resources, they also

	Cathedrals—Cultural Juggernauts, Large and Small	Extended Large Enterprises—Both Hierarchy and Networks	Fishnet Organizations	Entrepreneurial Startups
Characteristics, Examples	Family businesses, Chinese conglomerates, *Chaebots*, *Kurotzus*, TNOs with strong homogeneous cultures (Coca-Cola, IBM)	Complex global companies with networks of suppliers, alliances	Multiple small, often loosely interconnected networks that reform depending on marketplace; virtual organizations; professional services	Highly focused, usually externally funded
Innovation Strengths	Big resources for key innovators	Vast resources; diverse talent	Freedom to experiment—able to launch many small experiments; flexibility	Fast movers; passionate people; high risk tolerance; resilient
Innovation Weaknesses	Bureaucracy moves slowly; culture limits innovation to politically correct; don't tolerate failure	Large legacy investments to protect; biased toward efficiency; excessive diversity; failures killed slowly	Scaling up; internal competition; diffuse and disorganized	Scaling up, attracting top talent; finding investors; building brand
Key Innovation Gaps	Diversity climate failure; don't tolerate mavericks	Identify innovators; diverse external relationships	Rapid learning; time for innovation; stopping failures early	Finding resources; getting market share

Table 4.1. Organizational Innovation Framework: Closing the Gap.

Source: Global Foresight, 2004.

suffer from an overabundance of bureaucracy, which tends to smother innovation. A key issue for such organizations is attracting and retaining innovators. Fishnet organizations, by contrast, are loosely interconnected networks that create temporary hierarchies to support a specific piece of work and can disband quickly and reform around a new idea. They are quick to generate new ideas and test them but have trouble scaling them up once they are ready to roll out. Regardless of your organizational type you want to engage in *Learning Rapidly* and initiate strategies to accelerate closing your innovation gap.

BUILDING ORGANIZATIONAL READINESS FOR THE JOURNEY

Few organizations have sufficient resilience to meet the continuous challenges of the Badlands. They need to be ready to morph quickly as their best opportunities quickly emerge.

New Capability: Create Systemic Innovation

No silver bullets can instantly create the capability of Systemic Innovation in an organization. You cannot engineer it—but you *can* improve conditions so that it can grow. Systemic Innovation means that both the conditions and the urge to develop new ideas are active at all levels and in all departments within the organization. No longer does innovation happen only in one business unit or another, nor does it come from a distinct group of people; rather, innovation is part of the corporate identity and a bullet on everybody's job description.

Interestingly enough, most people in organizations already think they have the job to innovate. My research on innovation consistently showed that knowledge workers believed innovation was part of their job. More than half of those I surveyed indicated that the proportion of innovation in their jobs was over 40 percent, and a quarter put it above 60 percent.

Most barriers to imagining systemic innovation lie at the top of the organization and are erected by key leaders of existing core competencies. As my research indicates, the desire for widespread innovation exists, but the conditions for more people to act are poor (Figure 4.2).

Think of Systemic Innovation as a network of ecological niches that strives to maintain a balance of diverse elements, people, resources,

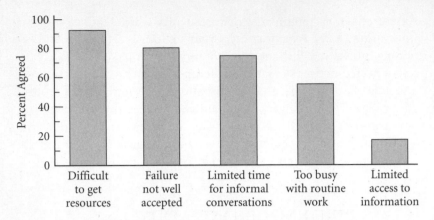

Figure 4.2.   Perceived Barriers to Innovation.
Source: Global Foresight, Innovation Study, 2003.

connections, and information so that it can thrive and keep re-creating itself. The most important attribute of Systemic Innovation is an abundance of people with an attitude of curiosity and a passion for making things better. These passionate, curious people are highly resilient and flexible, not just toward the work but toward each other. In the end, human factors really do count most. Companies must systematically review their knowledge workers and realistically assess whether they have the right mix of talent. If they don't, they must move quickly to resolve that key issue. Having curious and passionate people who can learn is not optional.

It will take time to develop this capability for Systemic Innovation, and no twelve-step program will help you do it. Nonetheless, I see three major initiatives that will help you jump-start the process:

• Mobilize the organization around innovation by creating a compelling view of its benefits.

• Change the context—the interrelated conditions the organization exists in, the key elements in the environmental setting of the organization.

• Seed a social movement within the organization that creates an epidemic of innovation.

Mobilize the Organization

One of the best strategies for resolving Competency Addiction and laying the foundation for Systemic Innovation is for leaders to provide a powerful and compelling alternate vision of the future that is specifically linked to the innovation imperative of this new environment. Although it is true that most innovations will not come from the top of the organization but from the fringe, top leadership nevertheless needs to create a robust climate for innovation so that the opportunities that come with this changed environment can be exploited. To mobilize for innovation leadership, the organization must communicate a bold new sense of destiny that attracts people so strongly that they are motivated to move forward no matter what gets in their way.

Gary Hamel, in his remarkable book *Lead the Revolution,* provides a simple, clear framework composed of four criteria critical to gaining a robust point of view that people can buy into: the vision must be *credible, coherent, compelling,* and *commercial.* Gone are the days when CEOs and other top leadership could rely primarily on rhetoric. These days credibility begins with good data about the changing environment and the organization's current and future position in it. Most people need leaders to paint the big picture and make sense of it with an insightful set of numbers. Complementing the data in Chapter Two with industry-specific data for your company is a great place to start. Although there are lots of uncertainties, which should be called out as just that, it is important to back up the big picture with strong numbers. As Hamel suggests, try to find some "data bombs"—hard facts that create urgency. There will always be people who will challenge the inevitability of a different future; a good data set will help you respond effectively despite their doubts.

What's critical is coherency: consistency between elements of the new innovation imperative. Top leaders should take this opportunity to systematically think through the new proposition clearly before presenting it. They should actively test its assumptions, considering all the alternatives.

Data is critical and speaks to people's brains, but leaders must speak to their hearts as well. Further, leaders must truly believe in the future they are communicating. They must *Act with Integrity* and passion. They must have made the decision that they want to lead in this new environment and make this call to action real. They must answer the questions, Why should people devote themselves to this huge effort? and How does it speak to a higher purpose worthy of their investment of themselves? And finally, the goal must be seen as commercially viable. Most companies will have to reinvent their business models, and some will even have to reinvent their entire industries over the next decade. Gaining buy-in means understanding that the devil is in the details of a sound commercial venture. People will want to feel reasonably secure that the new value proposition is viable in this uncertain, rugged landscape and must know it is better than what they have now.

Carly Fiorina, CEO of Hewlett-Packard (HP), is certainly a leader who made the call to action at HP very real for people. In 1999, Hewlett-Packard's board of directors broke from the company's nearly sixty-year tradition by selecting a woman as CEO. Fiorina, previously president of Lucent Technologies' Global Service Provider Business, had successfully led Lucent Technologies' spin-off from AT&T. Now Fiorina was charged to lead HP into the Internet Age.

She came into her new job with a clear vision for HP. On her first day she established that the company was going to undergo dramatic changes. She spoke often of "reinventing" the company and invoked its history of being started in a garage by two buddies. Fiorina used the image of the original garage to communicate her vision throughout the company. She developed the "Rules of the Garage," a list of ten principles such as "Radical ideas are not bad ideas," and "No politics. No bureaucracy. (These are ridiculous in a garage.)" Simple sentences that few people would argue with, the Rules were Fiorina's way of reaching employees' hearts to get their buy-in for change. Fiorina spoke with passion about her vision for HP's future as well as with reverence for its past. She even hired an advertising agency to build a replica of the original garage and use it as the backdrop for a television commercial, in which Fiorina herself declared, "The company of Bill Hewlett and Dave Packard is being reinvented. The original start-up will act like one again. Watch!"

Part of the reinvention of HP was its merger with Compaq in the spring of 2002. Fiorina's determination to make that merger happen showed the clarity of her vision for HP. One of the opponents to the merger was Walter Hewlett, the son of one of HP's founders. The proxy fight lasted for months, during which Fiorina continued her persistent persuasion of HP's board. She did not even offer an alter-

---

The Rules of the Garage

1. Believe you can change the world.

2. Work quickly, keep the tools unlocked, work whenever.

3. Know when to work alone and when to work together.

4. Share—tools, ideas. Trust your colleagues.

5. No politics. No bureaucracy. (These are ridiculous in a garage.)

6. The customer defines a job well done.

7. Radical ideas are not bad ideas.

8. Invent different ways of working.

9. Make a contribution every day. If it doesn't contribute, it doesn't leave the garage.

10. Believe that together we can do anything.

---

native if the merger were voted down, one more way of projecting her belief that the merger was the right and only course for HP. She tried to convey to HP's employees that their commitment to the merger was critical to the future of the company. When the votes were counted, Fiorina was rewarded for her tenacity.

The merged company of HP and Compaq totals over $87 billion in sales and, just shy of its two-year anniversary, appears to be successful in a number of areas. Research firm IDC reported that HP took Dell's place as the leader in the PC business in the last quarter of 2002. The new powerhouse is also challenging IBM's dominance in services. In the second quarter of 2003, HP announced that it had beat out Big Blue for a $3 billion services contract with Procter & Gamble.

Top leaders must, like Carly Fiorina, make clear that leadership will change in this new environment, and that everyone is needed to perform their best. She called her colleagues to action: "Are you an inventor? Want to come along?"

No CEO can change the company alone. Some top leaders are better than others at cajoling people to change because of their position and the resources they control. But even they need coalitions.

Change the Context

Creating a new and compelling story of the organization's future is essential but nowhere near sufficient to launch the journey. Unless yours is one of the few organizations that have already developed the advanced capability of practicing Systemic Innovation, you will have to strategically and deliberately make changes in the social and physical environment surrounding the organization. This context includes the patterns and flows of communication and work. Part of every person's context lies in the people they see every day, the things they hear or read, the place they sit, and the information that flows to them. Unless you rearrange, eliminate, and add new things to the organizational context, the environment will continue to support all the old habits and will therefore not be able to innovate much, if at all.

A very simple example of context change comes from Japan, where an executive of a semiconductor company instructed his employees to stop the long-held tradition of addressing colleagues by title. The CEO implemented this simple yet enormously symbolic change in tradition in an effort to open up communication and to prevent workers from feeling inferior or inhibited. The CEO believed that using titles like "department chief" impeded decision making and innovation.

All human behavior is influenced by environmental cues, often subtle ones. This is what makes Competency Addiction so difficult to extinguish. People draw a million subtle environmental cues every day that encourage them to keep from changing. It follows that if you want your people to change, you must alter the cues they receive. Most companies need a new social infrastructure that allows their members to self-organize and to move freely and efficiently in pursuit of innovations. People need the right social and physical context to do their best work.

Every successful future leader will need to understand the power of context. Malcolm Gladwell, in his seminal work *The Tipping Point,* provides many insights into how subtle and not-so-subtle elements in the environment powerfully influence people's behavior. He concludes that it isn't so much the convictions in your heart and the quality of your ideas that control your actions; it's the immediate context for your behavior. Robert Sutton, in his book *Weird Ideas That Work,* identifies several context changes that have major impacts on innovation. Luckily, we can transform context. It involves changing the way people and things are arranged so that old patterns of relationships are disrupted and variation is introduced. Changing the context is challenging, but leaders can do a few things early on to create the conditions under which systemic innovation can evolve.

REVAMP THE INNER CIRCLE. It is still too common for executive inner circles to be composed of like-minded people. Most executives still talk far too much to people who are like them. They are isolated from much of the organization and lack a direct feel for the marketplace. Most will need to change their inner circle. It is natural to have people who influence us, so that habit will likely not change, but the most successful leaders will design a new web of influence that brings them in touch with diverse sources of information. UPS shifted the context of strategic planning with the establishment of the ITSC, and it had a dramatic impact.

The context at Motorola suddenly changed when CEO Christopher Galvin, the grandson of the founder of Motorola, resigned in November 2003. And it was deep, subtle changes in context that had been taking place at the board level in recent years that most likely influenced Galvin's decision. The pattern of having family allies take positions on the Motorola board had shifted over the past several years to recruiting successful outside corporate leaders to help the beleaguered company regain its position. This was a major change of context. When Galvin disagreed with the board's pace of change and strategy, it didn't take long for this board to accept his resignation. The sentiment for family ties did not run deep, compared to the need for the company to change.

REORGANIZE PEOPLE AND PHYSICAL LOCATIONS. As I've discussed, one of the biggest barriers to achieving Systemic Innovation is that too many people relate to the same people and things day in and day out. Shake up the organization and move people around so that they are relating to new people in new places. Do this throughout the organization—not just once, but as a practice. Put people in jobs they don't know how to do and let them figure it out. To encourage innovation, Australia's Lend Lease drastically redesigned its headquarters building, eliminating personal space and creating interactive meeting areas in former executive suites. Through the center of the building they built a "vertical street," an open staircase that links themed floors and provides communal and meeting spaces to employees. Elevators are programmed to stop at every other floor, to encourage employees to interact with colleagues in other departments. Oticon, a Danish hearing aid company, encourages live interaction among its employees by limiting the amount of paper in the company: a single "paper room" is the only place in the building where paper is safe. The company also reduced the number of elevators in its building in order to increase impromptu meetings in stairwells, and built stand-up coffee bars and "dialogue rooms" where employees can exchange ideas.

REWARD MANAGERS FOR DOING LESS. "Less is more" when it comes to managing innovation. Innovation work depends on the flexibility of Self-Leadership. The growth of the knowledge economy means that companies will need fewer managers, since knowledge workers know what to do and how to do it—but they need the right conditions and resources plus the freedom to move about freely and get things done. More management simply doesn't yield many results in any knowledge work, and in fact can be a downright bar to innovation.

START A DRUMBEAT OF TEMPORARINESS. Permanency is the enemy of innovation and the fertile soil for mindless behavior and ultimately Competency Addiction. The best leaders for companies and industries that need continuous, fast-paced innovation are slightly paranoid ones. Such leaders stay constantly on the alert for outside innovations so that they can remain in business. Keeping people in a state of mind where everything is temporary is another strategy to ensure more variation. After all, if things are going to be discontinued, it is hard to engage in mindless behavior for very long. At Brazil's Semco, the drumbeat of temporariness is loud. Every six months, employees bid for new positions, and they are accepted or rejected based on their skill sets. This has worked at Semco to prevent any worker from falling into entropy and has created a fertile ground for continued innovation.

REWARD SIMPLICITY. The best innovations are always simple. Although divergent thinking is a critical part of innovation, in the end it has to be boiled down to something simple enough so that it can be focused on and created. Simplicity is important in communication and for getting resources. You don't need elaborate processes to guide people or fund programs. These are legacy ideas from the past. Instead, you want fast learning and disciplined execution in an extremely straightforward environment. Too many masts and jibs and spars take the wind out of the sails of innovation.

Seed a Social Movement—
Create an Epidemic of Innovation

First and foremost, realize that creating the capability for Systemic Innovation depends on your organizing the equivalent of a social movement within the company. Some call it a revolution, others a campaign. I call it an epidemic, because the goal is to infect the organization with innovation. Just giving people information doesn't make them change. Systemic Innovation will not be created by events or proclamations from the top, and you don't learn about how to do it in an MBA program, at least not yet. However, one of the core competencies of future organizations will be creating social movements as part of continuously renewing cutting-edge knowledge work. Leadership needs to be much more savvy about how to create social change and must follow through. Given the overreliance on technical science in the twentieth century, and the existence of corporate cultures with an ingrained belief in the primacy of facts and technical solutions, people will find it very uncomfortable to make the shift to add a competency such as social movements. *They should just get over it.* They can't be successful without it. Yes, business runs on facts—not just hard scientific and economic facts but also social facts, as in the challenging climate of the future.

So how do you do it? Systemic Innovation can only be diffused throughout an organization through a word-of-mouth epidemic supported with a little knowledge from social movements. The goal is to inoculate the whole organization with the fever and capacity to innovate. In *The Tipping Point,* Gladwell describes the three factors needed to create a successful social epidemic: the law of the few, the stickiness factor, and the power of context. Appling this knowledge to systemic innovation is very useful.

The key part of seeding an epidemic is to apply the law of the few, focusing on three important roles: the mavens, the connectors, and the salespeople. Gladwell says that the person who spreads the word is critical; not everyone can do it. He further states that these three key roles have to be in place for success and that it is important to focus on them rather than being distracted by others. *Mavens* are passionate information accumulators and brokers. They are obsessed with finding knowledge and just as obsessive about passing it on. They are people with no personal agenda, but it is part of their personality to want to help other people. They are exceptionally skilled at passing the word along and being believed. People take their advice almost without exception. Companies need to identify the mavens in their midst and enroll them to become information brokers about innovation in the company, get them busy spreading the word about who is doing what and how it can help the one they are sharing that information with. This will build a sense that innovation is indeed a good deal to get involved in. Think of mavens as the data banks of innovation in the company.

Connectors are people who have relationships with many if not most of the units in the company, inside and out, and they move freely between these different worlds. They are insatiably curious, very self-confident, very sociable, and full of energy. They have an impulse to know everyone, and they find everyone interesting. They revel in casual, friendly relationships and have the ability to bring all sorts of people together. They have "weak ties" with many, many people. Gladwell points out that weak ties are actually more powerful than strong ties in providing access to innovation opportunities. Strong ties do not provide the variation needed for innovation. Approval by connectors is very powerful because they connect diverse parts of the organization. Connectors are important to growing Systemic Innovation because they will weave all the innovators together in never-ending patterns. This prevents innovation from becoming siloed and keeps optimizing diversity, ensuring a continual source of variation.

The third key role is that of *salesperson*. Neither the maven nor the connector is a persuader, and sometimes you will need to persuade some people to join in the innovation movement. Salespeople are able to build trust and move people quickly to participate or buy in to the new innovation thrust. They will help prevent and cure Competency Addictions and the formation of groups that could undermine the development of this new capability.

In addition to these exceptional people needed to find ways to get the message of the innovation imperative to stick with all sorts of people, *the stickiness factor* is the second key factor in seeding an epidemic. What makes a message stick is not the content but how it is packaged. Some simple ways of packaging messages, under the right circumstances, will make them irresistible. The message has to be memorable, and the way it is packaged has to move people to action. This takes lots of tinkering with the message and repackaging it for the different groups it needs to stick to. How you get it to stick with engineers is likely to be different from how you get it to stick with the marketing department. But there is a way in both cases, and you have to keep tinkering until you find it.

The third factor for seeding an epidemic is *understanding the power of context*. Context is the environment in which an action, in this case, an epidemic of innovation, takes place. Epidemics are exquisitely sensitive to the environment, and small changes can tip or prevent the tipping of an infection into an epidemic. The urge to engage in the process of innovation will probably come from something small in the environment. Gladwell cites many fascinating examples of how small things ended up increasing or decreasing crime in major cities, such as removing graffiti from subway cars, which turned out to be a symbol of a broken system that tipped people into more crime. Once graffiti was removed, crime fell even without any other changes. What this means to companies is that they must focus on changes in context to get their innovation epidemic to take hold.

The second part of context is understanding the power of the group in human behavior. To get a big epidemic you will need to seed lots of little epidemics in small groups. People do not bond to an idea but to each other, and the size of the group matters. People cluster in small groups. Let connectors be the links between them.

One word of caution is in order. Beware of an immunity developing to your epidemic. One of the greatest facilitators of immunity is e-mail, because it gives the illusion of making everyone a connector. The types of connections made through e-mail of busy people cannot substitute for the more organic face-to-face roles played by connectors. Information overload is a barrier to stickiness and true human connectivity. People tend to need and trust personal relationships more in the Information Age.

Semco, the Brazilian industrial equipment manufacturing company I've mentioned from time to time, doesn't have a fancy social theory. Nonetheless, CEO Ricardo Semler started nothing short of a social movement when he took over the reins at his father's company.

At first glance, it might look like Semler had no concept of management and no strategy for leading Semco. After all, he fired two-thirds of Semco's upper management on his first day of the job, saying, "The key to management is to get rid of the managers." He then removed himself from the position of top decision maker, calling himself a "counselor." But his actions proved to be far from naive; they were deliberate and strategic moves to revolutionize the social structure of the company. By eliminating bureaucracy, he gave employees an opportunity to share in leadership. He essentially made all Semco employees equally responsible for the future of the company. Workers formed small groups that were each charged with setting their own budgets and production goals. In place of managers, peer pressure and self-discipline guided the employees. They could decide their own salaries, but they had to demonstrate to their peers that their contributions justified their income. They focused on their professional development, learning new skills from their colleagues. An epidemic of shared leadership spread throughout the company.

Building preemptive skills was critical for each Semco employees. As noted earlier, every six months employees bid for new positions in the company, and their bids are accepted or rejected based on their skill sets. For any worker, falling prey to entropy is a sure recipe for losing a place in the company. Entrepreneurial spirit is fueled by the formation of "satellites," small work groups that set their own research agendas. Semco has an army of scouts in its satellites, exploring new opportunities. Today, in fact, the bulk of Semco's new products are the result of satellite innovations. By inoculating the organization with a fever of entrepreneurialism, Semler has proven that "worker involvement doesn't mean that bosses lose power"; instead, it removes "the blind irrational authoritarianism that diminishes productivity."

Another social movement example comes from BP Amoco. In 2001, BP Amoco was preparing to merge with ARCO. Barely a year had passed since the earlier merger of BP and Amoco, and management wanted the integration of the BP Amoco and ARCO workforces to result in a more innovative company. They used strategies similar to Gladwell's, building support from key employees and creating a context for change. Prior to any physical relocation of employees, BP Amoco funded a comprehensive internal study of both companies to identify key human resource issues that might occur in the merger. Through interviews and focus groups with employees, BP Amoco found influencers and salespeople throughout the company who could help make the integration a success through their social networks with their colleagues. Connectors helped management identify and connect with those in both companies who would need to be coaxed to become part of the social movement. The company used input from employees to develop a white paper that outlined the benefits of the merger; this became a tool for the salespeople to use in discussions with nay-sayers in their business units.

Along with seeding a social movement, BP Amoco's management created a new context for the epidemic of innovation. To create greater openness and collaboration throughout the workforce, BP Amoco redesigned its office buildings, adding state-of-the-art conference rooms, informal team spaces, and whiteboard areas for brainstorming sessions. Employees were given portable phones and access to high-speed connections throughout the office to encourage interaction among departments. The open floor plan allowed employees to see their colleagues more easily and encouraged face-to-face interaction. It also provided stickiness for the message of innovation through teamwork, since all employees had to do was look over their low cubicle walls to be reminded that they were part of a collaborative effort.

PARTING THOUGHTS

Creating Systemic Innovation is an ongoing process that is both exhilarating and extremely frustrating. It takes courage, creativity, and persistence to find the right people and all the little things that make the difference in getting the epidemic of innovation to spread. Here are some pitfalls to avoid and some insights to help close your innovation gap and move on to the rest of the journey.

Avoid These Pitfalls

While an organization develops its capability to innovate, it must be careful to avoid the following common pitfalls.

THE ILLUSION OF ESCAPE. The first pitfall to avoid is the illusion of escape. As you study the map in this book, you will note that several routes open up from the bottom of the first ravine. The direct route ahead looks similar to the path you have been on, a continuation of the roadway from the Great Industrial Plains. In reality, though, it is a box canyon that provides only the illusion of escape. Everyone has to pass through the Badlands. The leadership principle of *Acting with Integrity* must be applied at the very start, particularly when it comes to facing brutal facts. The leadership challenge here is not to try to figure out how to get out of the journey but instead to go forward and embrace it. Leaders at all levels of the organization need to show the courage to be different and the heart to take a turn up the pass beyond Competency Addiction into the heart of the Badlands. Despite the challenges along this route, they must passionately believe they can make it—and convince everyone else in the organization that they can make it too.

DENYING YOUR ADDICTION. Treating any addiction is difficult, a long-term process that is fraught with obstacles as well as both progress and failure. Denial of the addiction is an ever-present danger. With luck and the right conditions, some addicts can go "cold turkey" and thrive. But it is particularly difficult to cure Competency Addiction once and for all in companies today, given all the false starts and broken promises of making changes that litter most organizations' recent past. The meteoric rise of management consulting gurus who have packaged one-minute solutions and one-day transformational events mirrors the short-term thinking and short attention spans of many companies, particularly over the last few years. Thus at this historic moment, when major change is imperative and when more innovation—often of the radical kind—is required (right *now*), organizations must face their addiction to the familiar feel of the old ways and continually guard against it.

GETTING LOST IN FAMILIAR TERRITORY. Following your own tracks, ritualistically applying tried-and-true behavior strategies, trying to make sense of the Badlands with old assumptions and beliefs—all these patterns are comforting at first. For a while they can be useful to gain time as you figure out how to get ready for the long journey ahead. But there is danger in staying too long in one spot. You can even lose your opportunity to make the journey. Other companies—your competitors—are moving on, and new ones are entering the game, so you could lose talent, hemorrhage revenues, even go bankrupt. At no point will you ever be totally ready to march into an inherently difficult, uncertain, and frightening terrain. Prepare in the ways that we've discussed and take the plunge.

LISTENING TO OLD SAGES ON THE STAGE. The fourth pitfall to avoid is the old voices and passions of well-meaning gurus both inside and outside the company, as well as the legions of well-meaning management consultants who provided a stream of advice throughout the heady days of the last decade. The truth is, you can't rent a guru to help you get through your journey through the Badlands.

RELYING ON OLD INTUITION. Another pitfall is relying on intuition that was honed in the previous era. Much of this tumultuous new world of the Badlands will simply not respond to your gut feeling. Until you develop a new kind of intuition that meshes with this new context, you must obsessively test your intuitive impulses. The Badlands environment is changing in real time, reconfiguring itself under the power of potent driving forces and new social arrangements between humans inside and outside of business. To become "Badlands smart" is to become an activist designer of what you want to achieve in the next decade, based on understanding the cues and subtleties of this ever-changing landscape.

NOT SUPPORTING FAILURE. Eliminate the idea of failure, or at least soften its costs. No organization will survive the Badlands unless it creates a safe way for its people to fail, as well as a fast way to fail. It is better to have lots of fast failures than a few that are long, drawn-out affairs.

SUMMARY INSIGHTS

- Entering the Badlands is scary but very exciting. Getting a grip on Competency Addiction allows a company to move on and discover the opportunities in this turbulent environment.

- Most companies have major innovation gaps along a number of dimensions. Many companies simply don't have enough variation to generate innovation and few are anywhere close to having their optimal diversity. It is critical to get beneath the talk and specifically define what the innovation gap is in your company, not just today but in the near future. Nothing is more important than truly creating a climate where innovation can take off.

- The good news is that most knowledge workers feel that innovation is part of their job and are anxious to engage deeply with it. It is only legacy organizational practices, processes, and cultures that hold them back. Much of their creativity is now being expended in working around obstacles rather than focusing directly on innovation work. Partner with them in new ways to get breakthroughs.

- Address and resolve Competency Addiction and create Systemic Innovation simultaneously. It won't be possible to create Systemic Innovation in an organization without exposing and addressing powerful Competency Addictions. In both of these major thrusts you have to learn about the social networks in your organizations. They are what holds Competency Addictions in place and, ironically, also serve as the means for facilitating the context and climate for widespread innovation.

- Heretics are important, especially at the beginning of the journey. They can quickly provide insights into major innovation gaps and Competency Addictions, and have often thought through ways to resolve them. Even though you may not find heretics likable, get up close and personal with them. They can lead you through the innovation gap.

- Go whole hog and create an epidemic of innovation. Partial responses won't do the trick. This takes courage and learning a whole lot about social movements and epidemics, not knowledge usually resident in most companies. Bone up, get mentors, and seed your epidemic smartly and widely.

CHAPTER FIVE

Weave the Web

Create a Resilient Organization

It is no secret that the hierarchal structures of organizations from the Industrial Era are too rigid for this disorganized economy, characterized as it is by creative destruction and waves of disruptive innovation. In fact, savvy leaders (those who are born again in the Badlands) will experience the current organization as being increasingly dysfunctional in this environment. It is neither nimble enough to respond to fast-evolving opportunities nor sufficiently resilient to recover from the inevitable problems. As we move forward, hierarchy won't totally disappear, but it will be used more sparingly and on an ad hoc basis. And increasingly, bureaucracy will be a thing of the past.

> *The future organization is a web that will weave itself. Multiple networks of individuals and organizations, constantly being woven, will morph their relationships to respond to the constant flow of both opportunities and threats.*

PAIN #3: NETWORK ANGST—BETRAYAL AND RISK

The shift to social networks as the means for getting work done inside the organization causes anxiety, particularly among senior executives who mostly view networks as an invisible enemy: they are neither observable nor controllable, and they change continuously. Externally, companies are also being pushed by changes in the market to engage in all sorts of new alliances with suppliers, customers, consultants, and independent knowledge workers, and even, like Sony, with competitors. These are multiple, loose, temporary relationships with little assurance of fairness and protection.

Senior leaders in established companies feel betrayed, as long-term, established partnerships and employment relationships are gradually replaced by a new way of doing business, and all their years of hard work to reach the top seem threatened. The organization itself feels as if it is being pulled apart by exposure to uncomfortable risk and more ambiguous, looser relationships. Success depends on knowledge workers you don't control generating new knowledge that results in innovation. Traditional competitive assumptions are challenged and boundary and ownership confusions arise. The anxiety is palpable.

New Capability:
Engage and Support Social Networks

Social networks are rapidly emerging as the major source of leadership and innovation. Social networks, left alone, tend to act like tribes that include similar people and exclude those who are different. Therefore they need to be identified and shaped both internally and externally to ensure that they produce positive and dynamic relationships and have a strategic direction. You want the network to work for you; you do not want to work against it. At the same time, Networked Leadership must be free to self-organize in pursuit of strategy and innovation across internal and external networks and alliance webs. All companies need to climb quickly up the learning curve to build this complex new capability. Future competitive advantage will come from vibrant social networks, the dynamic new business infrastructure.

As the sustainability of the organization as a whole comes under scrutiny, anxiety about its future is palpable, especially among those with the most to lose—the winners under the old rules of the Industrial Era. This is often the first sign of the third pain, Network Angst, with its attendant feelings of betrayal and risk. I use *network* as an umbrella term to characterize the more flexible, loosely joined, and impermanent internal and external relationships between people and organizations that are the major defining characteristics of new organizational forms. As traditional, more stable, and more defined relationships ebb, old winners will feel abandoned and betrayed.

Global driving forces are all posing a challenge to conventional organizations, but none so much as the new technologies of connection, which make information accessible to the many on demand, allowing dispersed knowledge workers, suppliers, customers, partners, and competitors to interconnect outside traditional channels. Furthermore, and most important, these technologies unleash the power of the internal social networks to share knowledge and create new business independent of the traditional power and decision-making structures. These networks are far more nimble, resilient, and innovative than the old hierarchal structures. As they coexist side by side in the transitional terrain of the Badlands, these two kinds of structures are likely to result in increased tensions between the organization and the individuals who work in it, and between divisions and departments working in different systems.

As this shift begins to take place, companies will need to develop the capability of Engaging and Supporting Social Networks. Even though people have been forming social networks since time immemorial, the process and how it can be influenced is not well understood by most people in business.

The enterprise as a web is emergent, which means that what we have now are primitive life forms at the beginning of the organizational metamorphosis that will take place in the Badlands. This profound transformation, from a highly controlled and vertically integrated hierarchy—a cultural juggernaut—to an agile networked enterprise, is extremely challenging. A key organizational imperative is to make it easy for knowledge workers to go whole hog and freely develop personal microsocial networks within and outside traditional corporate boundaries.

Altogether these form a vital new and growing social infrastructure for business that is very powerful. How does a networked company come into being, let alone stay interconnected and resilient?

A social network is an invisible web of interconnected nodes, each node being a person or a social group that shares a common communication code around such values as commitments to keep promises, patterns of reciprocity, and the safety to contribute freely and openly. It is based on and held together by trust.

TRIPLE JEOPARDY: THREE BIG SHIFTS UNDERLYING NETWORK ANGST

The pain of Network Angst will be hard to resolve in the short term. The following three ongoing shifts underpin Network Angst and will contribute to a tense work environment for much of the decade ahead, as they erode of the traditional rules of engagement between organizations and individuals:

- The end of the old social bargain
- The restructuring of employment
- The disintegration of corporate culture

The Old Social Bargain Ends

The old social bargain—with its lifelong employment, worker benefits, full-time work, and employer responsibility for workers' careers in exchange for their work—is coming to an end in most advanced economies. The breakdown of the Industrial Era social contract between companies, employees, and labor sets up powerful new tensions. The new economic context steadily renders knowledge and skills obsolete, fosters global competition, and gives rise to new technologies that outdate business models overnight. The long and the short of it is that both employers and employees feel vulnerable. Employers find it difficult to find and maintain a competitive advantage if they are saddled with traditional labor arrangements, while workers feel insecure and at risk without a new contract in place to spell out the nature of the obligations between them and their employers. Both sides feel they are part of an unplanned experiment in finding new ways to work together. The old social contract for work will not be replaced with a simple, single new model. Instead, an entirely new set of principles and practices and multiple models will evolve through the dynamic interplay between organizations and knowledge workers. Angst comes from the need to act despite the absence of new rules.

Restructuring Employment

The rising importance of the knowledge worker and the precariousness of jobs, knowledge, and skills account for a significant amount of Network Angst.

THE RISING IMPORTANCE OF THE KNOWLEDGE WORKER. In the Industrial Era, average, ordinary people drove business results. Standardization and repetition were the keys to mass production and to high-quality manufacturing. Companies wanted people who would show up on time and do what they were told. Today things couldn't be more different. The knowledge economy of the Information Era depends on innovation from highly talented people. These workers create the new knowledge that serves in turn to create Radical Innovations that ultimately produce new wealth, positioning the company for the long term. The importance of these workers in every industry and discipline from high technology to architecture to financial services marks a huge, far-reaching shift in the type of talent a company depends on for its success.

Knowledge workers bring to the table certain essential characteristics that define their value to companies:

- The ability, as lifelong learners, to add new skills and knowledge quickly as the environment shifts
- The strong cognitive skills required to create knowledge and recognize emergent patterns
- A high degree of techno-literacy, with a continually updated technology tool kit that matches their specialized talents
- The ability to actively grow their own particular portfolios of knowledge and to create and maintain personal networks
- The ability to move fluidly among the many new leadership roles

The rising importance of this high-end talent brings with it new risks for both organizations and for the knowledge workers themselves. Their flexible yet more intimate relationship will be much more demanding for both parties and will be challenged further by the volatility and uncertainty of the Badlands.

NEW RISKS FOR ORGANIZATIONS. The fast pace of economic change and global competition means that companies will always be competing for these highly mobile, talented workers. If companies lose highly talented workers—and they will—they not only lose the person's intellectual capital, they also lose critical working relationships to which the person was linked through social networks. And this naturally means a loss of some of the specific information and business intelligence channels of information that flowed through the knowledge worker to the organization.

On the opportunity side, organizations have much more flexibility as to the people they hire and for how long. They can staff up in one global location and slim down in another, as business dictates. They can cut costs by sourcing labor in varying locations around the globe. They can minimize health and pension benefits by offshoring jobs and outsourcing at home. They can match people to strategies and retain them for as long as those strategies are working. They can let them go when having them no longer adds value, although they want to do so in a way that allows for the possibility of reengagement later on. They know that worker-company relationships need to have a Velcro-like quality—a strong attachment while needed that is also easy to disengage without damage when the time is right.

NEW RISKS FOR INDIVIDUALS. The downside risks for individual knowledge workers in such arrangements include less job security, less protection of their rights as workers, and fewer employer benefits. On the upside, they get to be their own bosses, and they gain the freedom to determine where, how much, and under what terms they will work. They become activists and advocates for their own growth and development, empowered to choose working assignments that bring them myriad rewards, from higher compensation to new knowledge and skills. They can link to a larger number of social networks, increasing their ability to employ an ever-expanding reservoir of business intelligence, enhancing their long-term value in the global talent marketplace. They can design for themselves a work life that better accommodates their personal and family needs. Part of the tension for a knowledge worker comes from balancing two conflicting needs: staying on the job long enough to complete good work and moving on soon enough to avoid getting stale.

Both sides know that the future success of businesses will depend largely on the creativity and productivity of their knowledge workers. This means that what is good for business also needs to be good for people, otherwise the business will fail. But how do companies build these new bonds of trust and negotiate win-win arrangements with their workers? We are in that awkward stage, when neither side has developed the sophistication to put together this new dynamic. To craft the deal effectively, each side will need to constantly clarify the value proposition it brings to the table. Each party will want to make sure it can deliver on promises and avoid both hype and unrealistic claims. The stakes are far too high to permit a mismatch.

The Disintegration of Corporate Culture

Corporate culture is a relic of the twentieth century.

The erosion of these important features in the work landscape permanently undermines traditional corporate culture, with its hierarchy, command-and-control orientation, and stability-seeking features. This old culture is anchored by people appointed to fixed roles and by patterns of routine work—all underpinned by old-social-bargain work arrangements. As the economy churns faster and faster it clashes with these old structures, eroding their effectiveness. As the old social bargain ends, so goes the trust and reciprocity for producing work. It dissolves all the shared identities within the organization. This is not to say that all hierarchy goes away—rather, its power will be diminished as it shares responsibility for the success of the organization with heretofore invisible social networks and with different leaders functioning in the new culture. In its simplest reduction you might imagine a future organization where some form of hierarchy supports routine work, and social networks generate the innovation that creates new wealth for the company.

The culture of networks is worlds away from the culture of hierarchy; it supports people self-organizing and moving freely in the pursuit of innovation. The business transactions that networks undertake occur in the context of interpersonal trust among small numbers of people, not through formalistic processes of hierarchy with all their legalistic overtones. Trust does not necessarily mean a deep personal connection but instead is based on commitments for the duration of the business agreement. This gives rise to a temporary project identity. Networks are dynamic; when the business is done, the players move on, but in the meantime they have built a relationship and trust that supports further reconnection. There is no mastermind at the center. That is the power of these networked, de-centered forms of organization. They do not just organize activities, they also produce and distribute cultural codes. Over time these interactions create a history of trustworthiness and credibility. The reputations of the players extend the reputations of their companies and, in the global context, of their countries too.

Reciprocity and trust form the glue holding the networks together. Trust is hard to build and maintain in an environment that is rapidly changing, yet it is imperative, since knowledge work is so highly interdependent. Such work creates opportunities to think together, solve problems together, and innovate together. Trust, learning, and innovation all go hand in hand and occur over a series of conversations where people share tacit knowledge with one another that results in innovation.

The organizations of the future must be able to create the context for trust among people in all their networks. This is where the second principle of transformation comes into play: *Act with Integrity.* If fast, positive changes are to take place, people have to feel safe enough to have candid conversations with each other about their analysis of markets, problems in core processes, and ways to change business models. Each organization must learn how to cultivate and increase the amount of trust throughout its structures and along the full extent of its reach. Many companies have cultures based on fear. These may prove effective in some models, but the stark truth is that innovative people simply do not produce their best work when they are suspicious of each other and where risks and failures are punished instead of supported and learned from.

RESOLVING THE PAIN OF NETWORK ANGST

It will take a long time to fully resolve the pain of Network Angst. The first step is to understand the shift taking place and its impact on the whole organization. Next we must find ways to accelerate the demise of the old while easing people's fears, and to create an opening for new organizational forms and cultures to emerge. Slowly the future of the organization will come clear. Throughout this process nothing is more important than moving quickly to establish the capability of Engaging and Supporting Social Networks.

New Capability: Engage and Support Social Networks

Social ferment feeds commercial innovation:
Historical lesson of innovation.

Although everyone, from the chairman of the board to the messenger in the mailroom, knows that people are interconnected in informal networks of influence, most executives think of networks in negative terms; they perceive them as bottlenecks for getting work done and believe they work in mysterious ways to undermine decision making. They either ignore them or try to navigate around them; both of these strategies seldom provide good results.

Social networks have performed all kinds of functions, so it's not unlikely that at some point they did undermine authority, but this is far too parochial a view of such networks; it is not just outdated but dangerous. Social networks embody an organization's social capital, and in a knowledge work economy are as important to understand and measure as human, intellectual, and financial capital. Because these social networks are critical to a company's success, leadership needs to engage strategically with them—not to try to control them or make them official parts of the organization, but rather to understand how they work and assess them regularly to ensure that they are functioning in support of strategic goals. If they are not, leadership needs to make deliberate moves to strengthen them. Engaging and Supporting Social Networks is not something many companies currently regard as a capability. They face a tough learning curve to develop it.

Candid and far-ranging conversations among knowledge workers on an ongoing, nonlinear, unplanned basis are what tap a company's reservoir for innovation and knowledge creation. Conversations are one of the key influencers of performance. These types of conversations will only occur in companies that have cultivated the climate for deep interpersonal trust. It doesn't matter how much knowledge resides in the heads of an organization's most talented people; they will not be able to develop that knowledge further unless they trust one another, particularly in the amorphous task of innovation. Networks glued together by trust can generate enormous wealth; conversely, those lacking trust can quickly drive a company to failure. In fact, this one quality will have more influence over the success or failure of a company in the future than will the rules and processes of the hierarchy. People who do not have trust are suspicious of each other; people who are suspicious of each other don't share much. Companies that do not share are freighted with many rules and a tight management style, which further retards innovation, forthright conversations, and risk taking.

My recent work on innovation confirms the importance of social networks. All knowledge workers worth their salt will have a complex set of informal and formal networks to leverage for innovation. People, information, and resources flow in idiosyncratic paths within and across the boundaries of organizations as knowledge workers use their relationship webs to perform their work. In the future, an organization's best opportunities will probably come from the networks of people with which it is connected. Most knowledge workers rely heavily on their own personal networks inside and outside their company to support both their innovation and routine work. As shown in Figure 5.1, they report the need for an extended network, often one outside their industry, for both inspiration and development of new ideas.

Most reported that conversations are the most important source of support for innovation. They need informal access to a wide variety of people. This makes them concerned about creating and maintaining a reputation within their companies and about nourishing their external networks as critical to performance—at least 80 percent strongly agreed with the following assertions: "I need to actively network to keep up to date," "I need to help others in order to get the help I need," "I need to be able to speak freely with people who will challenge my ideas," and "I need a good reputation in order to have access to key people and information." (The last point was nearer 100 percent.) There has been a shift from company-appointed teams to more spontaneous groupings for innovation work as well as routine work: only 40 percent regarded formal teams as very important and about 50 percent said the same of ad hoc task forces, as opposed to just under 80 percent for self-organized groups and 100 percent for personal networks. Despite these trends, however, people also report that their office workspace supports routine work but not innovation (Figure 5.2).

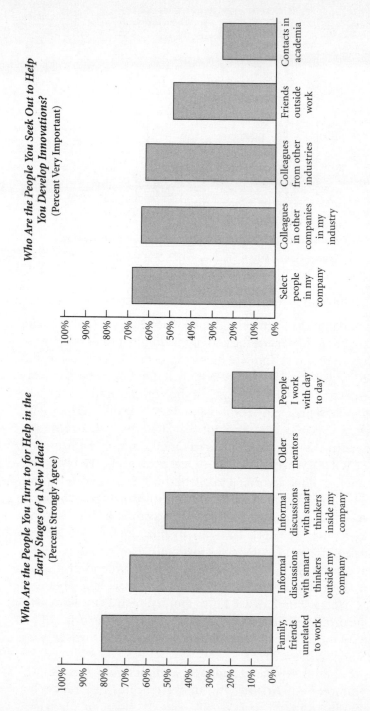

Figure 5.1.   Sources for Innovation.

Source: Global Foresight, Innovation Study, 2003.

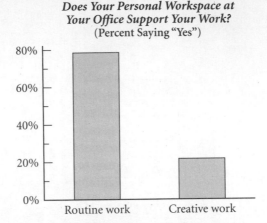

***Does Your Personal Workspace at
Your Office Support Your Work?***
(Percent Saying "Yes")

Figure 5.2.   Personal Workspaces Don't Support Innovation.
Source: Global Foresight, Innovation Study, 2003.

The End of Hierarchy?

The rising importance of networks in companies does not mean the end of hierarchy, but it does mean the end of the dominance of this type of organizational structure. Think of hierarchy as the skeletal system and human networks as the circulatory system. Karen Stephenson (a Harvard professor and founder and CEO of the very innovative firm Netform), a pioneer in mapping networks and describing their relationships with hierarchy, describes organizations that lack synergy between hierarchy and networks as having Acquired Organizational Dysfunction Syndrome (AODS). When organizations reach this gridlocked state, real work does not get done according to established processes; instead, the workplace becomes a giant trading floor for informal favors between people that enables them to get routine work accomplished. These time-consuming detours are hugely costly to organizations—the antithesis of a climate conducive to Systemic Innovation.

So hierarchy as we know it does not come to an end, it just becomes one alternative—to be used when it best serves the organization's goals. Most hierarchies will be temporary, such as the leadership in a specific project. No one knows exactly what all the forms of organizations of the future will be, but we can forecast there will be more networks and less hierarchy.

To create conditions where networks and hierarchy exist in productive symbiosis, you first need to understand the differences between them (Table 5.1).

Features	Hierarchy	Networks
Visibility	Explicit	Tacit
Flexibility	Rigid	Elastic
Knowledge	Rules	Roles
Relationship	Transactional	Trust
Diversity	Heterogeneity	Homogeneity
Discipline	Bilateral	Betrayal
Rate of change	Slow	Rapid
Disruptive change	Heretic	Maverick
Accountability	Transparent	Opaque

Table 5.1.   The Distinct Differences Between Hierarchy and Networks.

Source: © Karen Stephenson, 2003. From a paper presented at Leadership California Graduate Issues Program, November 2003.

Networks are held together through tacit relationships built on trust. In contrast, hierarchy makes structure explicit and relationships more transactional. Disruptive change in hierarchy comes from heretics, while in networks it comes from mavericks. Heretics operate on the fringes of organizations, often in stealth mode. Part of their modus operandi is criticism as well as innovation. Their job is to drive some of the initial stages of organizational metamorphosis. On the other hand, change is inherent in networks, where it occurs rapidly and flexibly. Mavericks are opportunity hunters, applying the principle of *Scan, Scout, Steer* to move the organization toward potential new wealth through Radical Innovation. It is important to remember the specific complications that networks bring into play: their tendency toward homogeneity, which could limit innovation; their difficulty with assigning accountability, which means that theirs is a culture where the principle of *Act with Integrity* must always be applied.

MOVING TO ACTION

Three puzzle pieces form the foundation for building the new capability of Engaging and Supporting Social Networks with an eye toward innovation. Ultimately they will work together to support the metamorphosis demanded of organizations in the Badlands. It will be difficult indeed to weave the web of your new organization without these pieces in place:

- Engage social networks.
- Adopt networked leadership.
- Build an external alliance capacity for innovation.

ENGAGE YOUR SOCIAL NETWORKS

Understanding your social networks is no longer optional; you don't have the choice of ignoring them. If you want to produce networks that support your strategic goals, you have to engage with them. This involves three specific actions:

- Map the networks.
- Identify key people and their connections.
- Optimize and align them with strategic goals.

Map the Networks

Mapping social networks makes key people and their connections visible; it transforms the diffuse nature of these powerful phenomena into concrete diagrams you can work with and more readily understand. There are a number of recognized experts in this field, but I'm particularly impressed by the work of Karen Stephenson, CEO of Netform and a Harvard professor, who has invented a methodology for mapping these networks that includes a nifty computer program. Her ideas have been extensively tested by work with such diverse clients as the Pentagon, Merrill Lynch, Steelcase, and IBM, and her unique background in anthropology, chemistry, fine arts, and computer software gives Stephenson a particularly diverse and dynamic viewpoint and capacity for analysis. After collecting data points through confidential surveys, direct observation, and interviews, Stephenson gathers them into her proprietary software program, which produces a number of maps of different kinds of networks. People in organizations are often members of several networks and play different roles in each. Creating an overlay of these maps provides an insightful look at the culture and who the key players are. Six primary networks are commonly mapped:

- *Work Network:* The people you habitually interact with daily to do routine work.

- *Social Network:* The people you contact to find out what is happening. These include contacts you make at work and outside work.

- *Innovation Network:* The people who regularly hold conversations to talk about new ideas and improvements in core business models and practices, as well as seed radical new ideas and experiment with them. Expect to find heretics and mavericks here.

- *Expert Knowledge Network:* The people both inside and outside the organization who are the resident experts on core knowledge and practices. This network often clashes with the innovation network, and its members are usually quite different.

- *Career Support Network:* A resource for people looking for advice about their futures and for mentoring as well as looking out for the organizations future.

- *Learning Network:* The people who take the lead in improving existing processes, practices, and methods. People tell them the truth about what works and what doesn't, allowing them to target improvements accurately.

It becomes evident by looking at the maps that the network as a whole possesses more intelligence than any one person in it. It provides a data-rich visual tool to hold a strategic conversation about how these networks process and influence the work of the company.

Identify Key People and Their Connections

Part of Stephenson's social network mapping includes identifying people in three key roles—hubs, pulse takers, and gatekeepers. These people are part of every network and have the trust of large numbers of people within the organization. In short, these people are the new culture carriers. Looking at who and where they are and to whom they are connected to provides an essential understanding of how well the company's power networks are supporting its strategic direction. CEOs will want to be positively connected to all the key hubs, which they often aren't. If a CEO or other leader feels undermined, mapping social networks can provide intelligence about how these networks may be organized to support that effort.

Hubs are the most interconnected people because they enjoy a very high level of trust across the organization and because diverse networks connect through them. For an organization to run smoothly

A CASE STUDY OF FLAWED
CEO SUCCESSION PLANNING

The CEO of an R&D subsidiary of a major telecommunications company was nearing retirement. Three direct reports to the CEO occupied the critical roles of hub, pulse taker, and gatekeeper. Diane was the hub in the work network; she had superior knowledge of the company's key technologies and was critical to day-to-day operations because she was so well connected and because of the high degree of trust she inspired by her way of working with key people. Everyone prayed that nothing would ever happen to Diane because she was critical to generating knowledge. What many people didn't know, including the CEO, was that Diane wanted to be promoted and was thinking she might need to leave the company to achieve her ambitions. Joe was the pulse taker. He and Diane did not see eye to eye and avoided each other. Joe did not have a deep understanding of the company's knowledge and technology and was not well connected or trusted in the organization. However, he had cultivated a strong relationship with the CEO and not only had he become his most trusted adviser at work, he also spent a lot of time with the CEO outside work.

When the CEO retired and Joe replaced him on the basis of the CEO's strong recommendation to the board, Diane left the company. Joe tried to use his very weak connections inside the company to steer it forward and failed. He was fired after three months. Enter Stan, who did not have a close relationship with the CEO or with Joe but did with Diane. He had a very strong career network that regularly took on strategic thinking and plotting for the future of the organization. He was trusted by many people. He was appointed CEO and did reasonably well, but the subsidiary never regained the performance and profitability it enjoyed under Diane's direction.

The CEO erred in putting too much faith in his relationship with Joe as his retirement neared. He was not aware of how critical Diane was to the success of the company and how unimportant Joe was. When Diane left all the social networks where she was so vital, innovation and efficient work became radically weaker and began to lose their resiliency. Had the CEO understood the social network structure of the company, he could have prevented its decline.

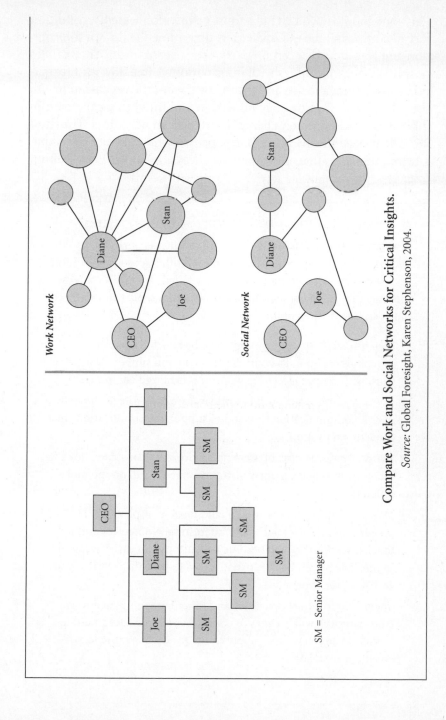

Compare Work and Social Networks for Critical Insights.
Source: Global Foresight, Karen Stephenson, 2004.

(let alone innovate), all its hubs must be interconnected, a condition rare in companies today. Gatekeepers determine the flow of information and resources to a certain part of the organization. They can do positive or negative things with information. A free flow of information allows innovation to arise from any part of the organization. On the other hand, Competency Addiction and infighting can result in information and resources being diverted from new ideas. The third key role is occupied by pulse takers, people who cultivate a few specific relationships that allow them to always be "in the know" about

---

NEW TECHNOLOGIES SUPPORT SOCIAL NETWORKS

New connective technologies will enable social networks to stay connected and engage productively with each other and across boundaries with ease whenever and wherever needed. They will contribute mightily to making the social network structure robust and will facilitate weaving the web of the new organization.

- *Peer-to-Peer Technologies:* People will be able to create work groups across boundaries in the moment and support real-time work with active file sharing without centralized computers.

- *Wi-Fi:* Multiple places will become information-rich experiences, that is, communication "hot spots" supporting conversations that generate innovation.

- *Battery Power:* Microbatteries will last longer than a day, allowing individuals to manage their own power needs and do their jobs differently.

- *Displays:* Smaller, lighter weight, and flexible displays will help people make information more interesting. No longer confined to a flat screen, they will become ubiquitous and easily accessed in multiple places. Look for "hot spots" to have displays ready to embellish the experience.

- *Digital Tags:* Industry partners and other companies in any specific value web will use tags to communicate and coordinate activities up and down the supply chain, producing more focused collaborative relationships.

Source: Global Foresight, 2004.

how the organization is really doing. Stephenson likens them to prairie dogs, which are invisible most of the time but pop up every so often to see what is happening. They are a hidden source of influence, given their connections with key power brokers. They are also a critical source of intelligence. Mapping these social networks brings to light patterns of relationships within a company, and in the process, seemingly inscrutable successes or failures become far less mysterious.

Optimize and Align Networks with Strategic Direction

Leaders must engage with social networks to optimize their function. Understanding how best to influence social networks is still in its infancy, but certain actions are clearly useful. One is to encourage speed in response to communication between key people. Quick responses send the message that the sender is important, and this builds trust. It also communicates a sense of reliability—that you can rely on someone to participate in certain ways. Top management can also weaken social networks that they feel are adversely affecting the company by removing key people from hub, gatekeeper, and pulse taker positions. Mapping personal social networks of key people in the organization can help management see where their connections are weak or strong.

All this may sound like manipulation, but that is old thinking. People should want both themselves and their company to be successful. Using social tools and social theory to improve business is a critical success factor. Yes, some people in power will abuse this knowledge, but that happens in any system. Networked Leadership will drive manipulative leaders from power more than hierarchal organizations can.

ADOPTING NETWORKED LEADERSHIP

Social networks are filled with leadership potential that can benefit the organization. Knowledge workers, with their advanced education and highly developed capacity for learning, can lead in many different ways. This new leadership for the organization will emerge from networks not in a permanent role but as a function that comes into play when conditions are right. Networked Leadership is the self-organized relationship among leaders that provides the shared vision and inspiration to create knowledge across the social web (the interlinked social networks inside and outside the company) to accomplish strategy and innovation as well as aggressively lead the needed organizational metamorphosis.

One by-product of Networked Leadership is that instead of creating more followers, it creates more leaders. Networked Leadership emerges because it is essential to sense-making and to mobilizing action. It is tightly connected when called to action but easily disbands once any one specific piece of work is done. Out of this process comes a new sense that relationships are temporary. The ability to interconnect and perform seamlessly across boundaries—whether they be organizational, generational, or cultural—is the new leadership paradigm for these turbulent times.

Networked Leadership: Vital to Disruptive Innovation

As organizations experience networks' taking precedence over hierarchy—or, as we say, move from cultural juggernauts to fishnets—their borders become more porous. New leaders are making multiple connections both within and without. This environmental imperative for dynamism and interconnectivity makes solo leadership and management from the top irrelevant and ineffective. Everyone must be engaged in strategy and creating new business opportunities or the organization will consistently underperform and ultimately perish. Unfortunately, the Badlands offers no road maps, templates, best practices, or replicable models. Every company's emerging weblike structure will necessarily be unique. It will be distinctive to a given company's style of conducting business, and it will showcase the company's innovative drives and burgeoning talent. Out of this new culture a "leadership brand" will emerge.

One factor that will support the Networked Leadership imperative is people's general readiness for a change. Many workers are tired of organizations run by celebrity CEOs, where most of the benefit flows to a handful at the top and to traditional shareholders. People are tired of the knowing-doing gap, where the changes that need to be made are clearly understood but simply aren't implemented because the leadership is too cautious for the times or has too much to lose if change is made. Top talent want to achieve their goals. They want to break free from innovation-quashing cultures and dysfunctional bureaucracies that impede forward movement. They know that in the Badlands, "You can get in alone but you can't get out alone."

> The leader as solo flyer is a relic in the Badlands. There is too much complexity and turbulence for any one person to go it alone and thrive.

This change in leadership consciousness is a prerequisite to adopting Networked Leadership. Networked Leadership is a major vehicle for extinguishing outmoded organizational cultures. Power shifts to the bonds of interpersonal trust of the Networked Leadership as they create new channels of information and communication that bring business results. Old leaders who were carriers of the old culture and who can't join in this new social way of working will leave or become marginalized. Networked Leadership is a new concept and thus not well defined—it is developing phenomenologically.

Networked Leadership made a big difference during California's energy crisis of 2000–2001, when every leader of every persuasion experienced firsthand the pains of Leadership Insecurity and Network Angst. Some energy companies, like Pacific Gas and Electric, based in San Francisco, and Southern California Edison, based in Los Angeles, suffered near financial ruin. Southern California Edison teetered precariously on the edge of bankruptcy, while Pacific Gas & Electric entered Chapter 11 bankruptcy proceedings. Others, like Sempra Energy in San Diego, weathered the crisis fairly well because they were better prepared as a business; they had made earlier business decisions that allowed them to stay financially solvent and had a strong early form of Networked Leadership.

Stephen L. Baum, Sempra's chairman, president, and CEO, had cultivated a strong Networked Leadership model in the late 1990s, encouraging innovation from his diverse team. This empowered the many leaders within Sempra Energy and its business unit San Diego Gas & Electric to act independently and synergistically on the front lines, in areas ranging from government affairs and community relations to customer service and regulatory affairs. When the crisis hit, that style served the company well, allowing it to manage intense criticism and make rapid decisions on many fronts at the same time. Sempra Energy's leaders remained interconnected, united, and committed to weathering the crisis together. It was a heroic feat. As Molly Cartmill, director of corporate community relations at Sempra Energy, said, "We really took the heat during the energy crisis. We learned a lot of lessons along the way, but we kept in communication with each other and with everyone outside—government officials, our customers, our suppliers, and community leaders—and we stayed coordinated. We couldn't have done this without a leader like Steve Baum, who believed in the company and trusted all of us. We were fast, yet flexible, and we were united in our approach. That kind of coordination and consistency are rare during a crisis."

Despite success stories like that of Sempra Energy, adopting and supporting Networked Leadership is tough work. Changing the leadership model has a great many resource implications as well. For example, if innovation and new business ideas begin to flow from a multitude of nodes throughout the web, which ones get support in the form of actual resources to develop their ideas further? To have credibility, top management must model this type of leadership within the organization, as Baum did. Leadership will be truly networked only when top management embraces the imperative and leads the way.

When Symbol Technology, once an industry leader in wireless connectivity (via bar codes) ran into had times, the company brought in Bill Nuti as president and COO to help turn things around. Nuti quickly partnered with CEO Rich Braveman to rebuild trust by candidly acknowledging the company's problems, sharing new strategies to rebuild it, and enlisting ideas from both within and without for healing the damage. They moved to *Engage and Share Leadership* throughout the company. Symbol Technology still has a long way to go, but with Nuti and Braveman modeling Networked Leadership, as well as creating a climate where the truth can be told with impunity, they are positioning themselves for survival.

Multicultural Leadership: Generating More Opportunities

Innovation requires diversity:
Historical lesson of innovation.

The most important global divide is no longer between political ideologies but between cultures. Not only must leaders provide global outlooks and skills, they must also support the diversity needed to engage with other cultures, a capability still in short supply. Leaders from all cultures will need to participate in Networked Leadership and Self-Leadership, but attitudes and capabilities for both of these vary widely across cultures. Networked Leadership depends on trust, and trust building is not easy across cultures. The Americans and British are more comfortable with Self-Leadership, while people from Mexico, Japan, and Spain more naturally gravitate toward shared or consensus leadership. Networked Leadership is a new concept and set of skills that will challenge leaders from all cultures.

Cultures matter a great deal today and will matter even more as we journey deeper into the Badlands. Leaders from different cultures will want to express themselves in their own unique cultural ways. While people in most countries favor globalization, they do not favor homogenization of cultures and lifestyles; they do not want globalization to obliterate or even much alter their own cultural uniqueness and way of life.

Global leaders need to bring themselves up to speed on how leadership priorities differ across cultures. Although all leaders share many of the same desires and outcomes, their priorities may differ. For example, getting results and managing strategy to action is not seen as a top priority for leaders from many cultures, although it is the number one priority for Americans. Empowering others to do their best is more widely held as a top priority in most cultures. If not understood deeply enough and not managed well, these powerful but subtle differences can prevent companies from doing business with each other successfully.

CEMEX of Mexico, a global cement company, has actively adopted a Networked Leadership approach. Management actively organizes cross-cultural teams of leaders from its network of alliances, transferring them from one part of the company to another, as needed. For every acquisition, the company assembles a team that includes the best leaders and managers, always striving for optimal diversity. Its top management facilitate a Networked Leadership attitude by sharing innovations widely. They spend time learning from new people and companies and building trust by actively looking for innovations they can use across the company, immediately providing the new acquisition or alliance member high status. All this is simply standard practice that yields great results, continuously improving the entire enterprise. And it shows on the bottom line year after year.

The United States still takes few steps to promote leadership development across the spectrum of nationality, ethnicity, age, and gender. It is heavily skewed toward male leadership, predominantly in the hands of American and European men who are fifty and older. In Asia, top leadership is dominated by men, and often by men from a specific family. In the West, necessity, among other drivers, will ultimately reverse the dominance of white males, because as the workforce becomes more gender-balanced and ethnically diverse, there simply won't be enough white male leaders to go around.

Today's executives can facilitate sound leadership development by taking steps to push all kinds of people into challenging professional experiences and then giving them time to learn from those experiences. To make the Badlands a crucible for diverse leadership, companies need to do more than simply wait for the demographics of hiring to create it. Remember, in the Badlands speed is important. Target diversity as a goal, don't just leave it to chance.

BUILD EXTERNAL ALLIANCE CAPACITY FOR INNOVATION

What is driving the formation of alliances and this new business ecology? The smartest people never work for you. They're driving this ability to connect to other people, to try and connect the right intellectual capital together.

New approaches to creating and maintaining external relationships are just as important as the new efforts to engage internal social networks. In reality, the boundaries between companies are growing more permeable daily, increasing an organization's ability to move quickly, flexibly, and creatively in this fast-paced environment while maintaining the integration of processes across borders. In fact, the more resources, knowledge, strategy, values, and practices that flow seamlessly between business partners, the better. Companies have always talked to their customers, their suppliers, and their partners, but not always with the scale, interconnectedness, intimacy, and free flow of information and resources that will come to characterize their relationships in the future. The speed of globalization has transformed the traditional linear transactional value chain, based on the principles and culture of hierarchy, into a complex value web that is intrinsically more democratic than the one-way flows of the traditional value chain (Figure 5.3). Morphing a company's business relationships

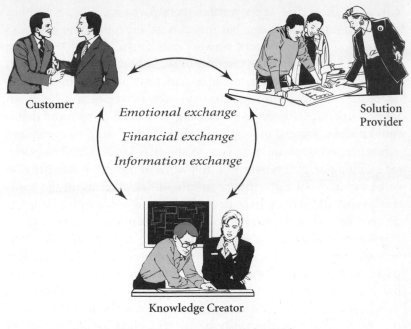

Figure 5.3.   Dynamic Value Web.
Source: Global Foresight, 2004.

into a value web changes the roles of its key members as well as makes the roles more fluid. Your customers become end users, who in turn become full partners in the innovation process. Suppliers become knowledge creators, anticipating the emerging needs of niche economies they serve. Manufacturers shift their roles to become solution providers. All members provide feedback freely, and everyone becomes invested in the solutions and innovations they helped to create.

> *Adopting the Networked Leadership Paradigm*
> *is critical to building a dynamic value web that*
> *supplies innovation.*

Amazon.com understands the power of the network and is successfully engaging and supporting alliance webs inside and outside the company to create value and innovation. Internally, Amazon.com has brought twenty-seven thousand new voices to the table by allowing friendly hackers to access its data and feeds, creating a fast-growing ecosystem. These developers, most of them part-timers and hobbyists, are doing innovative things that Amazon never would have gotten to on its own. This type of social network could help Amazon transform itself from a retail site and a provider of some hosting and transaction services into a key e-commerce platform, ensuring growth and long life for the Internet company. Amazon is also relying heavily on its social network of customers as advertising. In 2003 it announced that it would no longer spend money on television advertising. Management prefers to concentrate on three ways to appeal to consumers: low prices, free shipping on orders over $25, and word of mouth. It is betting on the power of the social network to spread the word about the company's value and service. In essence, this loose alliance with customers has become part of the value web of Amazon's marketing strategy.

It will be challenging to support the growth and dynamic development of a robust alliance web that yields innovation. It demands that you know the value you want and are getting from each member and that you maintain a sense of the web's overall value on an ongoing basis. The usual barriers to successful alliances will still exist—lack of trust, need for control, competition concerns, and legal and regulatory problems, to name a few. They are best managed by paying sufficient attention to making sure your value web possesses the characteristics that ensure success.

Characteristics of Great Value Webs

- Participation of customers, suppliers, and knowledge creators
- Nested diverse social networks connected seamlessly across boundaries
- Tiered structure of participation
- Frequent review and weeding
- Exit strategies
- Optimal diversity
- Free flow of knowledge
- Respect and sharing of intellectual property
- Negative and positive feedback flow freely systemwide
- Innovations that serve the whole community

Many alliances fail because participants have false expectations or lack clarity when it comes to risks and rewards. Sometimes it helps to create a simple tiered tool that defines clearly each party's desired level of participation in the value web (Figure 5.4). This need not be a legal document; rather, it can serve as the basis for discussion between members. There are a host of differences between a licensing agreement and a full strategic partner with whom you are jointly developing a product, yet often parties are not clear about the nature of their relationship, or they come to it with different expectations. Lack of clarity around risks and rewards leads to a breakdown in trust.

It is also important to conduct frequent reviews. Is the alliance still bringing value, and to whom? Is it the same value all parties expected? Has the relationship migrated up or down the tiers of participation? The review process should include an exit strategy for every relationship. What conditions would indicate that the alliance is over or not working, and what is the process for ending it?

The goal is to create a value web where diverse players, inside and outside traditional organizational boundaries, are interconnected and engaged in a free exchange of knowledge, information, and emotion as well as money. To continue to successfully grow the company (even in the face of a lot of doubt from financial analysts), Starbucks is engaging and supporting creative alliances in both U.S. and international

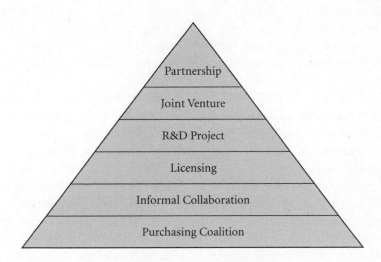

Figure 5.4.   Alliance Tiers.
Source: Global Foresight, 2004.

markets. In the United States, Starbucks has created small social networks by offering wireless Internet access via hot spots at 537 of its stores. When asked about this being a potential problem with people hanging around too long, CEO Orin Smith said, "It's never been a big issue." As it turns out, most people spend a couple of hours and have a few beverages. Starbucks is becoming the de facto office for some people. Starbucks is also trying to build a value web of loyal customers by introducing the Starbucks card. Over time, this network of loyal users will be accessing the Starbucks Internet site, offering feedback and becoming a rich source of new ideas and growth possibilities. This type of relationship with customers will definitely be an important part of the value web for Starbucks.

In its international markets Starbucks is learning that creating new alliances and joint ventures with local citizens and companies can provide a quick start in these new cultures. In China, for example, Starbucks has formed a joint venture with a potential competitor, Shanghai President Coffee Corp. Starbucks can apply the principle of *Fast Learning* by partnering with this Chinese company to learn quickly about the culture and norms in China, a country that is known more for tea drinking.

Knowledge flow—not knowledge management—stimulates innovation, but it requires both respect and sharing of intellectual property. One entity's ideas or products are usually only part of a solution for a customer, whereas innovating together by sharing intellectual property adds value for all parties. Making the value web a safe place to share involves ensuring that all members get value from their collaboration. Innovation requires both positive and negative feedback—both must flow freely in the system. The more knowledge that flows among all the nested networks in your value web, the greater the number of unpredictable opportunities that will emerge, creating the new markets of your future long-term success. These radical and disruptive innovations need to be nurtured and managed to become a new business model.

Achieving optimal diversity is a tricky proposition. You want to have just enough variety in the networks that combine and recombine in your value web to keep novelty and innovation popping up, yet not so much that you go below the minimum threshold for systemwide stability. Too much diversity can lead to loss of focus, while not enough can yield little innovation and creativity.

ALLIANCE FOR INNOVATION DESIGN PRINCIPLES

Ultimately, you will want innovation to spring up from anywhere, anytime, throughout all the multiple value webs that are nested and interlinked throughout the economic space occupied by your company. None of these individual value webs rely on a well-defined culture, either geographic or organizational, for stability or innovation. In fact, these webs seek not stability but rather fluidity among the sets of social interconnections of the participants. This fluidity is very skillfully managed by key individuals, just as in the internal social networks I described earlier in the chapter. As a traditional organization moves to create structures that are a match for the networked economy, leaders will realize they need a different kind of social infrastructure. Designing and maintaining them is the work of the Networked Leadership.

Here is a set of design principles to guide building alliances for innovation:

Make the purpose clear. The goal is to create new markets where all the participants are winners. The game is to bring companies together to create this marketplace and then participate in it. So you are after *Radical Innovation* that will create a marketplace you may not even understand, nor can you imagine what all the products could be or exactly what things might happen there.

Think of the alliance as a community. Innovation requires a sense of deep community ties. Only in that state is there enough trust to share and hold the kinds of conversations that generate innovation. Having enough trust to create a new marketplace means that diverse participants are willing to set up an interdependency that connects their fates. It is important to keep it a safe place to share. The net effect is always a surprise and unpredictable, but it quickly becomes part of the deep knowledge of the value web shared by all members. It is at this level that the disruptive innovations emerge.

Understand the personalities, cultures, and life cycles of the various participants. As with social networks, you need to engage deeply with the members and understand their values and styles so that you can feel comfortable enough to engage. You want to keep the tension of diversity alive and healthy and not allow the value web to default toward homogeneity and exclusivity. Out of diversity comes innovation.

Understanding the life cycle of the various collaborating companies is also important. Old companies and young companies are very different—you want the differences to be a feature, not a bug.

Allow it to grow organically. You want the web to continuously self-organize in response to specific environmental opportunities and threats. Alliance webs need to mutate and replicate quickly, adapting to a changing environment. They abhor central control and should never be so still that they have time to create it.

DRINK AT DANGEROUS WATERHOLES

The best alliance webs will create a whole new market. You can't create a new market without competitors, yet they don't like to drink at this waterhole for fear of attack. You have to entice competitors to participate, knowing they have secrets and managing participation so that efforts to keep secrets don't sabotage the marketplace.

PARTING THOUGHTS

The organization of the future will be a more social entity than the organization of the Industrial Era, when much of the work was done through people's use of machines. Most of the critical work in the new knowledge economy will be mediated through people-to-people transactions and conversations. Hierarchy will not disappear but will move to the background, almost becoming a back office for the organization while the new social infrastructure of social networks moves to the foreground. This is all part of the metamorphosis of organizations into more weblike structures.

SUMMARY INSIGHTS

The pain of Network Angst will persist through much of the Badlands, as the metamorphosis of organizations will not happen quickly or smoothly due in large part to the environmental churn. There will be lots of trial and error in the design of new organizational forms. They will remain emergent, but here are some insights about what some of their characteristics will be and how the metamorphosis will happen.

- An organization will become even more of a social entity as knowledge work happens on a person-to-person basis, not person-to-machine basis. A much different and more robust social infrastructure is needed—one that allows its members to self-organize and move both freely and efficiently in the pursuit of *Radical Innovations.*

- *Engaging and Supporting Social Networks* is a critical new capability organizations must hurry to develop to ensure they have a robust source of innovation and leadership. Going up the learning curve to understand them is critical. It will be a pitfall for an organization to think it can control or create them, but it can make them visible and engage with them, facilitating a good fit with purpose and strategic goals.

- A new value around temporariness will emerge from the constantly changing landscape. People and organizations will become more at ease with multiple temporary relationships and learn to move into them and out of them seamlessly.

- Hierarchy is not dead, but it will only be used as a tool when it fits the circumstances. Along with the diminished importance of hierarchy, the old corporate cultures will become relics of the twentieth century, pushed into oblivion by the demands of flexibility and continuous innovation in the Badlands.

- Trust is not just a nice thing to have; it is imperative. People do not innovate when they are suspicious of one another. Innovation comes from sharing knowledge in deep and spontaneous ways in multiple, rich, often unplanned conversations.

- The Badlands is a powerful context shift that will drive a new leadership paradigm. Leaders must be adaptable Self-Leaders who perform well in cross-cultural and cross-generational situations. But what is just as important, they must be able to engage in Networked Leadership for the benefit of the organization in pursuit of their shared purpose and innovation. You can get in alone but you can't get out alone. Today many leaders are still creatures of hierarchy—there will be lots of tension between the old and new leaders, which will slow down the metamorphosis. Top leadership needs to adopt and support this new leadership paradigm and hasten the demise of the old powers.

• It is critical that the Badlands crucible work to create the diverse leaders companies will need—leaders representing the human spectrum of culture, gender, age, and experience. We don't know much about how leadership crucibles work for this diversity; we mostly know about leadership development in older white men.

• Companies of the future must have a strong and flexible capability to enhance talent quickly and continuously. Although some companies have developed programs in this area, none of them are advanced enough to keep up with the need. A mismatch between the knowledge and skills of people and the needs of the economy will be a permanent feature for the foreseeable future.

CHAPTER SIX

Avoid Strategy Tragedy

ompanies can no longer simply work hard and expect to succeed. They have to dream big and become very different. This means building the capacity to put truly disruptive, innovative strategies into play and manage them to success in the marketplace. The Badlands is all about continually seizing new opportunities and creating new value, not merely coping with massive change by hunkering down and waiting for the turbulence to stop. The devil is in both the strategic details and in the unfettered imagination. This challenge is met best by organizations with reservoirs of resilience and creativity; it cannot be met solely through traditional planning responses and optimizing existing strategies. Creating new approaches and innovative business models is very hard work, but creating wealth in the future will depend on this type of *Radical Innovation*. Renewal of a company's core business takes speed and flexibility in a fast-changing environment. Many organizations lack the resilience to keep up with these changes and react too cautiously, which only worsens the problem. This results in doubting their capacity to compete, often disguised as denial, bringing them face-to-face with the imminent threat of Strategy Tragedy, our fourth pain and a close cousin of Competency Addiction.

PAIN #4: STRATEGY TRAGEDY—CAUTION AND DOUBT

Understandably, navigating the harsh environment of the Badlands with strategies that are running out of energy feels scary. No strategy lasts forever, but strategy decay occurs faster in the Badlands. Strategy Tragedy, accompanied by gnawing feelings of caution and doubt, occurs when well-worn core strategies simply fail to produce the expected business result and there is nothing on the horizon to replace them. Denial and excuses run rampant, and managers place too little emphasis on the distinct possibility that their business model is out of date. Strategy Tragedy strikes when leadership digs foxholes to defend against turbulent change and fails to act urgently and radically to ensure the organization's future success. Leaders continue to tinker with old strategies, showing little regard for the changing strategic context until it is too late.

New Capability:
Growth Through Disruptive Innovation

Creating new value, and ultimately new wealth, begins with vividly imagining a very different business future—in itself a radical innovation. Building this capacity includes changes in context and new habits and competencies. Make sure you have access to a healthy number of people who are contrarians—people who think outside industry norms and can express their views in strategic conversations to mobilize new business models. Many companies do not have a deeply ingrained, widespread capacity for real strategic thinking; for them, strategy is a ritualistic process that often occurs without much passion in groups far removed from the front lines. In the Badlands companies need an engine of growth that supports managing many disruptive innovations through to the market. Learning to invest in emergent strategy at the right time and then going whole hog to see you become the market leader takes smart, intuitive thinking and courage.

Over the last decade the art of strategy got lost. Strategic planning fell out of favor when it was relatively easy for both mature and young companies to make profits. After the free flow of venture funding dried up, new companies all too often launched untested strategies with unsustainable business models. Online grocer Webvan is a good example. During the dot-com boom, Webvan entered the online grocery business. The company launched a sophisticated marketing campaign aimed at the affluent customer. Because it was not a bricks-and-mortar grocery like Albertsons or Safeway, Webvan had to arrange for special high-tech warehouses to store its inventory and had to purchase and maintain a fleet of specialized trucks to deliver the goods. Webvan burned through $1 billion before shutting down in 2001. The company's expensive approach to delivering groceries was not sustainable. Ironically, in 2003 conventional supermarkets like Safeway and Albertsons are entering the online grocery business and having some success. They can fill orders from their own stores, not expensive warehouses. And they are not aiming to build a giant online grocery business; they are just trying to offer new options so their best shoppers will keep coming back.

In the 1990s companies spent millions of dollars on new technologies and consultants, but their investments in technology applications often failed to increase margins and never delivered on the hyped scale they had promised. During the dot-com boom, electronic marketplaces were heralded as "the next big thing." Web sites dedicated to business-to-business transactions proliferated, but of the more than fifteen hundred e-marketplaces that existed in 2001, fewer than two hundred remained at the end of 2003. After investing billions in technology that enabled companies to identify new suppliers and buyers from all corners of the globe, e-marketplace companies found out that users weren't interested in doing business with unknown entities; they simply wanted technology to facilitate the relationships they already had.

The frenzy to squeeze more profits out of existing business lines resulted in many companies' abandoning their investment in long-term foresight; systematic thinking about the future became optional as companies turned back to wealth creation from existing business models. But for many, sticking to old business models created only the illusion of wealth. This was particularly true in the telecommunications industry, which overinvested billions in laying down fiber-optic cable of which less than 10 percent got used. It will take years to recover from this strategic error.

Historical lessons remind us that a mismatch of scale produces instability and breeds innovation or dysfunction.

PREVENTING FATAL STRATEGY TRAGEDY

Strategy, planning, dreaming, thinking about the future—who has the time? In the heady days of the 1990s, everyone was busy creating wealth. Now almost everyone is in bunker mode, cautiously trying to sort out the consequences of past excesses, scandals, and the ongoing recession, while optimizing and squeezing out profits from old core businesses. Everyone, even industry leaders and stellar performers of the past, is just trying to make a buck and stay alive. This is business as usual in a recession, but these aren't ordinary times. Even the most venerable companies with the longest track records of success are struggling to deliver. Coca-Cola is one of these giants being heavily challenged to stay competitive as margins in the soft drink market are eroding. Coke has been suffering from both Competency Addiction and Strategy Tragedy. The company is addicted to "Coke" as its identity and the refreshment of choice. But not only is the carbonated soft drink market growing at less than 1 percent in North America, Coke's strategy has overlooked the discontinuities in the marketplace. These shifts include a hot youth sports market and consumers who are greatly influenced by health and fitness. When it comes to choosing liquid refreshment, more and more people are not thinking about a Coke. Bottled water and sports drinks dominate shelf space, and Pepsi has beaten Coke to a leadership position in these segments, having cultivated a wide portfolio of products such as water, juice, iced teas, and alternative sports drinks. Coke has been caught up in its addiction to being Coke, and has been slow to respond to the fact that consumers want new and different choices when it comes to beverages.

So how do you avoid a fatal dose of Strategy Tragedy? It starts with making a brutally honest assessment of both your current state of strategy readiness and your organization's resilience, its capacity to renew itself continuously and rebound from inevitable failures. Here are four actions to take immediately and to repeat often to stay in touch with the health of your strategic position:

- Diagnose your level of pain.
- Anticipate strategy decay.
- Get a view from 30,000 feet.
- Disseminate a sense of urgency for radical innovation.

Diagnose Your Pain Level

Start by making a quick assessment of your current Strategy Tragedy pain profile (Figure 6.1). This is not a metric to truly calculate your likelihood of fatal pain, but it's useful as a catalyst for in-depth conversation about the current symptoms of and preconditions for Strategy Tragedy within your organization.

Ideally, your answers to items 1, 2, 3, 4, 9, and 11 should be false and 5, 6, 7, 8, 10, and 12 should be true. If your score is less than 75 percent correct, you are set up for pain. This assessment, coupled with

	True	False
1. The same ten (or twenty) people have been talking to each other about strategy for the last several years.	☐	☐
2. Our strategy is more like that of other organizations in the industry than it is different.	☐	☐
3. We are better at optimizing our current strategy than creating radically new ones.	☐	☐
4. We use PowerPoint presentations as our main method to support strategy discussions.	☐	☐
5. Newcomers to the organization are listened to more closely than those people who have been here for a long time.	☐	☐
6. Our strategies defy industry norms.	☐	☐
7. Some of our recent strategies have changed customer expectation of our and others' products and services in the industry.	☐	☐
8. We have products that target customers' unsolved needs.	☐	☐
9. Our new ventures are managed by people who are confident they have the right strategy.	☐	☐
10. We spend time trying to think of ways to get our customers to change.	☐	☐
11. Our company expects new ventures targeting new markets to take off fast and grow big quickly.	☐	☐
12. Our organization is abuzz with spontaneous discussions.	☐	☐

Figure 6.1.   Rapid Assessment Tool: Diagnose Strategy Tragedy Pain.
Source: Global Foresight, 2004.

an analysis of how much strategy decay you have, can provide very useful insights about where you need to make big changes. Incorrect answers here each represent attitudes and behaviors that will cause Strategy Tragedy pain on their own—much less collectively! However, your score will provide you with a good indication of how much work you need to do to free up your people's thinking so that they can create better strategies.

Anticipate Strategy Decay

Most companies don't place enough emphasis on honestly assessing their strategies' rate of decline. This is especially dangerous in the Badlands, where the pace of change is very fast and strategies can become irrelevant much more quickly than in the Industrial Plains. New technologies can suddenly appear at any moment, savvy consumers can change their minds, or a new global competitor can enter the market quickly and grab market share. Think about Napster and the music business as an example of how swiftly a small group of unknown techies can bring an entire industry to its knees. Try to anticipate where your strategy is most vulnerable and consider alternative scenarios so you can put new strategies in place before what is merely a problem becomes a crisis. All strategy suffers from decay. There are few perpetually successful strategies, and even those that are extremely long-lived are sure to come under severe pressure someday from the driving forces in the business environment.

Take another look at the Coke-Pepsi rivalry. Coca-Cola has had incremental success by tinkering at the edge of innovation. Products like Vanilla Coke and Cherry Coke have been very successful but short-lived; when the marketing hype dies down, so does demand. The underlying trend of decreasing demand for carbonated drinks makes Coke's incremental innovation a strategy ready-made for decay. On the other hand, Pepsi has been planning for the eventual decline in the carbonated drink business, busily creating a diverse portfolio of beverages since the early 1990s. Pepsi has acquired brands such as Gatorade, the leading sports drink; Tropicana, with its array of juices; and Aquafina, the leading bottled water. In the face of waning consumer interest in colas and a growing preference for health and fitness refreshments, Pepsi is in the right place at the right time while Coke is now suffering the consequences of a serious *Strategy Tragedy*.

> *Rapid Decision Making and Disciplined Execution,*
> *two of the Principles of Transformation, are key to*
> *avoiding a Strategy Tragedy.*

How knowledgeable are you about the signs of strategy decay? Does your company have a systematic process for evaluating strategy effectiveness and provide you with the business intelligence you need to make an intelligent change? Gary Hamel, leading strategy guru, provides four common causes of strategy decays: *replication, supplantation, exhaustion,* and *evisceration* (Table 6.1).

Great strategies get *replicated* faster than ever today because everyone has access to vast amounts of information, not to mention the growth of the management consulting industry and the dissemination of best practices. Strategy convergence within industries is common, resulting in loss of margins, as illustrated by the PC industry. In the early 1990s PCs were fairly expensive. Over the next decade discounts, improved production, and streamlined supply chain management contributed to drastic price reductions. Dell came out on the winning side because of its ability to cut the costs of production and to dramatically improve supply chain efficiencies. HP acquired Compaq in order to stay competitive, but smaller companies like Gateway were forced out of the market because they could no longer compete on cost. Better strategies come along and *supplant* existing ones very fast. Pepsi's strategy to expand beyond the carbonated drink business into a diverse portfolio of beverages has supplanted Coke's one-dimensional view of the market: these days, fewer and fewer things go better with Coke.

Rapid prototyping is far easier with technology. With so many consumer marketing and sales channels, new markets can take off fast and get saturated fast, putting them at risk for *exhaustion*. The garment industry is one such example; consumers have so many ways to buy clothes—in the store, over the phone, online, or through catalogs—that retailers have had to work hard to maintain their margins. As noted earlier, Sweden's H&M has learned that fashion needs to stay fresh and to be replenished constantly. Levi's, on the other hand, has been slow to respond to market dynamics and has lost significant market share because it has stuck with a fixed view of its brand, with its history and

Replication	Supplantation	Exhaustion	Evisceration
Loss of distinctiveness	Discontinuities that reduce economic power	Performance metrics, slowing down	Customer power eating margins
What important industry norms are you defying?	Is your strategy in imminent danger of being replaced?	Is your strategy reaching the point of exhaustion?	To what extent do your margins depend on customer ignorance or inertia?
What is truly unique about your competitive advantage?	What discontinuities could reduce the economic power of your current business model?	Are the markets saturated? Are your customers fickle?	How quickly and in what ways are your customers gaining bargaining power?
How is your financial performance today—exceptional or average?—and is it rising or declining and at what speed?	Are there nascent business models out there that could render yours irrelevant? Do you have strategies in place to coopt or neutralize them?	Is growth decelerating, and if so are you doing anything about it?	Do your productivity gains increase margins or do you give them back to customers in lower prices? Or in better services at the same price?

Table 6.1. Anticipating Strategy Decay.

Source: Adapted and reprinted by permission of *Harvard Business Review*. Exhibit from "The Quest for Resilience" by Gary Hamel and Lisa Valikangas, September 2003. Copyright © 2003 by the Harvard Business School Publishing Corporation; all rights reserved.

quality. Consumer affluence has risen around the world, so people spend more money. Consumers are e-shopping for the best-priced goods across numerous categories. Web sites such as Shopping.com and BizRate enable consumers to read product reviews, check real-time prices, and place orders, all in just a few minutes. On any given day, Shopping.com alone facilitates $3.6 million in purchases.

This rapid evolution of cheaper prices can quickly *eviscerate* a strategy. For Sun Microsystems this hit very close to home. Sun called itself "the dot in dot.com" during the technology boom of the 1990s. Its strategy: build high-end servers and stay at the cutting edge of innovation by investing heavily in R&D. When the tech bubble burst, Sun's earnings plummeted—from a profit of $1.8 billion in 2000 to a loss of $3.4 billion in its fiscal year 2003. Sun's strategy of betting on high-end (and higher-cost) innovation was clearly in decay. The shift in the industry to standard, lower-priced corporate technology has Sun battling it out with Dell and HP in the small business market, and with IBM in the larger markets. Some analysts say that Sun is a niche company without a niche. Sun's CEO, Scott McNealy, is determined to turn things around. Sun is fighting back by rolling out new strategies such as selling software systems at $100 per employee and producing a faster chip, hoping to catch the wave on the next big thing in technology. Time will tell if Sun can survive.

Hold these lenses up to all your core business strategies and plot their decay frequently. You need to accept the inevitability of strategy decay, not deny it. Though you cannot prevent it, you don't have to be destroyed by it.

Not only does strategy decay happen faster in the Badlands, strategy itself is more complex there than it was on the Industrial Plains. The focus on new market share, a traditional metric of growth, is too narrow. Whole industries are in flux today, and tomorrow's industry leaders are investing strategic resources in reinventing their industries and creating new standards. Successful strategies will depend on a number of factors—from influencing government regulations to getting suppliers to apply more technology to their part of the value chain to supporting higher margins through both productivity and efficiency gains. Wal-Mart, known for its use of technology and supply chain clout, is promoting a new tracking and identification system called radio frequency identification (RFID). RFID employs intelligent bar codes that can talk to a networked system via radio frequency waves. This technology will eventually eliminate the need to scan merchandise with the UPC (Universal Product Code) bar code that we know so well. Its implementation will require Wal-Mart's suppliers to conform to tagging their products with the new RFID codes if they want to stay on the shelf at Wal-Mart. Wal-Mart has already gathered its top hundred suppliers (giants like Procter & Gamble and Unilever) to discuss implementing a plan to attach RFID tags to every box and pallet shipped to Wal-Mart by January 2005. Smaller suppliers will have until 2006 to comply. Retail analysts estimate that Wal-Mart could save $8.3 billion annually by using RFID, mostly in labor costs for inventory.

As organizations become more highly networked, strategy crosses multiple organizational boundaries, increasing the complexity of collaboration. Getting a big-picture view of your long-term strategic position vis-à-vis these two tools, Diagnose Pain Level and Anticipate Strategy Decay is vital.

Get a New View from 30,000 Feet

Once you have your completed strategy decay analysis in hand, the next thing you will want to know more about is the new business context of the Badlands. Despite the fact that you can't see very far into the Badlands, you *can* fine-tune the art of helicopter thinking and take frequent 30,000-foot views of your company and your industry. Most executives view their companies solely through the close-focus lens of current business strategies or processes—so taking the expansive view from this lofty perspective gives a very different picture.

Disseminate a Sense of Urgency for Radical Innovation

Armed with new insights about your present strategic position, you need to sound the alarm so that you can make critical changes, and fast. Creating radical new ideas and business models needs to be everybody's job. Unleashing this potential begins with bringing everyone up to speed on the big picture. The legacy of isolating strategic thinking to small corners of a company means that most companies are not very good at creating conditions for disruptive innovation. As noted in Chapter Four, most knowledge workers believe that innovation is part of their job, but they are constantly fighting to participate effectively. People need more support and also need to be brought up to speed on the rigors and opportunities of the Badlands. Communicate to everyone the new imperative for disruptive innovations, along with sufficient knowledge about the turbulent environment so that people can scout smarter for opportunities that are likely to create new wealth. If people don't understand the new context, the big historical cycle of innovation and the transition zone they're in, they can't contribute ideas that make an impact.

A company armed with new insights together with a sense of urgency about strategy can quickly move to develop a game plan that targets the creation of new wealth. Apple's iPod is a good example of new wealth creation. This MP3 player, which can store hundreds of digital music files, is the top-selling digital music player—more than 1.3 million units sold. With a wholesale price of about $360, the iPod itself is a source of continuing revenue. But just as important, iPod users can visit Apple's iTunes Music Store and purchase individual songs for 99 cents each. With sales of more than 10 million downloads in its first few months of business, iTunes is on track to bring Apple a new source of wealth.

ORGANIZATIONAL READINESS
New Capability: Create New Wealth

The ultimate goal of strategy in the business world is to create wealth. Profits are critical, but wealth creation also includes imagining a future for your organization that is both challenging and sustainable, exciting and achievable, competitive and compelling. A successful ongoing renewal includes engaging people with both their hearts and minds. The capability of Creating New Wealth is the next piece of the puzzle of organizational readiness, fitting neatly alongside Systemic Innovation.

Radical alternatives to current conditions are difficult to imagine, so leaders need to build vibrant visual bridges between their thinking today and thinking in the future. This can be done through stories, pictures, metaphors—any kind of mental prototyping that creates a shared understanding of the issues and knowledge gaps. These must be shared in conversations face-to-face, not simply in PowerPoint presentations or through e-mail. Just giving people information doesn't help them to think differently, particularly when it is done by well-worn methods. That only supports mindlessness. People need to experience new information in new ways—somehow feel it in their bones.

Good conversations are a key component of the lost art of strategic thinking; they are essential to engaging everyone—and you do want everyone engaged—in a creative look at the future of the company. Management at the Danish hearing aid company Oticon believes so strongly in the value of face-to-face communication that almost no other kind—e-mail, memos, or phone calls—takes place within the company's headquarters building. Employees do not have stationary desks; rather, mobile filing carts substitute for offices so that informal meetings can occur anywhere, any time. The open communication intrinsic to Oticon has led to many of the company's unique, innovative products, including the VoiceFinder hearing aid, which is speech-activated so that users can tune out annoying background noise when they are not engaged in conversation.

Inventing and Managing Radical Innovations to the Market: Success Stories from the Badlands

Creating an engine of economic growth from disruptive innovations is new territory, although a number of companies in the last fifty years have developed disruptive innovations very successfully: Charles Schwab with online trading, Southwest Airlines with its focus on small cities and low costs, and the University of Phoenix with its open-enrollment online college programs, to name just a few.

The Badlands demands developing an engine of growth for multiple disruptive innovations as structural shifts in the economy make old business models obsolete and generate opportunities to create new wealth. And it's not enough just to have new ideas—the emergent strategies need to be nurtured and managed to see them through to the creation of their new markets.

It's tricky business. Companies continue to be challenged by creating processes and teams expert in managing disruptive innovations right alongside more mature business models. It is hard to keep both old and new business robust and to balance the allocation of resources to each. According to my research, many companies still struggle to create a climate for disruptive innovation. Less than 25 percent are good at generating radical new ideas, funding small experimentation, and have trouble killing losing projects fast (Figure 6.2).

Most companies are still going up the learning curve of managing disruptive innovations through to market. The biggest challenge is deciding when to invest in an emergent strategy. Only about half of my

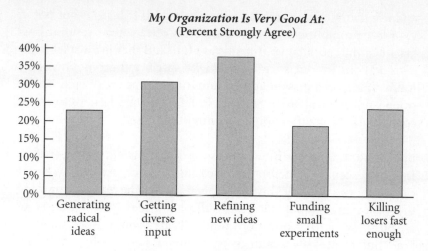

Figure 6.2.   Climates for Generating
Disruptive Innovation Still Need Work.
Source: Global Foresight, Innovation Study, 2003.

respondents strongly agreed that their companies were good at picking the right manager for new ventures, and about a third did so for the propositions that their companies were very good at testing and refining new strategies and deciding when to invest in them.

Generating New Ideas

It is absolutely essential to make a habit of the following practices if you are serious about building the capability to Create New Wealth through disruptive innovation. Since economic turbulence is not going to go away in the near future—at least a decade—these processes need to become automatic behaviors, visible and in action throughout the organization. They should not be packaged as a workshop, nor relegated offsite. They need to become part of everyday conversation.

Sephora, a French cosmetics company, is thinking and acting very differently from most cosmetics retailers. In fact, it has been accused of ripping up the rule book when it comes to cosmetics retailing. Sephora stores are the destination resort of retail cosmetics, offering everything: books, videos, and a full array of cosmetic products. The stores are expansive and inviting with a creative open display approach to cosmetic merchandise. You can pick the products up and sample and test them to your heart's desire. The staff is solicitous but not in your face promoting the latest scent. They offer you a shopping basket when they see that your hands are full, and they are available for consultations. Products are not sold with special gift promotions. Premium brands and mass-market brands of perfume are offered side by side in alphabetical order. Sephora is definitely taking steps to create change and think differently in cosmetic retailing.

DREAM FIRST. The traditional tools for long-range thinking, such as forecasts, scenarios, vision exercises, and wild cards, need to be set aside until you do some dreaming. Then you will be ready to summon the fresh thinking that will make radical new ideas possible and create business model innovations that will carry you through the Badlands and create new wealth. Most companies err on the side of not having enough ideas, but you will need many, many ideas to ensure that just a few will fit in the new landscape.

Start by imagining how you could create new customer expectations, or perhaps even new industry standards. Dream about the day when you are considered the creative genius behind your reinvented industry. Somewhere out there someone is working on reinventing your industry. Think about the impact of Amazon.com on bookstores, or the effect of low-cost providers like Southwest and Jet Blue on the airlines industry. Why shouldn't the next big idea come from you?

CHALLENGE DEEP-SEATED BELIEFS. Every company has its orthodoxies. And sooner or later most deeply held beliefs become tomorrow's blinders.

DON'T FORGET TO SEEK COLLISIONS

Variety and diversity are absolutely critical to creating new value. Applying the *Seek Collisions* principle of transformation is essential to avoiding Strategy Tragedy. All leaders need to *Seek Collisions* with as diverse a set of people as possible. You will never know what you need to know by staying put—you must continuously place yourself at the intersection of multiple pathways where new people and ideas intersect, to ensure that you take in whatever's out there to be learned.

In early 2003 when he decided to disband the company's executive management committee, putting an end to ninety-two years of tradition, IBM's CEO Samuel J. Palmisano challenged the deep-seated belief that strategy comes from top management. The IBM tradition of having this elite twelve-person group preside over IBM's strategy was just not working. The monthly meetings slowed things down. The best ideas were not coming to the table. Palmisano urgently needed to do something different if he wanted to return IBM to greatness.

Palmisano's new approach to strategic planning involved working directly with three teams that he had put in place earlier in 2002: operations, strategy, and technology—all made up of people from around the company and, in some cases, from several layers down in the organization. When he asked this team to come up with a bold new vision for IBM, they came up with so many ideas that they didn't know where to begin. Palmisano directed them to take ninety days to think through the specifics. The results helped Palmisano form a new vision for IBM: e-business on-demand computing. This idea proposes to join thousands of computers and applications in an enormous enterprise. It involves partners and customers. It is a huge technical and cultural challenge for IBM, a corporation where tradition has been king for nearly a century.

Companies don't review their assumptions often or deeply enough. This includes all aspects of the current business model, from the mission statement to how profits are made to who the customers are and what value the business brings to them. This deconstruction should be accompanied by in-depth discussions of why these beliefs are held, where they came from, and whether they still hold value. Next you need to challenge all those beliefs—assume that not all of them are true—and to ask what that would mean for the business. The final step in the process is to look at this fleshed-out set of beliefs extended over the long term in the ever-shifting rugged landscape of the Badlands; pay special attention to discontinuities in your industry and related industries. How are things going to change? How are they changing now?

Don't stop with your own company—go on to attack commonly held beliefs about your whole industry. What are the ten beliefs everybody shares? How will each one of those be affected in the Badlands? Which conventions should you jettison and why? What opportunity would that create for you? And how would customers benefit if you developed that opportunity?

> Applying the principle of *Disciplined Execution* is especially useful when it comes to digging deep to get the payoff from challenging assumptions. Much strategy fails because leaders don't fully delineate their critical issues based on a rigorous analysis of assumptions. Given the pace of change in the Badlands, many assumptions will quickly become obsolete.

The goal of challenging deep-seated beliefs is twofold. The first objective is to figure out which beliefs (if any) are still valid, which are likely to come under extreme pressure in the Badlands, and why. This process should fuel opportunities for *Radical Innovations*. The second goal is to begin to break up Competency Addictions around strategic planning so that you can unleash curiosity and heretical ideas. Many corporate cultures reward people for being right, which only stifles creativity.

Map the Future Sweet Spot of Your Core Competencies

All organizations have core competencies: how they do things and what they know; their people's unique skills and capabilities; their strategic assets, customer data, brands, patents, alliances, contracts, distribution channels, and core processes. Most employees have a vague notion of what these core competencies are, but few companies have done the necessary work to clarify them and instill a deep understanding of what they are throughout the firm. This understanding is the critical platform people need in order to link pieces of your core competencies with emerging opportunities. People need a familiarity and fluency with your core competencies before they can be smart about new ideas. Simply making a list is not enough. What is unique about these competencies, and what benefits do they deliver to customers, partners, and the larger society?

A few years ago, few people outside of China had heard of the appliance company Haier, let alone knew how to pronounce its name ("High-Are"). A key to Haier's success in the international market comes from the core competency it developed in distribution and logistics, which will continue to be a sweet spot for it in the future. The company has applied this core competency to create new opportunities for itself.

The appliance company's unlikely success story began in 1984, when CEO Zhang Ruimin purchased state-owned Qingdao Refrigerator Company in Shandong Province, on the northeast coast of China. At the time, the firm was in such dire straits that its employees were burning the factory's wooden window frames to generate heat. Zhang understood early in his tenure that one of the greatest challenges in serving China's market was establishing a dependable distribution network. As a result, Haier invested heavily in logistics systems. Today its network is so advanced that suppliers worldwide can receive real-time data from Haier's factory equipment and synchronize their shipments with Haier's needs.

Over the past few years, Haier has forged alliances with foreign companies, allowing Haier to market its products overseas in exchange for providing logistics services for its partners. Through one partnership, for example, Haier's wine coolers and washing machines are sold in Japan, and Sanyo sells its batteries and other products in China. Recently, Haier has capitalized on its brand name in logistics to branch into PC manufacturing; the company expects a 300 percent growth rate in 2003.

The principle of *Scan, Scout, Steer* is applied liberally here, along with *Seek Collisions.* You can't map the future sweet spot of core competencies without good, active scouts who bring vital emerging business intelligence from the hidden valleys, lost oases, and empty mountaintops of the Badlands. During their travels they need to ask themselves how they could apply these competencies in other settings, with other groups of customers in other industries. They also need to think about how the core business and its customers are changing and what new core competencies, skills, and strategic assets might be needed to better serve existing customers and their emerging needs, as well as identify new ways to take advantage of existing competencies, skills, and assets.

Toggle back and forth between new opportunities and what you already know, imagining new connections. For instance, Maytag, the well-known appliance company, is capitalizing on the "lonely Maytag repairman." Maytag decided to expand its repair business after market studies revealed a lack of trained technicians for the increasingly complex appliance industry. The studies also showed that consumers had confidence in the Maytag brand. The company is leveraging its well-known brand and tremendous goodwill by expanding into the service and repair of other appliance brands. This new line of business is a relatively easy extension of what has been one of Maytag's core competencies.

> *A new self-concept—identity—*
> *derives from innovation.*

Redefine Your Company by What It "Knows" That It Didn't Know It Knew

Companies collectively know a lot more than merely what supports their core competencies. Although this knowledge may not be useful in the current business model, it could definitely be an asset in the business model of the future. This information is known as *tacit* knowledge, and it can be invisible to the firm, so unearthing it involves charging people with the task of searching it out.

Any company has a diversity of ideas lying dormant within it that can be tapped by *Seeking Collisions*. Newcomers are a group notoriously not given enough airtime in strategy thinking. They are untainted by the groupthink of the company. Young people are new voices and have a huge stake in the future, and your future has a huge stake in retaining them in your company. They really do have a point of view very different from older people. Toyota has taken this insight to heart by leveraging the power of its own young knowledge workers as it developed strategies to roll out the Scion, a new car model. At the core of its Scion planning team was Jeri Yoshizu, a young sales manager who served as the company's eyes and ears for what Gen Y consumers want. She learned about trends among potential Scion owners by interacting with them at events such as DJ press parties, and she maintains steady communication with the Gen Y crowd when she is back in the office. Before Toyota offered its selection of colors for the Scion's optional stereo, Yoshizu polled potential Gen Y customers about what the colors should be named. The results? A hip assortment of shades emerged, from "lithium" and "blade," to "acid."

MANAGING DISRUPTIVE INNOVATIONS THROUGH TO THE MARKET

Organizing for disruptive innovations is a far different process from executing a strategy in the face of relatively few unknowns. It is a much messier, less precise, more diffuse process. When you are pursuing new opportunities, you hardly ever get strategy right the first time; you have to keep tinkering. Deciding when an emergent strategy is finally right is an art as well as a discipline. Under pressure from competitors, many executives think they have the right strategy long before they do, and as a result they invest in driving their product to market only to have it fail.

Emergent strategies face many challenges, not the least of which is attracting resources. Every organization, large and small, has gatekeepers who filter the allocation of resources according to criteria that may not be the best for getting innovations launched and developed. Such criteria can include everything from an opinion that the size of the opportunity does not warrant investment to focusing on investments that are most likely to advance the gatekeeper's own career within the company. This is why in most organizations' top management, CEOs need to stay close to the portfolio of emergent strategies to assure themselves that the strategic direction they have set keeps getting fine-tuned, and that resources are actually allocated to support the ones that fit the best.

You need to jump-start four critical areas in order to build an engine for disruptive innovation:

- Focus on improving customers' lives.
- Create a portfolio of small experiments.
- Reinvent the company and industry.
- Apply global intelligence.

Focus on Improving the Quality of Your Customers' Lives

People today, all over the world, are looking for a better quality of life. Your customers are in the Badlands too, although perhaps on different trails; they too are facing significant changes in their lives. People are going through more career and job changes, women have new roles in the household, divorce is changing the shape of families, and aging is changing not just people but entire demographics. Many consumers will develop new needs and desires as they experience this new context for living and working. Anticipating those first could provide you a new gold mine. In your industry customers and potential customers are grappling with many problems and issues. Could you solve any of these with a new product?

How many companies truly understand the lives of their customers? *Empathy,* according to the dictionary, is the action of understanding, being aware of, being sensitive to, and vicariously experiencing the feelings, thoughts, and experiences of another. CEMEX, for example, didn't just learn deeply about its core customers; it wanted to understand a customer it didn't have—the urban poor of Mexico. CEMEX leaders were impressed by how well poor urban dwellers could construct very modest but serviceable houses. They wanted to see if there was some way they could help. They sent a team of young managers to live and work in a poor neighborhood near Guadalajara for a year. Out of this experience came a novel financing project that allowed more than fifteen thousand families to participate in a lottery scheme financed by CEMEX to fund expanding households. CEMEX contributed small amounts of money in the form of microloans, as well as blueprints and construction advice. Mostly women participated, and there have been no defaults.

Act with Integrity as you Scan, Scout, and Steer
to understand and improve your customers' lives.

Successful companies are going to have to anticipate the needs and desires of their customers or risk losing them to others. They must come to understand a customer's value structure and how that is changing (or not changing) and must become an early mover with innovations. Tesco is the largest grocery retailer in the United Kingdom. Ten years ago, however, it was second to Sainsbury and determined to copy its more upscale competitor. But in the middle of this chase, Tesco's top boss had a revelation, or "crikey moment," as he calls it. As he was reviewing market research that showed that his customers had significantly less money because of the recession in the early 1990s,

Terry Leahy made a landmark decision to change the company's business model to follow the customer, not the competition. By introducing products that address its customers' needs for low prices—the Value line of products and the Clubcard, a frequent shopper program, are two examples—Tesco built a high-quality brand at affordable prices that brought its customers closer to it. Tesco has grown to three times the size of Sainsbury, and still Leahy continues to implement programs that anticipate his customers' needs. For the "One in Front" campaign of 1995, Tesco hired thousands of additional workers to reduce customers' waiting time at the checkout line. In 2003, the company took this sense of urgency in meeting customer needs to a new height: experienced inline skaters were stationed at each register, ready to zip through the aisles to retrieve any items that shoppers forgot to put in their carts. Recognizing the importance of environmentalism to its customers, Tesco has become a leader in recycling. Tesco is a careful innovator, always focused on what consumers seem to want but sticking close to its core. This gives it the cachet of innovation but leaves it room to move on quickly if things don't pan out.

Prior to the introduction of the Clubcard, analysts told Leahy that the program would lead his company into bankruptcy. Today, after returning millions of dollars to his customers in money-saving vouchers that they earn through purchases, it is Leahy's turn to laugh as card loyalty programs become standard among mass retailers, including Sainsbury and Marks & Spencer. Holders of the Clubcard essentially have a stake in the Tesco, receiving regular dividends. Leahy has yet another, more personal, reason to smile: he received his knighthood from Queen Elizabeth in 2002 in recognition of his efforts to serve consumers from all economic ranges.

Understand your customers' ecology of services and how yours fits in. What's the context in which your customer is using your service? Amazon is an example of a company that truly understands its customers' ecology of services. Starting as an online bookstore, Amazon has flourished into a vendor of almost any product or service a customer might want. Based on the customer's search, the site will present ideas of other products that might complement the purchase. For example, a home improvement book might be paired with repair tools or small appliances. With product partners in every area from apparel to cosmetics to pet supplies and gourmet food, Amazon presents its customers with a unified store that answers their every product need.

Maintain a Fresh Portfolio of Small Experiments

Central to building the capacity for creating new wealth is a fresh portfolio of experiments. Royal Dutch/Shell created an incubator for innovation by establishing its Exploration and Production (E&P) division. Parent company Shell gave the E&P group a budget of $20 million to invest. In what it calls the "GameChanger" process, E&P facilitates a brainstorming session to encourage creative thinking among employees in all areas of the company. The GameChanger team evaluates ideas that are submitted and gives seed money of $100,000 to $600,000 to those that seem to have the greatest potential. The originators of the ideas go off for several months on their projects and reconvene with the GameChanger team to review their progress. At that point, the GameChanger team decides whether to continue with the projects or set them aside. Innovations that emerge from the GameChanger process become formal corporate initiatives.

CEOs and top management play critical roles in shepherding small portfolios of disruptive innovations. They set direction, but—just as important—they need to stay close to the experiments and be ready to act fast when an emergent strategy is ready for the big investment it will take to move successfully into the market. It is easy to move too fast or too slow. The seasoned judgment of top management helps get the tricky timing for a new investment right.

Make sure to support little labs everywhere. It is ideal to have lots of experiments going on all over the company, rather than off in some isolated nook. If strategic thinking is everyone's job, then it should be visible in every corner of the company.

It is a myth, and an obstacle to progress, to think that the only good new idea is a big one. Large companies, in particular, overemphasize

---

Fast Learning is the principle to bring into play here. Don't expect many small ideas to succeed or scale up, but make sure they provide the kind of *Fast Learning* that will continuously position your organization to have a better chance of seeding those ideas that will pay off. This means aggressively testing the validity of assumptions. When a company moves to this small-experiment portfolio, it should do so as a learning strategy first and foremost. This stance paves the way for a strategy to emerge that can create the new wealth.

seeking the next billion-dollar idea to the detriment of investing in many smaller, lower-risk experiments. Some of the riskiest bets were taken in telecommunications. Think about the huge cost of Motorola's failed Iridium Project, satellite telephony that banked on being adopted by geographically remote customers. Hindsight shows that the world simply didn't contain enough potential customers to return the company's investment.

In the Badlands, all companies need to think more like good venture capitalists, taking lots of small risks, knowing that most will fail. You should expect to fail, and you will want to do it fast. To make sure

---

OPPORTUNITY AREAS FOR
NEW DISRUPTIVE TECHNOLOGIES

Not only will single new technologies cause strategic challenges, combinations of new technologies will interrupt markets and create new platforms for further innovations. Here are just a few to consider:

- What impact will nanotechnology have on your business? Are you at risk for disposable electronics' affecting your business?

- How will your supply chain be affected by digital tags? Combine digital tags with peer-to-peer technologies and supply chains begin to self-organize.

- Any chance smart materials will cause your strategy to decay? As more embedded computer power ends up in materials from paint to clothes to household appliances—making them intelligent—do they make any of your products obsolete?

- Any impact of the decoupling of the production and distribution of energy on your business? How about small, cheap, long-lasting featherweight batteries? What happens to you when fuel cells scale?

- Miniaturization of technologies facilitate embedding them in all sorts of things—as environmental monitoring for pollution and quality of air, water, and poisons—or for assessing and managing health. How will this affect you? Look for big impacts at the intersection of health, fashion, and cosmetics.

- What impact might genotyping have on your business future?

Source: Global Foresight, 2004.

you fail as quickly as possible, it is critical to aggressively test assumptions that support the disruptive innovation, assumptions in new markets being much less certain than those in more mature markets and business models. The approach should be to invest in Radical Innovations so that the upside potential will be much greater. A portfolio filled with truly new ideas and engaged in small, hypothesis-testing experiments reduces risks while increasing chances of finding a breakthrough. Be sure to keep a lookout for new disruptive technologies.

Reinvent Your Company and Your Industry

Luckily, in most organizations an amazing number of people at least muse about how the organization might change. Find ways to bring these imaginations out into the open. Encourage people to paint a new picture of the company in as many ways as possible. Imagine your core business being totally superseded. How did that happen and how did you respond? Did you actually become extinct?

Another way to reinvent your company is to think about its boundaries—how do you draw boundaries around your business, and is there an opportunity here to make a major shift? How are you different from, or the same as, other companies in your industry? What are the forces under way that could cause shifts in boundaries among all firms in your industry? What alliances could you form to create new markets and services?

Remember PC maker Gateway, the company famous for the cows in its advertising? This $3.5 billion-a-year PC maker has totally reinvented itself. You won't find a cow print anywhere near their new retail stores, nor will you find a PC. The company was edged out of the competitive PC market by giants like Dell, but instead of going completely under, Gateway has reinvented itself as a major player in the consumer electronics industry. ("It was a gut-wrenching level of change," according to Rod Sherwood, Gateway's executive vice president and chief financial officer.) As a result of this reinvention, Gateway will employ 6,700 people by the middle of 2004, down from 25,000 in the year 2000. Gateway stopped manufacturing its own products—except for a few large custom accounts—and it has hired outsiders to handle everything from manufacturing and shipping to employee benefits. In the past year Gateway has become a serious contender in the flat-panel TV market and has also entered hot categories like digital cameras, camcorders, and music players. Its strategy is to undercut well-known brands with prices similar to the no-name brands found in Wal-Mart and other discount retailers. Its target market is budget-conscious families and "zoomers," empty nesters with disposable incomes who have relatively little technology savvy.

Since launching its first plasma TV in November 2002, Gateway has become the largest seller of such TVs in the country. The jury is still out on whether or not this radical makeover will be successful. It won't be long before Dell will be breathing down Gateway's neck again, but Gateway management hopes that this time there will be enough room for both of them.

In the Badlands the massive structural shift that is under way will erode at least some of the fundamentals of most industries over the next decade. Leaders will have no choice but to consider reinventing their own companies *and* the industry in which they function. Are hybrid industries in your future? After all, this is the age of combination science, so start to imagine which other industry might partner with yours. Applebee's, the world's largest casual dining chain, has combined with Weight Watchers International to offer healthier, low-calorie alternatives on its menu. In an age in which obesity is a growing health risk, this looks like a strategy that will benefit business and public health. Imagine the different roles your company could play. Imagine becoming an industry leader, if you aren't already. What would you have to do to get there? What new resources would you need to alter the competitive dynamics of the industry?

Just think of how Napster changed the music industry. The Recording Industry Association of America, dealing with a 31 percent slump in sales between 2000 and 2003 caused largely by piracy, sued Napster, the Web site where users could download music for free. But neither the RIAA nor technology companies have been able to offer a solution that consumers liked as much as Napster. Napster completely changed customer expectations, and as a result the industry is being reinvented. Innovators like Apple are entering the field and creating a new hybrid, the computing-recording industry. With the launch of iTunes, Steve Jobs not only started a new business for Apple; he found a successful business model for legally selling music online. A solution like iTunes, which is far simpler and more user-friendly than any of its predecessors, has been needed for a while. The success of iTunes has turned around the recording industry, which has given its blessing to Apple in the form of licensing agreements from the five major labels. And a revamped Napster is reentering the game, this time having adopted Apple's model for selling music.

Apply Global Intelligence

Global companies are filled with diverse knowledge workers who can contribute to generating the disruptive innovations required in the Badlands. In addition, they can also provide innovations for transforming processes and expanding knowledge of the core business. Often the headquarters company fails to take advantage of this talent pool.

CEMEX has a core competency in integrating acquisitions rapidly through the use of a postmerger integration team (PMI), whose members are some of the most talented managers and functional experts in the company. Although it has a CEMEX Way, a standard set of processes and a scorecard for operations, the company continuously improves itself with contributions from anywhere in the world. It deliberately seeks ideas from its new acquisitions and has a history of taking good ideas and using them, openly acknowledging the contributors and asking for more.

It became common knowledge in the global company that CEMEX headquarters in Monterrey, Mexico, was in need of improvement in several components of its operation. Francisco Garza, the head of Venezuelan operations, suggested to the CEO that they organize a PMI team to send to headquarters to try to come up with some radical ideas for improvement. Needless to say, the CEO was a little put off by the notion of bringing a multinational team to headquarters, but he finally agreed. Garza assembled a team of forty-five highly talented managers and functional experts from several different countries—from Spain to Colombia—and turned them loose inside headquarters to design solutions to several major problems. Within six months they had found over $100 million in annual savings, including closing two plants and streamlining logistics. After this very positive experience, teams like this have been regularly cycled through the mother ship in Monterrey.

Similarly, Carlos Ghosn did not impose change when he joined Nissan; he chose talented managers to lead work teams to plot the company's new strategy. He brought in European managers from Renault and teamed them with their Japanese counterparts at Nissan to create cross-functional teams. In this way, Ghosn combined the consensus-building work behavior of the Japanese workers and the leadership experience of the former Renault managers. The move resulted in robust cross-functional teams with a broad perspective for forming Nissan's strategy.

PARTING THOUGHTS

Creating a portfolio of *Radical Innovations* and managing the emergent strategy process for disruptive innovations is very challenging but essential to master. Because of the Badlands environment, companies have the opportunity to create an engine of growth around multiple disruptive innovations, not just one. This is a new business condition—virgin territory. Ten years from now we will have some models of success and failure. Today we just have some principles, lots of risk, and lots of potential. We don't know all the pitfalls, but here are a few that you can take steps to avoid.

Avoid These Pitfalls

- Superficial foresight should not substitute for a systematic look at the future. Yes, we face lots of uncertainty, but those who are surprised by much of the future are those who didn't pay attention.

- Expecting your business model to age gracefully is a legacy mind-set, as is holding on to the delusion that success is self-perpetuating.

- Depending on visionaries and gurus for strategy (you can't buy a strategy from the outside) is dangerous.

- Don't discount small, new, and weird ideas.

- Imitating others is seductive, but new strategies that target the same markets and customers as your competitors will get you nowhere.

- Matching successful managers of old products to new ventures often results in a big failure. Staffing new ventures with the right talent in the right structure is critical.

- Unrealistic growth expectations from disruptive innovation often lead to trouble, especially in big companies. The dot-com

bubble aside, usually it takes time to create wealth. Don't
get caught needing to make big profits fast from new ventures.
Support their potential by having ongoing income from other
businesses.

- Investing too early in an emergent strategy before it is clear what
  the strategy should be can blow your chance to be the leader.

SUMMARY INSIGHTS

All organizations that want to survive for the long term will have to
engage in *Radical Innovation;* business as usual will ultimately lead to
underperformance in the market. It is also not a time where one disruptive innovation can serve you for a long time—you will need a
steady stream of them, which means you must build an engine of
growth that generates them and manages them successfully through
to creating the new market.

- Begin by understanding where and when you are likely to experience the pain of Strategy Tragedy. That means anticipating
  strategy decay for all components of your core business, how it
  is likely to happen, and at what pace. This is not a one-time exercise but an ongoing assessment process—things change fast
  in the Badlands.

- Build the habit of frequently testing the assumptions of
  every business model. Old models will become obsolete more
  quickly in the Badlands, and you want to anticipate shifts, not be
  caught by them. Emergent strategies should never fail because
  the assumptions were wrong. Figure out if the assumptions have
  validity very early in the process and be quick to let things go if
  they don't pan out.

- Engage regularly in "helicopter thinking" and use the intelligence you pick up to educate everyone in the company about
  what lies ahead. Instill a sense of urgency for *Radical Innovation.*
  This will help all the people scout smartly.

- Refine the art of strategic conversation as a habit everyone en-
  gages in. Don't let PowerPoint presentations and routines drive
  out the creativity you need. Most people do not know how to
  identify the difference between disruptive (radical) and sustaining (incremental) innovation. Most *Radical Innovation* will

emerge from the tacit knowledge embodied in all the talent. Conversations that lead to radical innovations and ultimately new markets won't happen in the culture and structure of hierarchy. Your social networks need to be vibrant and free to self-organize for the pursuit of innovation.

- Foster the spirit and principle of *Seeking Collisions*. Creating disruptive strategies for the future is hard work and depends on running into unanticipated opportunities. Strategic variety is key—you need options that match the magnitude and variety of change in the environment. You won't find them sitting at your desk or just talking to the same old people in the same old places.

- Focus on your customers' present and future. How could their lives be better through products you create? How can you change the competitive landscape with radical innovations that thrill customers?

- There will be a sweet spot in your core competencies in the future—scope the possibilities out fast and start playing the game where they are likely to be.

- Creating and sustaining an engine of disruptive growth is very difficult. Few companies have done it, and even fewer have done so more than once. This is new territory. Learn to manage the emergent strategy process actively and well. Once you take the plunge and invest in your first batch of innovative ideas, make sure you have several more in process.

CHAPTER SEVEN

Engage People Deeply

T he global workspace is swirling with options for individuals and organizations from Munich to São Paulo to Beijing. Both are scrambling up the learning curve of creating flexible work arrangements. These new relationships are not being crafted in the culture of past times but in the maelstrom of the Badlands, where needs of both employers and knowledge workers seem to change perpetually. Of the many variables at play none are more important than the array of personal, cultural, and generational characteristics of an increasingly diverse global knowledge workforce. The stakes are high—everyone needs to find a good fit time and time again. The rapid obsolescence of knowledge and skills means both individuals and organizations need to become habitual learners. Individuals look for opportunities that advance the trajectory of their careers in wholly new ways, and organizations must adapt to both the generational and cultural needs of their most critical talent. This creates a complex match-making environment, filled with new risks. Increasingly, knowledge workers in all cultures and generations are more reluctant to share their creativity without new scrutiny of the organizational environment. These new rules of engagement give rise to the fifth pain, Talent Tantrum, which is often accompanied by a strong feeling of being unfit and undesirable. This is a highly chronic pain, multifaceted and persistent. The very phrase "Talent Tantrum" communicates the breadth and depth of people issues resulting from the environmental upheaval under way.

PAIN #5: TALENT TANTRUM— UNFIT AND UNDESIRABLE

As organizations are forced to rethink and reconfigure how they create and deliver products and services, innovate in their business models, meet the challenge of global competition, and come to grips with Competency Addiction, they experience gaps in essential skills, competencies, and attitudes. Organizations feel that they are *unfit* to compete for the talent they need.

The complexity of engaging with a far-flung, multigenerational, and multicultural knowledge workforce demands much more sophistication than most organizations have cultivated to date. Large organizations in particular feel *undesirable* to the vibrant knowledge workers they need to attract and retain, especially the younger Gen X and the Net Generation, who dislike traditional hierarchy and corporate culture.

New Capability: Engage People Deeply

To achieve the desired business results, organizations must get to know key talent at a much deeper level and negotiate the terms of engagement across generations and cultures in a more customized fashion. To do this well, they must also know and clearly communicate their own value proposition to a diverse global workforce. Young people are just as apt as more senior workers to have the skills needed, and they are just as likely to live in Asia as they are in the United States or Europe. Knowledge workers, including young, global ones, are highly aware of the increasing importance of their human capital to organizations, and will be equal partners with organizations in shaping new work arrangements. The stakes are high for both, and a good fit is critical to success on every side.

THE GLOBAL TALENT TANTRUM:
UNDERSTANDING THE PAIN

As the future unfolds, the Talent Tantrum becomes more global. In this chapter I provide insights and strategies from my ongoing research with the emerging cross-generational, cross-cultural global knowledge workforce. Over the next ten to twenty years it will be commonplace for businesses both large and small to employ three, even four, generations in a single workplace, and perhaps as many cultures. Until recently, the workers with the most knowledge and advanced skills were Veterans and Boomers, who had been in the workplace for many years. They grew their knowledge and honed their skills over time as they climbed the career ladder. This profile no longer holds. With the rapid transition to a knowledge economy, highly qualified workers are a part of *all* generations. Knowledge and skills change quickly in this environment, demanding that all knowledge workers, regardless of their age, continuously stay current. Since younger workers are just as likely to have a good match of competencies as older workers, they have similar expectations when it comes to challenging, advanced opportunities. However, despite the leveled playing field for skills, differences still occur among generations that will affect both their work and their relationships with each other.

> *Historical lessons remind us*
> *that innovation requires diversity.*

Although a significant effort has been made to improve understanding across generations and cultures, this remains among the biggest stumbling blocks to successful global business. Cross-generational teams and groups can be a rich source of innovation if they manage to take advantage of their synergies and diversities, but getting team members to trust one another is challenging indeed. Organizations that develop and apply their many gifts will be able to complete the organizational metamorphosis demanded by the environment over the next decade. But without this capability, they will simply not count themselves among the long-term survivors.

FIRST A LITTLE CONTEXT:
THE VIEW FROM 30,000 FEET

No matter what generation or culture you belong to, your world of work is undergoing rapid changes. Two particularly potent trends that will keep the global environment uncertain for the next decade or more are the precariousness of jobs, knowledge, and skills, and the rising importance of Net Generation knowledge workers. These forces, in turn, will cause people across generations and cultures to adapt in significant ways, developing a more fluid sense of their own identities that will contribute to their readiness to innovate. This will be a decade marked with strong feelings of vulnerability for both people and organizations, creating the potential for dramatic growth and transformation.

Precariousness of Jobs, Knowledge, and Skills

Even when we look out over the long term, the prospects for finding the right knowledge workers, attracting them, and retaining them appear daunting. The continuous flow of opportunities from new knowledge and technologies will continue to outpace the workforce for the foreseeable future. Despite the rapid global growth of the college-educated population, antiquated curricula and undertrained teachers will hamper the future workers' efforts to gain the skills necessary in the knowledge economy. Companies will be forced to outsource globally and develop talent-enhancement programs to maintain a qualified workforce. This means both the worker and the organization will always be changing—adding to the churn and tenseness of the environment.

Unfortunately, some education gaps will take time—perhaps decades—to close, so companies cannot expect the shortage of specialized knowledge workers to be remedied quickly. Many advanced countries, including the United States, simply have not made sufficient investments in education to ensure that enough people are prepared to participate in a fast-expanding knowledge economy. Emerging economies like China, India, and Mexico are educating increasing numbers of people at the college level, but that education may not be well matched to the economy's ever-changing needs. In the emerging economies, problem-solving skills, in particular, are in short supply due to educational methodology that overemphasizes rote memory, such as we see in China and Turkey. Further problems include the continuation of credentialing requirements in many countries, especially in Europe, that postpone any real employment for youth until their late twenties.

Substantial cost savings will encourage companies to look for high-end talent in low-wage countries. Transnational companies of all sizes will create new jobs around the world, where educated labor can match their needs, and where vital new markets are poised to grow. Advanced economies like that of the United States will see a dramatic increase in the number and type of jobs being sent offshore.

Many jobs in advanced economies that were lost in the recession will not be replaced domestically. Thanks to their large and rapidly growing science and technology workforces and their voracious consumer markets, the two Asian giants, India and China, will be among the major beneficiaries of high-end global jobs flowing away from advanced economies; they had surpassed U.S. production of college graduates in the natural sciences and engineering as early as 1999 and were rivaling U.S. production of postgraduate degrees, and the totals are continuing to rise. But it is not only Asian countries that are gaining newer and better jobs: countries such as the Philippines, Costa Rica, and Romania are also providing new global sites for white-collar work.

This is why for countries like the United States there has been so much talk about a new phenomenon, "jobless recovery," at the end of the recession in 2004. Until the U.S. economy responds by creating new industries that will in turn trigger the need for a new wave of high-end jobs, unemployment rates will remain high. In the long run, the globalization of jobs is a positive development for the world, yet there are no guarantees that it will settle out equitably. Some workers in advanced economies whose jobs get sent offshore will not find new jobs of equal worth, pay, and status, and at the same time failures of offshoring will contribute to volatility in employment in emerging economies as companies close down unsuccessful operations.

Rising Importance of Global Net Generation

By the end of the Badlands, in 2020, all but a few Veterans will be gone from the workplace, as will most of the Baby Boomers. The majority of experienced knowledge workers will be the young Net Generation from the emerging economies, particularly from Asia.

U.S. AND EUROPEAN JOBS GO OFFSHORE

China

China is becoming a key product-development center for General Electric, Intel, Philips, Microsoft, and other electronics giants. Strengths are hardware design and embedded software. Call centers for Japan and South Korea are growing in coastal cities.

Philippines

More than eight thousand foreign companies source work in nine different Philippine IT parks with fiber-optic links. Strengths include huge supply of English-speaking, college-educated accountants, software writers, architects, telemarketers, and graphic artists.

Mexico

Mexico is becoming a favorite IT and engineering outsourcing haven for U.S. companies that want to keep work close to home. As car and electronics companies move manufacturing over the border, they are boosting demand for engineers.

Costa Rica

Cheap telecom costs and an educated workforce make San Jose a thriving spot for call centers, targeting Spanish-speaking consumers in the United States and Europe.

South Africa

Well-educated speakers of French, English, and German from all over Africa staff growing call centers in South Africa, catering mainly to European companies. Deregulation of telecom could speed development. Other call centers are opening up in Mauritius.

Eastern Europe

Indian and American IT service providers are opening offices in Hungary, Poland, and the Czech Republic to tap abundant German and English-speaking workforce for European clients. Romania and Bulgaria are growing as IT workshops for German multinationals.

Russia

Some hundred local Russian software service exporters employ up to ten thousand engineers specializing in complex projects. Boeing, Nortel, Motorola, and Intel have small R&D centers. The country still has an enormous untapped pool of people with master's degrees and doctorates in sciences, IT, and math.

India

IT services, chip design, call centers, and business backoffice work already generate $10 billion in exports for India, and the total could hit $57 billion by 2008. Indian providers like Tata, Infosys, and Wipro already are global leaders, and U.S. IT service firms are piling in.

Source: Global Foresight, *BusinessWeek.* Used by permission.

One of the biggest shifts in human resources over the next ten years will be the rapid increase of young knowledge workers around the globe, particularly in Asia. They are the elite (about 12 percent) of the more than one billion people who are between the ages of fifteen and twenty-four years old. Companies must capture the hearts and minds of these young global knowledge workers; without engaging them it will be difficult to drum up sufficient resources to expand in the knowledge economy. By 2010 there will be approximately 128 million Net Generation knowledge workers around the world, and the majority of them will be women. By then, China will have more Net Generation knowledge workers (about 23 million) than the United States (about 20 million), and that disparity will grow (Table 7.1). India will have about 18 million. There will be another 320 million Net Generation members with secondary schooling. Most of these skilled workers (completed secondary education) and knowledge workers (completed college) will live in Asia.

	Number of Gen Ys with College Degrees in 2010		
	Total	% Female	# of Females
China	15,917,200	41.0%	6,526,052
United States	14,125,320	57.0%	8,051,432
India	11,361,360	36.0%	4,090,090
Russia	6,826,200	40.0%	2,730,480
United Kingdom	2,854,400	57.0%	1,627,008
Poland	2,756,880	66.0%	1,819,541
Germany	2,014,100	52.0%	1,047,332
Turkey	2,022,450	43.0%	869,654
South Korea	1,019,100	49.0%	499,359
Brazil	4,465,110	61.0%	2,723,717
Mexico	3,643,740	52.0%	1,894,745
Japan	5,635,000	49.0%	2,761,150
Rest of world	55,220,340	29.9%	16,503,921
World	127,861,200	40.0%	51,144,480

Table 7.1.   China and the United States Will Lead in Supplying Gen Y Knowledge Workers.

Source: OECD, *Education at a Glance,* 2003.

> *The Net Generation is ready to engage in the*
> *Principles of Transformation. They will actively*
> *Scan, Scout, and Steer and fearlessly Seek Collisions*
> *to make Rapid Decisions.*

Luckily this growing, dispersed pool of smart young people is eager to feed the success and growth of the global economy. However, they will not be passive partners; they have their own agendas and because of their better education, strong social networks, technological savvy, and access to information they will demand a lot in exchange for their work. These natives of the Badlands will be to the global economy what the Baby Boomers were to America—they will change everything they encounter to suit their needs and interests.

New Capability: Engage Knowledge Workers Across Generations and Cultures

The new capability of Engage People Deeply will need to be constructed in the midst of the global maelstrom of the Talent Tantrum. Over the past few years I have completed several cross-generation and cross-cultural studies of work attitudes in the United States and other regions. Most recently I collaborated with TakingITGlobal, a company devoted to bringing young global leaders together that was founded by Jennifer Corriero and Michael Furdyk, two young Net Generation leaders from Canada. Together we explored the attitudes of younger generations in several different countries. There is no global standardized language or age range for the various generations. The research that underpins the rest of this chapter is one of the few studies to make global comparisons, and for purposes of my research I have defined the generations using the following age ranges and terms:

- Veterans: born between 1920 and 1942
- Baby Boomers: born between 1943 and 1965
- Gen Xers (Sandwich Generation): born between 1966 and 1979
- Net Generation (Gen Y's): born between 1980 and 1995

THE WAR LENS. The twentieth century was marked by many signature events, but none more significant than war. War has shaped the global outlook of different generations, particularly for the two older generations. As time passes we see a profound shift away from the global view, sculpted by the two world wars and the cold war, that believes the world should be managed and that countries should remain separate to avoid further wars among cultures. The younger generations—and particularly the Net Generation—are questioning the benefits of war as a tool for managing modern global problems, and rejecting separation as a strategy. Their experience of war is that it is essentially not winnable, and therefore pointless. The Net Generation is connected every day to people all around the world; its basic impulse is to integrate and collaborate.

- Veterans: Win a War
- Boomers: Why a War?
- Gen Xers: Watch a War
- Net Generation: Winless Wars

CROSS-CUTTING THEMES. The following themes stood out in my research as important to understanding some of the key similarities and differences within the growing global talent pool. Given that the majority of tomorrow's knowledge workers will be young people from the emerging economies, I place a strong emphasis on understanding them.

- Each generation will experience different challenges and bring different gifts to the Badlands.
- The global Net Generation is ready to participate.
- Finding deeper meaning in work is becoming more important.
- Workers feel the innovation imperative and want to be focused on creative work.
- Cross-generational leadership is a must.

DIFFERING CHALLENGES AND GIFTS

Each generation and culture brings to the workplace diverse formative life experiences. Each holds different values and behaves differently in most dimensions of the workplace. In stable environments, like those in the Industrial Era, these unique generational characteristics remain steadfast throughout an individual's career. My research showed that all generations, these days, are feeling the pressures and uncertainties of globalization and are personally concerned about how it will affect them. They expect big changes and feel both fear and excitement. The Badlands provides an experience as powerful as the original formative experience for each generation, and it will challenge long-held beliefs and attitudes. Here is a window on what each generation wants in the Badlands, what its members think their key challenges are over the next decade, and what gifts they believe they bring to the table.

The Veterans: Mentors

Veteran knowledge workers range in age from about sixty to eighty-five, so few Veterans are still active in the workplace, and those that are have retirement on their minds. In many countries retirement is mandatory between age fifty-five and sixty. Most Veteran knowledge workers are found in advanced economies. Emerging economies have a few Veterans, but for the most part they did not have access to advanced education in large numbers. Most such countries are still rural and industrial.

Many advanced-economy Veterans left the workforce with early retirement packages during layoffs and downsizing in the 1990s and the early part of the current decade. Across the globe they place great value on hierarchy, order, and working their way up the ladder of success. Despite their small numbers they will continue to have influence, although it will wane in the Badlands. Those gray-haired sages who are choosing to work past retirement feel they have much to offer. They possess *neotony*—the ability to learn like a youngster, with fresh curiosity. Companies should try to keep those special Veterans actively engaged.

The Veterans' Badlands challenge is to move from a time-based metric to a value-based metric, as well as adjust to the new demands for customization. Those who stay in the workforce want to have an important role, but the rapid pace of change and continuous stream of innovations is new territory for them; they feel a sense of loss about the decline of seniority as a value. *The gift they want to give* is their wisdom born of experience and their power to facilitate contributions from the top younger talent.

The Boomers: Older Worker Pioneers

For the next decade most of the experienced knowledge workers in advanced economies will be aging Baby Boomers. The first of them are just reaching sixty years of age and the youngest are forty. They are still a relatively small group in emerging economies, where they are far less educated than their advanced-economy counterparts. However they share the experience of pioneering, this being the group that has led the way in globalization and has experienced huge societal changes from leadership positions that they continue to hold today. They have weathered several recessions. These are senior managers of the global economy and see themselves as its stewards going forward—particularly those Boomers in their forties. They feel challenged to make it all work.

This is the first generation to realize in middle age that sixty-five is no longer old. Their personal challenge is how they are going to spend the extra twenty-five years of life they can now look forward to. Work has always brought meaning into their lives; in fact many are workaholics. Extending work life into their seventies will be the choice many make, particularly the younger cohort. For companies to keep the skilled knowledge workers they need, especially early in the Badlands trek, they must engage deeply with talented Boomers.

The Boomers' Badlands challenge will be to give up control. They are keepers of the old corporate culture, which needs to give way to the new. Given the propensity of this generation to dominate and reinvent everything they experience, they will be reluctant to pass the baton of leadership and will struggle with the democratic nature of social networks and new forms of collaboration across borders. *The gift they want to give* is commitment in tough times, and the ability to get work done.

Gen X: Cautious, Self-Reliant Skeptics

Gen X, age twenty-six to forty, is a sandwich generation, caught between two eras, two worlds of work. This generation can't (in China) or doesn't want to (in America) use older generations as mentors. In America this generation is dominated by former latchkey kids, who had working mothers and lived in neighborhoods with high divorce rates. Gen Xers entered the workforce at the end of the Industrial Era's dominance, just when the knowledge economy began to take off. Their independence comes from having to take care of themselves. In China, this generation was the first to grow up in "capitalist China" in the 1990s, experiencing the tension between the old ways and the new. Their lives are so completely different from those of their parents that they cannot view them as role models and mentors. The Chinese experience of radically different lifestyles between parents and children is common to many other emerging economies. South Africa's Gen X was caught between apartheid and the new South Africa of Nelson Mandela. Their formative teenage and young adult years were shaped by this struggle and by the early years of transition away from apartheid.

Although it varies between cultures, this generation is far less impressed than its predecessors by the wisdom of elders and bosses in the workplace. Since fewer of its members attained college educations, this generation has fewer knowledge workers in it than the Net Generation.

Gen Xers are focused on building their skills and expanding their learning. They want challenging work but find older Boomers difficult to relate to, partly because Boomers enjoy power politics and can be poor delegators. Organizations will be challenged to get Gen Xers fully engaged with corporate goals and to think beyond their own pursuits. Intolerant of old corporate culture, this generation looks for informality and freedom at work.

The Gen Xers' Badlands challenge is to engage fully in teamwork, which this generation has seldom experienced as efficient or rewarding, especially across generations. Their fierce independence makes Gen Xers entrepreneurial, but solely on their terms. They are flexible because they have been forced to adapt to old and new ways in their societies. *The gift of this generation* is its self-confidence and "fast" ways. Gen Xers like to get things done every day, and they are not risk averse.

The Net Generation: Eager to Innovate and Change the World

These children of the Information Age grew up immersed in technology—connected to the Internet, attached at the hip to their mobile phones, and reliant on their PDAs. They are interconnected via multiple social networks that cross many borders and move seamlessly between real and virtual worlds. *Their formative work experience will be the Badlands.*

The Net Generation enters the workforce embodying all the tensions of organizational life in a fledgling global economy. This is the first generation to pass through its early years deeply influenced by globalization. Net Gens will struggle with the meaning of a global identity as opposed to a national identity. As a global group they are clear about wanting to earn good incomes, and they are far from ambivalent about the importance of money. They also are interested in sustainable economic development; they acknowledge that their lives will be better in the long run only if they help to resolve some of the larger social issues in the world around them. Organizations will be hard-pressed to provide them as much challenging work as they want, and they will be impatient with corporate rhetoric that does not convert quickly to action.

The Net Gens' Badlands challenge is to avoid getting frustrated. Even though they are self-confident, they remain embedded in their social networks and will find it difficult to connect with other generations quite different from their own. They are fiercely dedicated to a work-life balance that will be tested in the maelstrom of disruptive innovations. *The gift they bring* is their positive attitude, work efficiency, and social consciousness.

THE GLOBAL NET GENERATION: READY TO PLAY

Today's global youth is the most educated, sophisticated, and techno-savvy cohort ever to enter the knowledge workforce, and its members are eager to participate, not just at work but in a wide variety of roles in society. These young knowledge workers have grown up during the Information Revolution, and they have been influenced by myriad forces through their interconnectivity with each other and society via the Internet. They share a mind-set that the best decisions and problem solving take place through interaction and the inclusion of many voices. In addition to these shared attitudes, young knowledge workers possess many unique stances and attributes, shaped by the cultures they live in, that in turn shape their expectations of work. To apply this rich diversity of knowledge workers across cultures, we must gain a deeper understanding of how they differ from other generations and where they are similar.

Commonalities Among the Global Net Generation

Despite many cultural differences, young global knowledge workers widely share the following attributes:

- Self-confidence and the expectation of good wages and jobs
- Nascent global identities, strongly influenced by nationalism
- Sophisticated technological skills
- Pragmatic idealism
- Expectations of multiple jobs and careers
- Desire for a balanced life
- Inability to see upper-management Boomers as role models
- Expectation of gender equality

This group brings specific, unique demands and desires to the workplace that will differ from region to region. Although cultural, political, and structural barriers to beginning their knowledge work career are globally diverse, the Net Generation shares a commonality without borders.

ATTITUDES TOWARD OLDER GENERATIONS. By and large global youth have an ambivalent attitude toward adults (Table 7.2). The results of our research strongly suggest that young people expect to struggle getting their voices heard and to experience a large communication gap. They feel disengaged but also optimistic that they will be able to break down those barriers because they believe they have greater opportunities than the generations before them to empower themselves and define a new relationship with older generations. Although some aspects

Associations with the Word *Youth*	Associations with the Word *Adult*
Lack wisdom, need guidance	Caregivers, standard setters
Dreamers, visionary, hope for the future	Criticial, dream-killers, few idealists
Freedom, experimentation, playfulness	Burdened, busy, full of responsibilities
Open-minded, flexible, innovative	Rigid-thinking, stuck, conservative
Rebellious, free-spirited	Professional and traditional
Innocence, naive, full of potential	Greedy, corrupt, selfish
Disadvantaged, vulnerable, unheard voice	Decision makers, position of authority

Table 7.2. The Global Young Are Wary of Older Adults.

Source: TakingITGlobal, Global Youth Survey, 2003.

of this gap can be attributed to traditional gaps between younger and older generations, the Net Generation attitude toward how to resolve it is quite sophisticated and deeply held. As this global group pours into the workplace, older generations must engage with its members in new ways to ensure they can make their contribution as quickly and freely as possible, unencumbered by outdated work conventions.

KEY INFLUENCES. These young knowledge workers are grateful for all the opportunities that have influenced their development and prepared them to participate more effectively and at a higher level than generations before them (Table 7.3). They have a clarity about exactly what these factors are and how they impact their lives. They want to harvest these inputs as fast as possible in the workplace and their communities.

Factor Influencing Change	Result or Outcome
Technology—access to information	More knowledgeable
Technology—ability to communicate	Open-minded, exposed to different views
Technology—access to opportunities	Diverse range of experiences and skills
Rise in democracies	Greater amount of freedom and choice
Lowering voting age to eighteen	Increased civic participation
Demographics—large population	Greater concern for youth involvement
Access to education	Higher literacy rate, better able to participate
Social movements	More rights, privileges, and voice
Rise in consumerism	Materialistic and self-centered
Increased life expectancy	Married and having children at older age
Increased migration	More contact with foreign cultures
Increased divorce rate	Broken families, more independent
Youth-led organizations	Meaningful engagement
Increased entrepreneurship	Economic empowerment
Stakeholder inclusion in decision making	Youth are being recognized as stakeholders

Table 7.3.   The Big Influences and Impacts on Global Young Adults.
Source: TakingITGlobal, Global Youth Survey, 2003.

TECHNOLOGY ENABLES YOUTH TO CHANGE AND PARTICIPATE. These young global knowledge workers are very positively disposed toward technology, and attribute access to it as the key to making many new things possible. They are keenly aware of how they believe it has changed their lives and society, both positively and negatively (Table 7.4).

Their negative assessments focus on pornography, consumerism, wasted time, overreliance on online relationships, and the digital divide. They also believe technology has allowed the rapid development of numerous benefits:

- Convenience and flexibility
- Entrepreneurial spirit and initiative
- Informal, interactive participation
- Freedom of expression
- Empowerment for the disempowered
- Ability to overcome barriers
- Access to untapped potential

Technology as an Enabler	Impact
Communications and connectivity	Reach beyond community, belongingness
Access to opportunities	Job or volunteer related
Information and knowledge	Able to make more informed choices
Learning (more available)	Distance education
Activism (more effective)	Outlet to implement change
Sparked sense of wonder and curiosity	Questions answered through click of button
Awareness of broader issues	International news, less national bias
Personal development	Ability to develop new skills
Modernization of agriculture	Reduced drudgery
Access to medicine, transportation, and other advantages	Increased life expectancy and mobility

Table 7.4.   Global Young Believe Technology Helps Them a Lot.
Source: TakingITGlobal, Global Youth Survey, 2003.

The participants in our research were all connected to the Internet and very aware of the digital divide. They feel deeply committed to closing it for other young people, given the personal experience of what access means to their lives now. This has driven a global effort to get more young people involved in community and societal decision making.

Differences Between the Generations

Most young global knowledge workers are concerned about their professional preparedness. They feel that the formal college education they have received is already outmoded and of little practical use in preparing them for the future, and they hope they can learn quickly on the job. Few countries have developed a multifaceted industry to train people for their careers and jobs outside traditional educational institutions, and few companies have formal training and educational programs for workers. This leads many young workers from emerging economies to want to work for TNCs that provide learning opportunities. A career itself is a new concept in many countries; many research participants outside the United States did not expect to change jobs a lot or to have multiple careers.

COMPARISON OF GEN X AND NET GENERATION. For the most part both Gen X and the Net Generation don't think about having multiple careers but instead think about having one, or possibly two. Americans have evolved a much different concept of career and job mobility that reflects the ease of changing jobs in the United States and the vast array of readily accessible learning opportunities.

"I hope for one career, but circumstances may make me have more." (Gen Xer, India)

This commentary was common across a number of countries. Often the Net Generation member interviewed would articulate a desire for two careers: one for work and one for giving back to society.

"Two careers. First is the career I choose and study for. After a while I plan to be a politician, after I gain some experience in my original career. I would like to be a politician in order to develop the city where I was born and raised. I believe I owe a contribution to the place where I have my roots." (Net Gen, Brazil)

Although both Gen Xers and Net Gens expect to have their employers participate in their career development, people in the Net Generation were more likely to see a strong personal career management role for themselves (Table 7.5). Respondents expressed a wide variety of perspectives on who should help in their career development.

Country and Culture	Generation X	Net Generation
United States	Think of themselves as sole proprietors of their careers, scarred by early work experiences	Have many careers in different industries, value diverse mentoring opportunities as critical to building portfolios
Brazil	The number of careers needed to meet personal goals; organizations should help develop careers	Two careers—a work and social career; person solely responsible for career development
China	Career is an ill-defined new concept, mainly job-centered; see jobs as stepping stones to more money	Career notion beginning to catch on, see it only possible with TNCs—a good career means you can leave China
Germany	Seek credentials and postpone careers until almost thirty; one-career-oriented, one-profession-oriented	Expect more than one career because of uncertain employment environment; ready to change
India	Success means an engineering career	Excited by the increasing options for different careers but one-career oriented; value for entrepreneurship is rising
Japan	Well prepared to fit in the traditional career pattern; aware social contract is breaking down but see few viable options	Multiple careers; career development is a partnership with many—family, school, community, employers
Mexico	One career, one profession; expect companies to play major role in development	Need to manage own career for social mobility
Turkey	One regular career and one as a backup—two jobs or more at one time common to hedge the bet; expect companies to help a lot in career development (part of strong paternalistic role)	Career is still a fuzzy idea—not linked to any one skill set; employers should use their vast resources to help build careers for their employees
South Africa	One career—has been a struggle; it is very hard to find good jobs	Two careers—one for income and personal growth, the other to help the community and nation of South Africa

Table 7.5. Global Comparisons: Career Expectations—Generation X and the Net Generation.

Source: Global Foresight, 2004; TakingITGlobal, 2004.

"My career development is a multi-stake partnership and cooperation. I believe that my mentors, friends, networks, professors, family, and adviser are crucial in shaping and making it successful in my pursuit of personal development and my social responsibility in my immediate community." (Net Gen, Japan)

The Net Generation is the first to face the daunting challenge of creating a work life that spans a period as long as sixty years. American Gen Xers and Net Gens see so much change occurring that they don't think long term; rather they view their work lives as a series of experiments with opportunities that suddenly arise. Most members of these generations, regardless of their countries of origin, do not see their parents as role models; instead they see their parents' views of work as outmoded.

NET GENERATION DIFFERENCES WITH GEN X. The younger generations experience differences between them, leading to the feeling that they are distinct from one another. We asked the Gen X and Net Gen participants in our research to give us their views on how the two generations were the same or different. They offered a wide range of opinions. Here are some of their comments:

> "The Net Generation is more progressive. We are more open-minded to innovation as part of our everyday lives. We are used to the speed and dazzling effects of the information stream." (Net Gen, Turkey)

> "I think Gen X is more rebellious and anti-institutional. The Net Generation is quite tired of the ills of previous generations— Third World debt, war—our generation is more peace loving and tolerant of each other. We see how far we have come. We demand to enjoy work and to find it challenging. We want self-actualization in the truest sense and to be rewarded for what we do." (Net Gen, South Africa)

> "It is very easy for the Net Generation to assimilate and be able to use new technologies, although they are falling into an all-solved-by-technology paradigm. On the other hand, Gen X tries to keep working in old ways. But definitely there are advantages and disadvantages in both." (Gen Xer, Mexico)

> "Today's generation has become more liberal and open minded towards their work. As an Indian, I feel that the newer genera-

tion is ready to work for odd hours, their expectations of work has changed. A twenty-year-old guy is willing to work a night job in a call center or a BPO firm which a person of Gen X would have hesitated to do. Gen X is more orthodox." (Net Gen, India)

"Gen X tends to use technologies from their time. Net Gen looks for the newest and best technology, especially like Wi-Fi. The mental and virtual needs of Net Gen focuses on high-speed virtual and network mobility and social connectivity. Net Gen has a high tendency towards cyber mental disorders like computer and technology dependency syndromes." (Net Gen, Japan)

"Our generation is cautious and tends to take small steps. Most of us were assigned jobs from the government so being on our own was not expected. We care about our coworkers more than the 'Me' Generation [Net Gen's name in China], who just want to get ahead. They will compete with us for the best jobs but will only stay in them until they get what they want. We are still more loyal to our employers." (Gen Xer, China)

"In Europe we still expect the same job security as older workers but the Net Gen doesn't. They don't believe as much as we did that the government and their employers will take care of them. I think they are confused and not adjusted to it yet." (Gen Xer, Germany)

THE MEANING OF WORK GROWS IN IMPORTANCE

Each generation creates meaning and identity through its unique educational and early work experiences, which in turn shape values about intellectual challenge, money, social good, and power in their work lives. These vary widely around the world. Today most people have legacy work attitudes cultivated during the Industrial Era, but this will change for all generations given the transformation under way in the economy. The participants in our research felt that work must be deeply, personally meaningful before they would engage in very high performance. Each of them could articulate a list of attributes that needed to be present at work for the work to really matter. They felt that it would increasingly be their responsibility to find work with meaning, but this response varied across countries. Almost all of them felt that building a web of personal work relationships was paramount. They found these relationships brought their work satisfaction and meaning, and felt the connections would last a lot longer than any one job. They felt that to be successful they needed to invest in creating good personal reputations and to be able to leverage personal networks to get their jobs done.

American Generational Differences

Many older knowledge workers from the Veterans' generation grew up in difficult economic times. Meaning came from making enough money to support their families. They felt respected and maintained their reputations by finding a good job and sticking with it, thereby providing long-term security for their families. At the end of their careers they derive much of their meaning from this seniority, as well as from their new roles as mentors. Boomers, by contrast, see work as an opportunity to do social good as well as to develop themselves. They have always wanted work to be *more than* just work. This has been a contributing factor to Boomers' being workaholics. Now they are challenged once again to find ways to connect their work to the greater social good, and to the new second stage of middle age they are inventing. Much of their future meaning from work will derive from being pioneers as the new older workers—a challenge they will relish. They also will continue to derive a lot of their meaning from traditional markers like titles and accomplishments, as well as the leadership they have shown in the development of the global economy and all the innovations they have contributed to since the first Baby Boomers entered the workforce in the 1960s. They also have a different relationship to money than Veterans have. Security is less important for Boomers—an exchange that bought this generation new experiences and freedom—although for older Boomers it still ranks high.

Gen X, by contrast, derives a lot of meaning from being recognized for personal contributions, because for this generation work is an important source of social status. Its members work hard to differentiate themselves from the generations above and below them. For Gen Xers it is important to make money commensurate with their status. It also means a lot to them to balance responsibility and personal freedom at work and to have a balanced work and home life. Unlike Boomers, they work to live rather than the other way around. They derive meaning from doing well in their personal lives.

Then there is the Net Generation, which grew up with instant information access and global connectivity. They derive meaning from continuing to learn and from meeting the endless intellectual challenges they expect the workplace to provide them. They also want to fit work into their lives so that it ensures a work-life balance. Balance is one plank in their sacred platform for meaning, complemented by making a social contribution.

Global Perspectives

Few people derive so much of their personal identity as Americans do from their work. Thus Americans struggle more with the meaning of work than others do. People from other cultures derive more of their identity from their primary affiliations of family, ethnicity, community, religion, and national culture, and overall they fix more distinct boundaries between work and home across all generations. But as knowledge work becomes a significant share of the economy in more countries, *all* cultures will struggle more with the meaning of work, for it demands significant intellectual and creative commitment to be truly successful.

The meaning of work is also influenced by the stage of a country's development, since the hierarchy of people's needs vary according to their economic status. Advanced economies have long, successful histories of wealth creation and consumerism. People who live in them take for granted that they can easily meet their basic needs, so they choose to pursue self-actualization. Not so in newly emerging economies, whose recent history includes a battle for the basic necessities of life.

The Meaning of Work: Comparison of the Net Generation and Gen X

Several common themes emerged, including one that was mentioned by every participant: the importance of finding meaning in work. Speaking for the Net Generation, most people mentioned the importance of work that contributed to society, of a workplace where they could develop personally—follow their passions and enjoy significant financial success. Net Gens are indeed pragmatic idealists. Gen X descriptions were more constrained, focusing on recognition and social status and contributing their skills in order to create a productive life.

There was a more tentative sense of idealism and concern about success. Gen Xers more often mentioned the role of the employer in shaping the work experience for them.

In every country each generation had a unique dominant theme that stood out (Table 7.6). Most of the participants from emerging economies, such as Mexico, placed some emphasis on the challenges of meeting basic needs.

"First, the economic situation in Mexico is difficult—work represents a source of income, a way to survive and to ensure basic necessities. Secondly, once work is satisfying household needs, providing food and health, then it can transform itself into a place where social networks and cultural backgrounds meet, developing new ways of relationships, attitudes, and knowledge." (Gen Xer, Mexico)

But they also were very focused on getting the personal growth they desired.

"I consider work as a tool for maintaining self-satisfaction, confidence, and respect. I work to prove my presence as a productive and intelligent advanced being. It is a ground to push my knowledge to the next level." (Net Gen, Turkey)

Advanced economies that have had persistent troubles, like Japan, were struggling with the issue of meaning, and where to find it. Their generations spoke seriously about being disillusioned and wanting to experiment with new ways of working that would bring more meaning to their lives.

"The situation is very serious in Japan. We need more innovative management, culturally and gender-sensitive environments, and dynamic responsive work policies." (Net Gen, Japan)

Many felt a workplace had to show empathy in order to provide the opportunity for a meaningful experience.

"Human coworkers, people with a heart. A healthy atmosphere where one can breathe, this means air, light, space to move around, space to take a break, a coffee maker and affordable food." (Gen X, Germany)

RESPONSE TO THE INNOVATION IMPERATIVE

Innovation becomes everybody's job in the Badlands, for change will be ubiquitous in that challenging terrain. Creative thinking and radical innovation become highly valued as the fuel for long-term

Country and Culture	Generation X	Net Generation
United States	Recognition and social status	Endless, thrilling intellectual challenges
Brazil	A comfortable place to realize goals	Being part of society and making an individual contribution
China	Dream of high-paid jobs, frustrated by poor education, concerned about stability of work	Chance for personal independence and financial success; connect with the world
Germany	Still heavily influenced by old social contract and by employer and state paternalism; have idealism and hope to gain personal expression	Persistent unemployment has given some a cynical attitude; tension between desire for exciting personal development and fear of not finding good work experience
India	Practical and self-development	Follow your passion, purpose in life, realize full potential
Japan	Disillusioned with their economy, finding a new meaning; loss of old meaning with nothing clear to replace it	Want to experiment with identity beyond the traditional borders of Japanese corporate life, desire global experience
Mexico	Attach meaning and identity to education and company position; pragmatic concerns for salary and security—but satisfy household needs first	Get ahead—social mobility
Turkey	Achieve status; be engaged in the global culture	Wonder what it means to be a young successful Muslim in a global economy; embody tension between Jihad and McDonald's
South Africa	Source of satisfying basic needs; some opportunities for contribution if employed in a social organization	Grow self as a person; make a social contribution

Table 7.6. Global Comparisons: Meaning of Work—Generation X and Net Generation.

Source: Global Foresight, 2004; TakingITGlobal, 2004.

prosperity. There will be more customization of products and services, plus a move away from mass production and toward innovation in the ways organizations and their work are arranged. Without exception all the knowledge workers in our research wanted to be creative. They experience the wrenching changes in industries and the constant demand for innovation and most welcome it. They are keenly aware that they need to keep learning right on the cutting edge so that they can keep their skills honed and fresh. In fact some of the need for innovation drives knowledge workers to abhor routine work. They feel that if their job has too much routine they will fall behind in learning what they need to learn to be successful in the long term. They also expressed concern, some of them disgust, at the poor climates for innovation in many companies. They find work practices and the cultures of many organizations restrictive for innovation from everything from office arrangements and hours to dress code. There was a spirit of forging ahead to innovate—almost an impulse to innovate despite difficult and constraining conditions. This seemed to be driven by both the personal excitement to be creative and the need to keep ahead of the game.

American Generations Differ on Innovation

Despite some shared cultural values around innovation, America's generations also have significant differences. Innovation during the Industrial Era was usually more incremental than radical. Radical innovation is considered too risky by most Veterans, many of whom are also hampered by their lack of technological prowess. Because they feel behind they hold back.

Boomers have contributed many of the startling scientific innovations of the last fifty years, from human genomics to the microprocessor. They have also produced their share of heretics in companies. Yet they are also great talkers, not always willing to make changes. They like their status and their power in the workplace, and can be obstacles to systemic innovation. Despite their considerable skill and spirit of innovation, if they didn't invent something themselves, they are less inclined to believe in it. Getting them to move beyond the "not invented here syndrome," preventing them from becoming obstacles to growing the systemic innovation that companies need, is the challenge of dealing with Boomers.

*Historical lessons remind us that new self-concept—
new identity—derives from innovation.*

Gen Xers are quite entrepreneurial as well as innovative, and they do their best work when they are on their own and with their own. They are the Internet dot-com innovators. Their cynicism and lack of trust of management often gets in the way of their pursuing innovation within large companies. Their lack of tolerance for the old corporate culture and disdain for the skills needed to change it get in the way, both of organizations' benefiting as much as they might otherwise from this generation, and of Gen Xers' realizing their full potential. The Net Generation sees change as a way of life. They feel well prepared and expect to have work lives filled with opportunities to participate in important innovations. They like diversity and group work but want to be treated as equals.

Global Perspectives

The process and style of creativity varies between cultures. For some people, ideas come not so much from brainstorming in teams as from intimate discussions with a peer or a mentor. Taking advantage of the diversity of cultures and learning how to maximize their contributions will offer a key competitive edge. Americans tend to be more egalitarian than other peoples about possible sources of new ideas and innovation. In the United States a good idea can come from anyone. Americans also tend to be comfortable with lots of trial and error. Compared to that of other countries, American education typically consists of less rote learning and more emphasis on creativity and problem solving. Thus young Americans are better prepared for creative thinking than many young people from other countries.

In this era America has been the major leader in innovations. Americans have been able to commercialize innovations quickly. However, this leadership will erode as other countries quickly climb the learning curve. No one culture has a corner on innovation. In the future expect more innovations that swiftly become globalized, and expect lead industry transformations to come from a variety of different countries. Cultural twists will be added to innovation as well, such as those the Japanese demonstrated with quality cars and electronics and the Scandinavians showed with innovative technical features for mobile communications.

Young Generations

As natives in the Badlands, Net Gens are hopeful that the future will not resemble the past. They feel they are well prepared to contribute innovations and solve problems creatively because their attitudes and ideas have not been institutionalized. This generation approaches things with fresh eyes (Table 7.7).

Linking innovation to social change was a commonly expressed theme among our research respondents.

"We live in a poor country. Innovation and creativity are everything." (Net Gen, Brazil)

In general, both young generations were eager to be engaged in innovative work, and spoke passionately about it and what they needed so that they could do their best. They derive a lot of personal satisfaction from innovation.

"Creativity is indeed important to me, because I am a very inventive spirit, and this inspiration has to be lived. I need freedom for designing projects in a holistic manner. Freedom includes freedom to move around, how to dress, how to speak and think, and when to take a break. Actually it means freedom of self." (Gen Xer, Germany)

"Space, time, ability to listen to music and work flexible hours if need be. Ability to work from home occasionally. Whatever feeds my creativity." (Gen Xer, South Africa)

Cultures will vary in their comfort with taking big risks, but in general the Net Generation is much less risk averse than the older generations, including Gen X. But within a given generation this reaction varies widely, and the Net Generation embraces some highly risk-averse people.

"I may take risks if I believe it is really necessary. If it is not necessary I feel more comfortable and don't take risks." (Net Gen, Turkey)

"I enjoy taking risks. I strongly feel 'only adversity introduces a man to himself.' My firm belief is that with every failure you expand your dreams." (Net Gen, India)

"I feel excited but these practices are risky. This because you go against the established rules, and can have a social disapproval. I think this kind of attitude is safe when the costs are the same and lower than the benefits." (Gen Xer, Mexico)

Country and Culture	Generation X	Net Generation
United States	Innovation comes easiest in small companies where they are the boss and can excel in out-of-the box thinking	Want innovation, believe the world has to change in both business and community, see that as their job
Brazil	Take risks if it doesn't harm any people; want mostly innovation work in their jobs	Only through innovation can you be proud of yourself; there is no choice but to take risks
China	Still constrained by the culture of "conformity"; cautious risk takers	Open and desirous of new ways, eager to learn but constrained by outmoded educational system, still vulnerable to old cultural ways
Germany	Comfort with incremental innovation but not as much with radical; feel that time pressures of today's work world stifle innovation and creativity	Impulse to innovate from need—see society changing and want Germany to become more competitive and create new jobs
India	More important to do innovative work later in career—early in a learning mode	Very important—personal pleasure in innovative work; prove your worth
Japan	Pretty stifling corporate cultures, more resistance than innovation; poor climate for failures; routine work valued	Willing to take more risks; can adapt to changed conditions but corporate environments a problem; desire creative and innovative work; patient with old ways while trying new ones
Mexico	Feel barriers—need organizations to open more pathways to facilitate innovation; difficult if not your job	Feel they are key to their country's future and more capable of innovating than senior workers
Turkey	Linked to learning and new ideas, not implementation; cautious about risks—need support from boss; innovation not a deeply held societal value	Feel tension—want Turkish, Muslim, and Middle Eastern innovations—don't want to imitate the West; risk-averse; increasing curiosity about creativity

Table 7.7.   Global Comparisons: Innovation Attitudes—Generation X and Net Generation.

Source: Global Foresight, 2004; TakingITGlobal, 2004.

Net Gens also commonly state that they will refuse to stay in workplaces that do not reward their creative contributions often and generously.

CROSS-GENERATIONAL LEADERSHIP IMPERATIVE: NEW VOICES, FRESH INSIGHTS

Finally, we must engage all generations in leadership, tapping the talents of leaders without prejudice to their age, weaving members of all age groups into a rich tapestry that values social progress. Each generation also has unique experiences that shape its leadership styles. When many of our older leaders were coming up they were intensely focused on making a living, learning the ropes, playing according to the rules, and getting ahead in their careers. Reading was thought to be the key to acquiring knowledge, and gaining a college education was considered the cornerstone to success. These leaders were patient about becoming truly successful. In stark contrast, today's young leaders have big visions about changing the world. They want work-life balance, have no celebrity heroes, and expect to have multiple careers over their lifetime. They don't think that past experiences matter very much because things are changing so fast. And in fact many of their experiences have prepared them better than those of older leaders to lead in this environment. Whereas the old generation worked hard to get rewarded by the system, the new one works hard to write its own rules. Both have fundamentally different orientations to wealth and money.

It is not uncommon to see organizations that are generationally dysfunctional. Either they allow a single generation to dominate leadership values and styles, or they facilitate a homogeneous culture in which harmony and differences of all sorts, including generational ones, are kept at bay. The result is a potential for innovation that is never fully achieved, plus a fossilization of leadership that will lead to an organization's demise.

Within the category of young leaders, differences loom large between those in the Net Generation, born between 1980 and 1995, and those from Gen X, born between 1966 and 1979. The Net Generation is the most highly educated generation ever to enter the workforce and its members want to lead. They are smart and have many ideas that they do not want to wait to see implemented. They are self-confident and collaborative. They grew up with a networked mind-set and in many ways are an ideal fit for Networked Leadership. They admire certain leadership characteristics, and others really turn them off. Although there are cultural variations, the Net Gen likes to get things done without a lot of drama, so it values active, focused leaders. This generation shares leadership well with those who are inclusive, empathetic, collaborative, and intelligent. It will not engage with disorganized, hierarchal, and unethical leadership.

Companies are becoming more diligent about getting input from these younger generations. Microsoft, for example, felt it really didn't understand the Net Generation well enough, despite having a fairly young workforce. So the company cast a wide net and hired two young Canadians, Jennifer Corriero, then nineteen years old, and Michael Furdyk, eighteen. These two young people advised both top management in Redmond, Washington, and product development teams throughout North America as to the needs and desires of their generation. Microsoft benefited mightily from their tenure, as did Michael and Jennifer. In many ways they are typical of the top talent of this generation. They found Microsoft a good environment but soon left their high-paying, high-powered jobs there to found TakingITGlobal, a new company that wants to help young people "change the world." They didn't think they could do that inside a large corporation.

Jennifer and Michael write, "It is essential to develop the capacities of young people to enable them to face challenges in life, express themselves and have a sense of self-confidence, and to take initiatives on issues they are concerned about." Jennifer and Michael find compelling the demographic that more than 50 percent of the world's population is under the age of twenty-five, and that youth is the major untapped resource in the pursuit of sustainable development.

Jennifer and Michael embody the spirit of other people their age: the Net Generation links meaning at work with contributing to a better world. They will not stay in companies for long without the opportunity to provide leadership in meaningful ways.

SUMMARY INSIGHTS

Most of this next decade will be spent in a painful and frustrating transition, during which companies will realize they need to deepen their capability to engage deeply with key talent to recruit and retain those who have the best fit with their need for innovation and high-quality knowledge work. It will also be a time when, adding to the turbulence, two huge demographic trends will hit the marketplace for talent: global aging and the coming of age of the Net Generation.

- The global aging driver provides Boomers around the world the possibility of an extra twenty-five years of life. They are well aware of their potential longevity and will not seek retirement at the conventional age. Look for a big discontinuity with regard to when and how work life ends, not just in America but also around the world.

- The majority of tomorrow's knowledge workers will come from the Net Generation of emerging economies, and by 2010 most of them will come from Asia, principally China and India. Global companies are unlikely to meet their innovation and knowledge work needs without attracting and retaining the Net Generation. A highly competitive marketplace will develop to attract these talents as their own native countries become more attractive places to work.

- Deeper understanding across generations and cultures is critical. Differences are deeper and more common than companies usually acknowledge and these will be more prominent among knowledge workers than they were with skilled labor. Cultural literacy and generational savvy are crucial for a successful Badlands journey. All other Talent Tantrum challenges will get resolved much more easily as this new capability comes to be fully developed.

- Of all the work dimensions I studied globally, three stand out as the most important to young knowledge workers—the meaning of work, career growth needs, and opportunities for innovation. The Net Generation has a strong desire to have an exciting work experience and make a contribution to society, all the while living a balanced life. They have a strong orientation toward innovation that can be readily tapped, and they expect to learn as much on the job as they provide in work effort for the company. Of critical importance are the different cultural orientations as to what that means.

- Knowledge workers must find a clear connection between their personal values and their experience in the workplace, and that connection must link to a higher purpose—usually, social responsibility. As more work products become in effect *knowledge* products, people will have more of their own intellectual property invested in their work. This degree of personal contribution will cause people to ask higher-order questions about value and the purpose of the work. The rapid creation of new knowledge and value, and the continuous obsolescence of skills, will cause them to rethink meaning over and over again.

- High-end talent will seek work in places where they can participate in creative endeavors at the edges of their knowledge. They want to work for organizations that value their special brand of creativity and skill sets in ways that personally appeal to them. The big winners will be organizations that celebrate failure and learn from it, and that provide sufficient resources so that workers can develop ideas into projects.

- Building the trust needed to engage different generations and cultures demands a variety of approaches. Knowledge workers are not the same across cultures—or in any one generation. They have many similar issues and desires, but what is of most importance to any one group is different. Companies must engage them on what is in the foreground for them.

- Many knowledge workers, particularly those in Gen X and the Net Generation, find the legacy hierarchies and cultures of organizations to be truly oppressive. They will not stay and do the workarounds that the innovators in the older generations have done. They will leave organizations that they perceive do not support their special skills and work environment needs. This challenge presents a big opportunity for companies; these younger generations can be a great help to companies in changing the culture and creating new organizational forms and practices that accelerate innovation.

- Cross-generational teams can provide organizations with some of the variation they need to enhance innovation, but such teams won't form automatically or find their synergies for innovation easily. Knowledge workers and organizations need to learn about each other to realize this potential. Companies need to make this a high and visible value by creating climates and specific activities where work can take place across generations.

• Knowledge workers will come attached to their personal networks, and the whole package has high value for companies. Companies will learn how to evaluate the value of the business intelligence and innovation potential this provides. On the downside, when key knowledge workers leave they take their networks with them.

• Young people can provide much-needed new voices at the leadership level. There is a cross-generational leadership imperative in the Badlands. Young people around the planet are better prepared to provide leadership than any generation before them. They have a huge stake in the future and the capacity to make significant contributions to creating a better one for us all.

CHAPTER EIGHT

Create the
Corner Store

~~~

The global economy is becoming increasingly consumer-centric as the middle class expands throughout the world. Today, with increased disposable income, access to information and the Internet, consumers everywhere are better educated, increasingly sophisticated, and more demanding. With their intensive use of information while making decisions, these are *"activist"* consumers—in contrast to the more passive consumers of yesterday who primarily responded to marketing information. These smart, demanding consumers are also

---

Activist New Consumer

- College educated
- Income equivalent to $55,000
- Online information user
- Self-directed seeker of diverse information
- Proactively shares information with others

---

the high-value workers that companies are so actively seeking. Companies must engage expertly with them in both their roles. Although this shift began in the United States, it is a global phenomenon.

Most companies now are struggling to manage a challenging, multidimensional, and costly relationship with their customers. The increasing diversity of products and services, supported by plentiful information about them, has fragmented the consumer market into

---

PAIN #6: CONSUMER CONUNDRUM— CONFUSED AND FRAGMENTED

Smart, "informed," demanding, and highly discriminating customers drive the shift from mass markets to multiple niche markets. Intersecting this shift are some big trends that further complicate relationships. Women have become the major purchasing decision makers around the world. People around the world like globalization, but they do not want it to obliterate their preferences and lifestyles—culture matters more than ever now. People are living longer, driving a whole new active lifestyle for people between sixty and eighty years of age. In the Badlands, as your concept of who you are shifts, consumer behaviors shift along with it. People and organizations feel *confused,* and markets feel *fragmented.* These shifts and trends are still in an early stage, so much of what's happening will confound even the best market research.

New Capability: Customizing Personalized Relationships

Coddling customers by creating the feeling of a friendly neighborhood store will become a highly sought-after competitive edge. This requires listening to customers and remembering their preferences, engaging culturally diverse people within and between countries, and targeting the needs of different generations individually. The shift from passivity to activism gives consumers more control in the marketplace; information is a great equalizer between seller and purchaser. Consumers will increasingly want to interact with salespeople in order to make decisions with information they identify as important to them. They will want to engage in intelligent conversations in which information flows both ways. Money exchange will only follow information exchange. Sales will take place in the context of a new type of relationship, with the consumer—not the salesperson—driving closure.

multiple niches. Increasingly, successful businesses will be defined by how they manage these relationships and use them to differentiate themselves from competitors. Today's consumers drive a lot of rapid strategy decay by forcing deep discounting and by switching brands rapidly and frequently. All this adds up to our sixth pain—Consumer Conundrum—with its attendant feelings of confusion and fragmentation. Companies are struggling up the learning curve to interact with their customers in smarter ways and to create adaptable business models that can respond quickly to rapidly growing consumer experimentation with information, channels, and relationships.

Online companies such as Amazon pioneered in creative uses of customer information to build relationships. By using detailed records of customers' previous purchases, Amazon could suggest related items that might be of interest. Following a purchase of a historical biography, for example, a returning customer might be greeted with offers of books or music related to that time period. Now all sorts of online and bricks-and-mortar companies are experimenting with new strategies. Nubella, a health and nutrition start-up, has found a way to interact with grocery shoppers in a very personalized way. The company makes scanning software that reads barcodes when a customer checks out at a grocery store register. Based on the barcode information, Nubella's system determines what nutrients are missing from the shopper's purchase, and it sends out coupons for products that will fill gaps in the shopper's diet.

FOUR TRENDS SHAPING THE FUTURE OF CONSUMERS

The use of information in new ways by consumers is the most powerful short-term trend in the marketplace, and the impact of these activist consumers goes far beyond their own personal consumption. They are driving changes in how the economy and society function by mediating more purchases with technology and shopping 24/7, demanding access to information any time, any place. They no longer wait at the end of the supply chain to engage in purchasing but interact with multiple players from wholesalers to manufacturers.

Over the long term this intensive use of formation will be augmented by three other trends. Together these four forces will transform consumerism into a diverse environment full of multiple niches. Nowhere will keeping the big picture in view be more important for companies than here, in this emerging, unpredictable new consumer world.

These are the four long-term trends:

- Growth of activist consumers
- Changing roles of women
- Rise of a new lifestyle for older people
- Increasing social consciousness about sustainable growth

All four of these trends are dynamic, constantly evolving, bringing surprises to companies each year.

Activist New Consumers: The Information Seekers

Activist consumers already make up 50 percent of the consumer market in the United States and will be the dominant European consumer group over the next decade. In technology-oriented emerging economies like China and India, with their rapid rise in education and income, the number of activist consumers will also grow rapidly. These consumers gather, process, analyze, and skillfully use information to support the myriad decisions they make in their daily lives.

RELISH TAKING THE REINS. Activist consumers feel empowered by information to control their lives, to make better personal choices along all dimensions, and to take risks. The more important the decision, the more sophisticated and diverse the information these consumers seek before deciding. Access to information gives them the self-confidence to take on riskier investments, job changes, and experiment with nontraditional insurance products. They are concerned about privacy but are willing to sacrifice some of it in return for the convenience of a relationship with their preferred vendors.

PREFER INFORMATION THEY FIND. As more and more channels of consumer information open up, information seekers have developed strong personal filters about what kinds of information are relevant to them. This information becomes prized more highly than information that they receive passively through common push consumer channels such as television, newspapers, and unsolicited e-mail, or through general discussions with friends and family. Activist consumers prefer highly tailored offerings, but they also like choice. They know what they want. They are annoyed but not daunted by the excess of commercial information flowing all around them. They tune it out. At the same time, they like to engage in comparison shopping, first seeking information on their own and then comparing what they've found with information offered by a salesperson close to the purchase. Only after consumers have carefully examined a source and decided that it seems trustworthy and potentially beneficial to them will they choose to interact with it and possibly share personal data to let it better address their needs.

Online dating is a good example of selective information sharing of very personal information. Web sites like Emode, Eharmony, and Match advertise personality tests and algorithm-based profiling tools that promise to find a perfect companion for the user. Consumers interested in finding a compatible mate will answer lengthy questionnaires and take psychological quizzes in hopes that this information will result in a good romantic match.

Despite their desire for customized information, activist consumers will also want to continue to have access to traditional printed materials—not to browse, but to use as an additional resource to inform their decision. Brochures, catalogs, and magazines will not go away.

EXPERIMENT AND LEARN. Information seekers like to try out new brands of products and services, but not until they have gathered some data and have taken on some comparison shopping. They are quick learners, ready and willing to switch brands in a nanosecond based on new information. They experiment as they build their preferred source lists, and they like sophisticated, well-researched sources that they can trust.

NOT VERY LOYAL. The new consumers are not particularly loyal to products and services in the long run; they are constantly searching for greener pastures, and if something truly better comes along, they will purchase it. This tendency, along with the many new choices provided by the Internet and the fragmentation of consumer markets, all combine to put companies at greater risk of losing customers.

SEEK TO REDUCE INFORMATION OVERLOAD. Information seekers are quick to adopt new technologies that will help them make their searches more efficient and convenient. Susceptible to information overload, they seek solutions, both technological and human, to help them sort through massive amounts of information. They are always searching for strategies that will help them cope with a complex modern life.

WANT A DIFFERENT KIND OF RELATIONSHIP. Activist consumers often want a personal interaction with a broadly knowledgeable seller before making a decision, particularly if the purchase is a large or important one. These consumers have considered the pros and cons, have their own point of view, and now they are ready to decide. This interaction does not need to be face-to-face but must be high-quality and focused. These consumers like their questions answered immediately. Even though they may have extensively researched a purchasing decision, this final phase of interaction with the seller can provide the impetus to buy or not buy, often triggered by some small, critical piece of information.

The context of buying a car, for example, has radically changed. Activist consumers can access a host of online resources to learn about the many different makes and models of cars, as well as pricing. Lists of dos and don'ts about car buying and tips on the best trade-in value for your old car are readily available. Certain online resource sites will compare and contrast similar vehicles side by side. When activist consumers walk into a dealer's showroom, they are ready to talk specifics, and in many cases they make their purchase online.

All this adds up to quite a bit of Consumer Conundrum pain for companies.

The old days of linear, one-way relationships are dying out, as consumers now demand to be part of a complicated value web with suppliers, manufacturers, and retailers to make sure they get what they want.

Creating the feeling of a twenty-first-century
corner store needs to be part of the business strategy.

CREATING CAPACITY FOR CUSTOMIZED PERSONALIZED RELATIONSHIPS WITH ACTIVIST CONSUMERS. Every company will have to come up with a multi-pronged strategy to develop the right mix of approaches to customize personal relationships with their customers. Regardless of the specifics, companies must ensure that they have varied channels of information, different content for messages to specific groups, and, of course, database technologies to keep track of it all. The ability to individualize messages is a key part of this new capability. The following stories illustrate some of the approaches that have been tried by different companies and show signs of success.

Retailers that learn to manage customer relationships across multiple channels will be most successful. REI, the recreational supplies company, has a Web site that has been profitable since 1998, helped in part by the e-mail announcements it sends to its regular customers. In June 2003, REI started offering a new option that allows customers to buy online and then go to an REI store to pick up their purchases. Customers like having the combined convenience of online shopping and faster pick-up along with the ability to see an item when they buy it. REI is benefiting from the program, too: company research shows that about one in three of the customers who come into the store to retrieve Internet purchases stays on to shop, spending an average of $90.

In the world of gourmet retailers, A Southern Season is known as the Nordstrom of specialty food. This company in Chapel Hill, North Carolina, started out in 1975 as a one-person coffee roasting company and is now a $250 million enterprise with 250 employees. A Southern Season is one of the largest specialty-only retailers in the United States. Totally focused on the customer's experience, the company solicits feedback from shoppers in a variety of ways, including direct conversation, fax, e-mail, and a Web site. A Southern Season is delighted to hear that customers feel as though they own the store. When A Southern Season recently expanded into a new flagship store—with 59,000 square feet of space that held 75,000 items and a fifty-seat state-of-the-art cooking school—its customers expressed apprehension about the store's getting too big and losing its warm, homey feeling. To address these concerns, A Southern Season designed the space with a cozy interior layout broken up into smaller spaces, like a collection of little shops. Areas titled Wine, Gourmet Groceries, Candy, House & Home, The Bakery, Deli/Cheese, and Floral/Gift are separate profit centers dedicated to the philosophy of individual ownership.

Successful companies will need to find ways to keep customers by building deeper relationships cemented by trust. Activist new consumers love the Internet, but they also enjoy the old-fashioned ambience of the local corner store. These same customers enjoy it when a store uses technology to save information about them and their purchases.

Harrah's Entertainment, the casino chain, did extensive work analyzing customer data and found that its most valuable customers wanted service that was quick and personal. Now regular guests are greeted by name as they drive up, brought their favorite refreshments, and paired with a personal host.

Mass marketing certainly is not dead; it is still the perfect choice for some products and some consumers. Businesses do not need the same intensity of relationship with every customer. That said, businesses must respect the sophistication of the information seekers. They must learn to use information as a tool for retaining customers. Activist new consumers are not swayed by mass-market messages and hype; in fact, these will drive them away. When acquiring a major purchase, they expect the seller to provide sophisticated information, including accurate comparison data. The information set needs to be broad as well as deep, educating the consumer about the product in attractive and memorable ways. Relationships between customers and vendors are far more complicated than the simple and undemanding "Here's my money for your goods and services" model of the past.

Wachovia Corporation learned about the importance of maintaining customer service as it integrated its operations during a merger. The bank used to aim to complete a merger within eighteen months. But since customers complained of poor service resulting from that aggressive timetable, Wachovia has elected to more than double the time it takes for integration. Driven by increased customer retention, the bank's profits rose last year by 121 percent.

In the Badlands attrition is inevitable, but the good news is that in a fluid marketplace it will also be easier to gain new customers. The single best way to lose a customer (or not gain one) is to fail to provide a level of service that matches the customer's information and decision-making needs. Businesses will find it hard to recover from a spiral into decreasing customer satisfaction. Activist consumers are less forgiving of poor service and simply move on to other choices. Home Depot learned this lesson the hard way. Its sales slowed because it was not meeting customers' expectations for service; often there were not enough representatives on the floor to answer questions or offer advice. Rival Lowe's took over some of the hardware giant's market share by being more responsive to customers' information and service needs. To get back in the game, Home Depot announced plans to hire more customer service representatives and to install computers so that their reps can learn more about Home Depot's products.

Consumer business relationships are not unlike other relationships; neither party expects to have the relationship last forever, unless it continues to provide reciprocal value. Leading diet shake and meal replacement company Slim-Fast may have the right model. Slim-Fast ads can be seen on TV and in almost every magazine. The company's nutrition bars and shakes are prominent in grocery and drug stores. But it is Slim-Fast's Web site that extends and deepens the relationship with the consumer in ways that go beyond just buying a chocolate Slim-Fast bar. The site is dedicated to creating a community of people with a common concern about weight loss and a healthy lifestyle. The online service offers personalized member-only options such as a weight chart, diary, and customized fitness plan. Members can create a list of friends to talk to about weight loss and can turn to the tip of the day for motivation. Recipe boxes and fitness features are offered daily. Members can also order replacement products directly from the site for ease and convenience. In 2003 the Slim-Fast site reported 1.5 million members.

And finally, each company will need to provide service 24/7. People's lives are busy these days. Households are much more complicated to run. Consumers want the convenience of shopping anytime, anyplace. This means that companies will need to adjust their workforces accordingly to provide the right mix of personal service and technology-mediated information that will satisfy and retain their customer base.

FORECAST AND LONG-TERM IMPLICATIONS. Over the next decade the activist consumer will come to dominate the global marketplace. Consumers in all countries are experimenting with new information and communication channels, forcing businesses to respond in new ways and transforming the business-consumer relationship. Today there is so much experimentation that forecasting the end result is not yet possible. Those businesses that adapt to the changing interests of these activist consumers will have a strong competitive edge in the future. These companies must be willing to learn right alongside their customers.

Changing Roles of Women

In every corner of the globe women's roles and lifestyles are changing at home, at work, and socially. The changing role of women is considered by many to be the most profound social trend of this historical cycle of innovation. In the 1950s these shifts in the fundamental roles of women began to accelerate and globalize, driving significant changes in how families, households, workplaces, and even societies function. This trend further took off in the 1980s when it became evident that women worldwide were delaying the age they married and had children, were raising children as single parents, and needed to work outside the home for wages. Now women compose nearly 45 percent of the formal workforce, and most new workforce entrants are women. In Europe they account for 80 percent of that growth. In many countries women attending college now outnumber men. Advanced education equips women with high-level analytical skills, enabling them to make more of their own decisions independently, increasing their self-confidence and helping them excel in the workplace as tomorrow's knowledge workers. Women form a significant proportion of the growth in the specialized and sophisticated global middle class, a change that is still being assimilated around the world.

WOMEN LEAD TOMORROW'S DIVERSE HOUSEHOLD. As women become empowered to work, attend school, and earn advanced degrees, consumer patterns change to accommodate the changing role of women as well as their new spending power. The household has always been the source of consumer decision making; this is not changing, but the dominance of women as the decision makers for all purchases is swiftly becoming pervasive worldwide.

Key household shifts:

- The number of households is growing, but their size is declining. There are fewer married couples with children as more women postpone getting married and focus on obtaining a higher education.

- Single-parent households are increasing in number as young women leave home and live on their own, and as middle-aged women are more likely to be divorced and live alone. In California, for example, our most populous state, more than half the women over fifty years of age are single, due primarily to divorce. The population of widows is also on the rise globally, since women live longer than men.

- Nonfamily households are increasing as a result of women's sharing households with other women along the age spectrum, as well as an increase in unmarried couples.

- Although women have been making more purchasing decisions than ever before, they have not been the major decision makers for big and important purchases such as cars, homes, and finances, at least not independently from men. As women achieve higher levels of education and take on greater roles as important income producers, they are taking the lead in all purchases.

WOMEN *ARE* THE MARKET.   Women are not a niche market, they *are* the market. Business behavior is severely lagging behind this dramatic social trend and the opportunity it provides. Women in the United States, the global consumer trendsetters, are responsible for 80–90 percent of all consumer purchases, either directly or through their influence. Their global sisters are not far behind. It is no longer true that the typical woman is spending her husband's money; women now earn a substantial share of the family income as their own incomes have risen more than 60 percent over the last thirty years. Since they now form the majority of graduates of higher education, their incomes will continue to rise while men's will remain relatively flat (as they have for the last few decades). Women are increasingly running their own businesses and contributing trillions to the global economy. Women are tired of not having their needs met and are not happy about having to purchase goods and services through processes that do not honor their preferences.

Over the next decade women will demand changes in how companies market and sell to them—they will vote with their wallets if they are not engaged in new more appealing ways. They will be the *most* empowered activist consumers. They have many unmet needs that savvy companies should rush to meet. By the time we reach the end of the Badlands, companies that don't realize quickly that women *are* the market will find themselves displaced by those that do.

BUILDING CUSTOMIZED RELATIONSHIPS AROUND WOMEN'S UNMET NEEDS.
Women want information and purchasing processes that are tailored to them. Here are areas in which women have major unmet needs:

- Life management
- Education and career
- Health
- Social support
- Survival

Life management needs: There is little doubt that "life management" will be a growth industry fueled in large part by women's need to juggle their increasingly demanding lives; women are taking on roles but not shedding any. They have little time to shop, so they want convenience and service—more time and less stress. Women's multiple caretaking roles along the life cycle cause time management problems, so they need help managing their overburdened schedules. Young women need to balance their professional lives and young families. Women are going back to work much sooner after giving birth, and they're finding few external supports in place to help them. Middle-aged women live under the most stress. Not only are these women sandwiched between caring for their families and work responsibilities, they also provide most of the care to aging parents.

A recent study in California gave the mean number of hours caregivers provided at 93.3 per week. About 18 percent of those caregivers had to quit work to provide the care required. Canada's Shopper's Drug Mart has produced commercials that resonate with middle-aged women and caregivers. One TV spot shows scenes of a woman going about her day, taking care of other people in her life. The ad ends with a message, "Take care of yourself." Another commercial shows images of strong, graceful older women and the tag line, "Growing old is good." The spot encourages the watcher to be proud of her age and to want to stay healthy to enjoy it. These messages speak to women's need for empathy and respect—and help with their enormously demanding lives.

What Women Want

- Relationships, not transactions
- Conversations that include emotion
- Respect
- Empathy
- Comfortable service environments
- Interaction with other women
- Products tailored to them
- Discernable value

Managing multiple roles means that women must practice effective coordination and collaboration, and in doing so they turn to information technology for help.

Women need devices and services that filter the world for them, and they dream of innovations that could act as a concierge and a task manager in their busy lives. Their unmet need is to find a way to be less involved in the day-to-day management of all the activities at work and at home. Educated women are fierce information seekers, and the way information is packaged for their convenience matters a lot to them. They need information to integrate their family, home, social groups, and work life. Some emerging electronic agent products, such as Oxygen.com and Women.com, will continue to mature and seem likely to come to provide access to real people offering those services as well.

Given how busy their lives are, women would love to have *bots* evolve faster to support their shopping needs; these automatic shopping programs exist in primitive form and search the Web for the best deal that matches a buyer's specific requirements. Not only must such services deliver, women must trust them with very personal information—and to make the right decision with that information. Agents will evolve over the next decade and will be adopted by more users to fill their unmet needs.

Women are adopting new technologies almost at the same rate as men. Young women often use technology as a fashion statement, but their deeper need is to build personal networks to advance their careers and social status. Middle-aged women are solid technology consumers, but they are driven to purchase their tools for practical reasons; they are not attracted to "toys for boys." They would rather have peace of mind. They want equipment to last a long time, work reliably, and have good service options. They have little interest and even less time to tinker with complex technology and poorly written instruction manuals.

Convenience is a critical factor for all the large and small tasks women must manage. It's no accident that salad-in-a-bag and washed, sliced fruits and vegetables are taking up more shelf space at the grocery store. These invaluable products are not only time-saving, they allow a working woman to put something nutritious and fresh in front of her family.

Businesses that understand what working mothers need will gain this segment's attention. Nissan, for example, started showing a commercial for its Quest van with an announcer's voice saying, "Moms have changed." These kinds of messages communicate empathy. They acknowledge that women with children have very active lives and need a vehicle that reflects their various needs. Toyota Canada developed a sales process specifically for women, to supply them with the information they need as car buyers while eliminating the stereotypical male atmosphere of the car dealership. The program, called Access Toyota, is what the company calls a "nicer way to buy a car." It speaks to women's desire for relationship, conversations, and comfort in the service area. The showroom is a no-pressure environment in which salespeople (called Product Advisors) help shoppers find a vehicle that best matches their lifestyle. Access Toyota allows buyers to do a feature-by-feature comparison with other brands of cars and to check online pricing information to estimate the trade-in amount on their old car. While the program grew out of an interest in better serving women customers, Toyota Canada has implemented it throughout the company, believing that it provides a superior shopping experience for all of its customers.

Many women are adding "homeowner" to their list of roles, and businesses throughout the hardware industry are slowly beginning to address their needs. Lowe's home improvement stores redesigned their layout to make it friendlier to women shoppers, using brighter lighting and more attractive displays. Manufacturers of tools and hardware are also wooing women by making tools that women feel comfortable using. Zircon Tools gears 75 percent of its products toward female consumers. Its stud locators, for example, come in a compact size and translucent colors.

Education and career needs: Women want exciting, prosperous work lives and lifelong opportunities to invest in themselves as professionals. Young women want to move up faster and gain access to careers that bring rewards similar to men's. They are aware of the gains women in the previous generation have made and are grateful for them, yet they feel progress has been too slow—and they are right. They are looking for help in accelerating gains while maintaining a better life balance than their mothers did. Women will be seeking educational experiences that provide powerful networking and competencies to make big career gains fast. Young women will take a lot more risks to speed up their progress.

Increasingly, middle-aged women are motivated to start their own businesses so that they can have full control of their lives. They want to earn more money more efficiently and enjoy a higher quality of life. For example, in the United States in 1977, fewer than 1 million firms in the United States were owned by women. By 2002 more than 12 million businesses were woman-owned, and the number is growing. More women are inheriting the family business and making a go of it. Although women mainly run service businesses, they are also penetrating such traditionally male-dominated industries as trade, construction, wholesale, transportation, and agriculture. These businesses contribute more than $3 trillion a year in revenue—more than the gross domestic product of most countries! As business leaders, women employ nearly one in four U.S. workers, and they want support in providing good working environments for their employees.

Some companies are making a commitment to meeting the business lifestyle needs of women entrepreneurs. IBM, for example, established its Women's Business Center, a Web site with technological tools and resources to help women expand their businesses. IBM has also forged alliances with several women's professional organizations. Along with firms such as AT&T and Providian Financial, Big Blue has sponsored work done by the Center for Women's Business Research, a U.S.-based nonprofit organization providing research and information on women business owners and their companies worldwide. These are valuable efforts, but there are still far too few of them, which means there are substantial opportunities here.

Women need to ensure their own long-term financial security, and their financial planning needs are complex. More often than men, they may pause a career—and the associated benefits and pension—to have children, and they have a longer term to plan for, as they may live longer than their husbands. In fact, according to the nonprofit Women's Institute for a Secure Retirement, the average woman spends 15 percent of her career stepping out of the workforce to care for children and parents. Major financial institutions such as Bank of America, Charles Schwab, and Citibank are offering educational tools and products to help women manage their finances to meet their goals. Women are looking for advisers to talk about how their money will help them and their families have a higher quality of life, not just how their money will grow in the market. With programs and advisory groups focused on women, these companies' aim is to teach women how to invest and plan better for retirement.

Even banks in Asia are becoming savvier about women as a new type of customer. They have been especially active in introducing products targeted at their female customers. In fact, more than ten offer credit cards just for women. One card, from AIG Credit Card Co. in Hong Kong, gives the bearer special discounts on a health plan called the Tiramisu Female Checkup Plan, which covers gynecological visits, as a marketing strategy.

Health needs: All women know that juggling their multiple roles causes stress, which can lead to health problems. Young women who have watched their mothers struggle to maintain their health are very interested in self-care to prevent illness. Middle-aged women's bodies change dramatically with menopause, making them more vulnerable to health problems at the very time their care-giving roles expand to include their aging parents. In many cultures menopause is still treated as a disease, when it is addressed at all. Many women suffer needless health problems as a consequence of hormonal changes during menopause, because they lack critical information. Women also work part time more than men do, which means they often do not have health insurance for themselves and their children. Women worry about the health of the entire family and are actively seeking innovations to close this gap.

The number of resources available to help women address their health needs is increasing. The women's portal iVillage has an extensive listing of articles and health tips on topics from birth control and pregnancy to breast cancer and menopause. To supplement their medical visits, women can research health issues, send questions to health experts, and use tools such as a "health calculator" to measure their level of fitness. Women are using "blogs," personal Web logs, to share experiences and insights about health problems. New informal consumer-to-consumer communication facilitated by technology will grow to be an important new source of health information for women.

In the bricks-and-mortar world, businesses and clubs that emphasize a convenient and holistic approach to women's health are increasing. Curves for Women, a diet and exercise center, offers thirty-minute exercise and weight loss sessions to fit women's busy schedules. Class participants gather in a circle with an instructor to work out and discuss dieting issues, reinforcing the social support the group provides. Well-known companies such as Weight Watchers and Jenny Craig have been joined in recent years by online resources that allow women to access up-to-date medical information and track their health on a daily basis rather than just focus on weight loss.

Beauty is linked to health in many women's minds. Women eagerly buy products that demonstrate sensitivity to the special needs of their bodies. In the apparel industry, this has never been more true. As women become more self-confident about being beautiful at any size, apparel merchants are designing clothes that fit different body types. Brands such as Banana Republic, J. Crew, and Victoria's Secret are introducing petite and plus sizes in their clothing lines. In 2002, designers Tommy Hilfiger and Eddie Bauer joined in with their own plus-size lines.

Traditionally referred to by the euphemism *full-figured,* plus sizes are now being marketed more prominently. Vanity Fair hired actress and musician Queen Latifah to advertise its Curvation line. The confident, articulate, and outgoing Latifah makes a bold statement: larger bodies should be celebrated, not hidden away. The new woman's self-confidence includes feeling good about a normal body.

Social support needs: Young women are not trying to have it all the way their mothers did. They want balance. They want to participate in the full range of opportunities that the increasing prosperity provides. (Middle-aged women have less time for friendships and for seeking advice from other women about meeting life's pressing demands.)

Oprah Winfrey, with her multimedia empire, is an example of the power of women's networks and meeting social needs. Five days a week, she gathers a large audience of American women from a variety of backgrounds in front of their televisions. Oprah's down-to-earth style and openness with her guests and audience members have created a strong following. Her influence is so great that she has made instant best-sellers out of books she recommends on her TV show. Using her popular Web site, Oprah.com, she reinforces a strong sense of community and support. Chat rooms, health and fitness recommendations, shopping and family-oriented resources are all offered under the Oprah umbrella. Cable networks Oxygen (also part of the Oprah group) and Lifetime are two channels focused on women, with programs and commercials that address topics such as women's middle age and special health concerns. In the United Kingdom, femail.co.uk is another valuable resource. This hip Web site offers show-biz and entertainment information along with more traditional topics such as health and finance. The site promotes building support via communities of like minds, and has numerous chat rooms. Users can also get expert advice on a variety of areas, from pregnancy and children to sex therapy and dreams.

While women wait for more advanced technologies to support them, they are enjoying technology products that do make their lives more enjoyable. Kodak caught onto this need with the introduction of its EasyShare digital camera. Recognizing that women now make up over half of all digital camera buyers, Kodak set out to design a camera that would appeal to this group. Through its research the company found that women were not drawn to technology for its own sake, but rather wanted an easy way to capture memories and share them with friends and family. The result was the EasyShare camera, which has a streamlined design and allows users to take pictures without having to adjust a lot of settings. And to print or e-mail photos, the user simply puts the camera into a docking station that comes with it and presses a few buttons. Kodak has reaped the rewards of meeting the needs of its women consumers: within one year of EasyShare's launch, Kodak rose to number two in market share, after not making the top three the year before.

Consumer market research is turning some gender stereotypes upside down. With sporting event commercials showing men chugging beer and slapping their buddies on the back as they watch a game on TV, who would have guessed that 38 percent of the people watching professional football are female? While the NFL has yet to address women's needs through its choice of advertisers, Nascar, which has roughly the same percentage of female viewers (40 percent), has partnered with many "women-friendly" brands such as Tide, Cheerios, and Rubbermaid. Encouraged by the recent success of golfer Annika Sorenstam, the Professional Golfers Association (PGA) is also trying to get a piece of the female market, with a multimillion-dollar marketing campaign to bring more women into the game.

Carmaker Alfa Romeo is also targeting its traditionally "male" products toward women. A new TV commercial showing in Europe features a woman driver who, after zooming around a series of obstacles on the road, steps out of her car door looking confident.

In the United States, women make up more than half of all business travelers, an increase that can also be seen as a trend in other countries. Globally, women are learning to expand their power by working together to address common issues. As they attract a highly educated and sophisticated group of women in business and major nongovernmental organizations (NGOs), groups such as the International Women's Forum gain visibility and clout. Women are growing to trust other women more than they trust men to help them advance. This is a new trend. Women are just beginning to realize that their own networks can act as far more potent forces for change than the old boys' networks that held sway for so long. For women, these networks serve as linkages for new ventures and as filtering mechanisms for purchases, information, and services.

Survival needs: The majority of women around the world struggle to meet basic needs. One of the most successful global programs for helping women has been the expansion of microeconomic lending programs innovated by the Grameen Bank, which pioneered lending poor women small amounts of money to seed new businesses in Bangladesh—and has seeded an informal global movement for other banks to do the same. Women leaders in transnational corporations are initiating new programs. For example, the African and Canadian Business Women's Alliance (ACBWA) is part of Klohn Leonoff Ltd., a forty-year-old engineering firm in Canada. A formal unit within the company, ACBWA is based on opportunities identified by traditional engineering projects in developing countries. By linking the business expertise of Canadian managers with African women leaders in local communities, the engineering firm started numerous joint ventures as well as new businesses, ranging from papaya plantations to textile mills to foundries.

Ugly social problems continue to plague women and threaten their survival. Trafficking in young women for prostitution is still common throughout the world. In Romania, Iana Matei is the director of a program called Reaching Out. Matei courageously devotes her time to rescuing and assisting young girls between thirteen and twenty-two years old who have been lured out of the country with job promises and sold into prostitution. Reaching Out rescues the girls and provides safe housing, counseling, and job skills training. These children and young women need tremendous emotional support to overcome the trauma they have suffered and to reintegrate back into society. Reaching Out is currently the only program in Romania capable of sustaining long-term support for trafficking victims.

Increasingly, women in their fifties or older are widowed or divorced or have husbands too sick to work. They need to work to keep their lives together, and yet they often face job discrimination or are the first to be laid off. Many older women in every society, from the United States to India, are poor, living alone, and extremely vulnerable.

LONG-TERM IMPLICATIONS. Despite the obstacles they face, women are growing more confident about who they are as they expand their roles and identities. During this next decade, look for women's power to shape the marketplace to grow as they fulfill their role as lead activist consumer. The most dynamic segments will be single women at both ends of the age spectrum, which taken together constitute a huge new market. Avoid the pitfall of thinking work takes precedence over family. Women are very concerned about the quality of their lives. They are willing to make trade-offs for long-term benefit, but expect to get their needs, and those of their families, met.

Rise of a New Older Consumer

The majority of Boomers around the world are slowly realizing that they will live long, healthy lives well into their eighties and nineties, and many women will live to be more than a hundred. Defining this new stage of adult development will be the Boomers' last big challenge, one they will relish. Most people who are eighty years of age today didn't expect to live that long. Having already gone through their retirement years *and* their old age, people in their late seventies and eighties are muddling through this time in their lives, extending their old age rather than expanding middle age (with a few exceptions).

> *The concept that we are used up at sixty-five is*
> *patently ridiculous. When sixty-five was identified*
> *as the retirement age, people were dying in their*
> *fifties. We have never updated this concept. It does*
> *not fit with today's reality.*

Global generational research points out a conscious awareness among Boomers of a new life stage, a gift of twenty-five more years of life for many. This generation is taking a stab at meeting the new definition of "middle age." A recent cover story in *AARP* (the magazine of the organization formerly known as the American Association of Retired Persons) declared, "Sixty is the new thirty!" Article topics cover sex, relationships, and active lifestyles. Editor Steve Slon says that his staff's objective is to reach "people poised for new discoveries, not decline."

A number of companies are experimenting with identifying and reaching these new older consumers. In the fall of 2003, Kia Motors sponsored a campaign to redefine Baby Boomers by state of mind, instead of by year of birth. The Korean car company sent a Baby Boomer couple across America in its new Kia Amanti to gather signatures from Boomers asking *Merriam-Webster's Dictionary* to change its definition. Kia's Amanti is less conservative than its predecessors and targets Boomers with its combination of style, comfort, and safety.

The profound impact of this new phase between what was formerly middle age and old age will take a generation or two to sort through. American Boomers will define this stage. There are 80 million of them, and they control about 70 percent of America's wealth and 50 percent of its disposable income; they have lots of assets, including their own homes. They defined the activist consumer in their middle age, and they reinvent everything they engage with.

CREATING CUSTOMIZED PERSONALIZED RELATIONSHIPS WITH NEW OLDER CONSUMERS. Boomers will experiment aggressively with new lifestyles as they search for new meaning and fulfillment in the years before they finally pass into their dotage. The only certain forecast is "expect a lot of change." Boomers will break traditional patterns in their choices of housing, health care, shopping, leisure, work, and family roles. They will be the quintessential activist consumers—learning in depth about what they buy and searching for information in multiple places before they make their choices. Their hierarchy of needs will change as they reinvent their identities. They will not resemble the generation before them; they will create an entirely new market.

Companies have traditionally focused most of their marketing and advertising on people under the age of forty, even though most purchases are made by older people, especially women. This will change as Boomers spend a lot of money on themselves in new ways.

What Do These New Older Consumers Want?
- Rich experiences
- Intimacy and happiness
- Meaning
- Health
- Longevity
- Mobility
- Community

EMERGING UNMET NEEDS. The place to start is where the action is going to be, not where it is now. Being the first generation to be aware of the twenty-five-year life extension will make Boomers even more significant demographically than they are now. The only certainty is that this will be a dynamic experience. They don't want to be bored and conduct lives devoid of meaning. Some Boomers will create new careers and stay in the workforce at least part time, but many will not.

A significant proportion will want to make a social contribution with their extra healthy years. This group will reevaluate intimacy in their lives. If they are married, how will they renew their relationships? And if they are not, how will they find the intimacy they seek? Boomers will want rich life experiences—golf won't be enough for most. They will value this precious gift of additional life, and they will be very creative about how they evolve their lifestyles to accommodate it. As they do, two major needs will emerge: health and community.

Health: Boomers will spend a lot of their disposable income on health care, but in new ways. They are focused on staying healthy and feeling good as they age, and they are interested in products that will help them do so. Realizing that their health will depend on themselves and not the medical care system, new older consumers will experiment with health care options and not depend solely on the traditional system to provide for their needs. As they pay for more health care out of their own pockets, they will analyze the value proposition of health care, particularly when it comes to health promotion and to containing morbidity from the onset of chronic diseases. Boomers will choose to spend more of their money on alternative therapies, appreciating them for their holistic emphasis and focus on prevention. Already the growth of alternative therapies outpaces that of expenditures on traditional health care (Eisenberg and others, 1997).

Some companies are experimenting with ways to define and serve this group. "Tweeniors," as the group of consumers aged fifty-five to seventy are sometimes called, are the target audience for entire lines of new nutritional products and supplements. Slim-Fast meal replacement shakes are milk-based, delivering the calcium that many tweeniors are missing in their diets. Dairy Farmers of America in Kansas City, Missouri, makes a drink called VitalCal for consumers battling with chronic illness.

Similar growth applies to *nutraceuticals* and *cosmeceuticals.* Nutraceuticals are natural, botanically derived products that can be purchased over the counter. They appeal to the midlife consumer as an alternative to powerful pharmaceuticals and surgical procedures (Figure 8.1).

Nutraceuticals include not only dietary supplements such as the antioxidants vitamins E and C and herbal remedies such as St. John's Wort but also functional foods and beverages such as breakfast cereals with soy protein as a source of phytoestrogens, or a sports drink formulated with the supplements glucosamine and chondroitin for

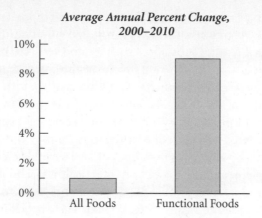

Figure 8.1. Functional Foods Market.
Source: Global Foresight, 2004; U.S. Census Bureau.

bone and joint health. Terms like *antioxidant* and *polyphenols* have become very familiar to informed and sophisticated middle-aged health consumers. Their strong desire to delay the effects of aging, to look great, and to feel younger drive the demand for nutraceuticals. Cancer prevention, cognitive function, and heart, eye, bone, and joint health are some of the major condition-specific categories for supplements, and companies are focusing their product development efforts in these areas. It's big business and only getting bigger. Demand for plant-derived chemical ingredients in the United States is expected to rise by 6.8 percent per year, to $2.7 billion in 2006. This is a major global trend as well. In Europe the United Kingdom leads the way with spending on nutraceuticals at £110 a year per person, and the number of people buying products has doubled in the past five years.

Equally dynamic is the cosmeceutical industry, a hybrid between the cosmetics and pharmaceutical industries. Companies in this industry are focusing their product development attention on the prevention and management of skin aging and the promotion of health, two primary concerns of the sophisticated middle-aged consumer. Cosmeceuticals, which focus on managing health and skin aging, are the fastest-growing segment of the cosmetics industry. Americans bought $2.6 billion of these products in 2002, and estimates for 2007 surpass $5 billion. Total department store skin care sales rose 2.6 percent in 2002, while the cosmeceutical brands jumped 62 percent for the same period.

Cosmeceuticals promise more than superficial improvements in appearance; they promote anti-aging through a variety of biochemical and nutritional natural substances such as aloe vera, vitamin C esters, and alpha lipoic acid. An emerging niche in the cosmeceutical market is physician-sponsored products. These lines attract droves of consumers because of the medical credentials of the sponsor. One of the most prominent physician-sponsored dermeceutical lines is put forward by Dr. Nicolas Perricone, a dermatologist who has gained celebrity status by selling his own lines of anti-wrinkle cream and nutritional supplements with a focus on total health. His books and tapes build on popular interest in looking good and tap into the deeper unmet need for better health. *The Wrinkle Cure* proclaims that you can "look 10 years younger in days, without surgery!" Critics question the science behind these claims, and Perricone himself has not published studies in peer-reviewed journals proving that the main ingredients in his products actually erase wrinkles. But he does point to other studies that can support his theories, one of which states that certain agents in Perricone's product line can increase skin firmness.

The Perricone Prescription lays out a very comprehensive approach to better health, and for many middle-aged, health-conscious consumers this offers enough hope and evidence for them to continue buying Perricone products. And they certainly are buying them. Perricone's sales soared in 2002 to $42.4 million, up from $11.9 million in 2001. Sales over the next three to five years are projected to double annually, fueled by the demand for new products, including a new anti-wrinkle cream that retails for $570 per two-ounce jar.

Our current medical care system does not provide a comprehensive approach to health and preventing illness. Dr. Perricone could well be one of the change agents on the fringe that we see during times of great innovation.

Ultimately, the American Boomers, turned off by the prolonged extension of poor-quality living as life comes to an end, will reinvent death itself. They will want to die the way they lived.

This group will want a different kind of community to live in between ages sixty and eighty. Retirement and old age will seem far away to many at sixty; they will not be attracted to the current configurations of most retirement communities. Boomers will have a tendency to want an urban lifestyle after many years in the suburbs. They will be attracted to condominiums with good services in support of an active lifestyle. They will also want to be part of a community and to be socially involved. Most won't want to be in gated communities locked away from the diversity of life and people of a variety of ages.

LONG-TERM IMPLICATIONS. Global aging extended by a long, healthy life will result in the permanent creation of a new stage of human development that has uncertain but huge impacts on consumerism. For companies it means that customers have another twenty-five years of consumption that will drive all sorts of innovation across all facets of life. It is hard to think of an economic sector that will not be affected, but there is no question that this will drive huge changes in health care.

EMERGING HEALTH TECHNOLOGIES
BENEFIT OLDER CONSUMERS

Technology innovations promise to transform health care over the next decade, offering many benefits to consumers—particularly older consumers, who suffer most of the burden of chronic medical problems. Older consumers will use technology to manage more of their own health. Watch for an increase in cyber-chondriacs. Some important areas:

- Genomics—map predisposition to disease as well as susceptibility.
- Gene therapy—common cancers—(breast, lung, colon), Parkinson's, arthritis.
- Tissue engineering—use of stem cells to grow new tissues for diseased organs (pancreas, heart).
- Cellular targeted pharmaceuticals—new biological advances allow targeted formulations for specific cells such as cancer cells.
- Bioinformatics—use of sensors embedded in the body and outside to monitor and track measurements for health or treatments and communicate them remotely.
- Home diagnostic testing—blood, urine, genetic, and molecular testing—for efficacy of various pharmaceuticals.
- Vastly increased access to health information—activist consumers will help transform health care as well as manage their own health much better.

Source: Global Foresight, 2004.

Increasing Social Consciousness
About Sustainable Economic Growth

The idea of sustainable development has taken hold in the global consciousness, particularly with regard to the environment and the treatment of workers. Although awareness and positive action are not evenly distributed, people from around the world are concerned about a whole range of sustainability issues (Table 8.1).

European governments are more active than American ones in addressing these issues and participating in global forums to set standards. The U.S. government as the global outlier is exemplified by its refusal to sign the Kyoto Agreement despite the nation's being the lead producer of carbon emissions. Consumers are increasing their demands that companies pay attention to these issues by addressing them with specific programs. And consumers are not alone as a voice for environment-friendly business. Several distinct driving forces are converging to create a broad, supportive context for more sustainable consumption behaviors and business practices. Yet obstacles remain that will impede progress.

SUPPORTING FORCES FOR MORE SUSTAINABILITY. First and foremost among factors promoting sustainability is the increase and accessibility via the Internet of high-quality information about the issue. This

Protect the Environment, Even If Economic Growth Slows			
	Agree (%)	Disagree (%)	DK/Ref
Canada	82	16	1
Italy	82	13	4
United Kingdom	81	17	2
Former W. Germany	82	13	4
Germany (total)	78	21	1
Japan	72	23	5
Former E. Germany	68	30	2
United States	69	26	4
France	66	33	1

Table 8.1.   Support for Environmentalism Is Widespread.

Note: Asked only in selected advanced countries.

Source: Views of a Changing World, The Pew Research Center for the People and the Press, June 2003.

has enabled consumers, businesses, and NGOs alike to develop shared understandings of the problems and various solution sets as well as their trade-offs. The Information Revolution and new communication channels allow for more transparency and communication regarding abuses, as well as widespread sharing of good approaches. This builds social consensus and awareness, and it even serves to change values. Increased channels of communication and free-flowing information have allowed a diverse distributed leadership to work together to craft standards and protocols to guide new action as well as to increase public accountability.

One example of new standards is the U.N. Global Compact that companies can voluntarily sign, agreeing to abide by nine principles of sustainable business practice. Thus far more than eleven hundred companies have signed, including such diverse businesses as BP Amoco, Cisco Systems, DuPont, Ericsson, Lufthansa, and Volvo. Access to better information in real time allows social advocacy organizations to reach audiences with their messages more effectively.

Corporations are creating new guidelines for environmental impact and for treatment of workers, based on better information and on successes that have also served to improve business results. Having had this experience, they are open to seeking new solutions to other sustainability issues. For example, companies had good success reducing pollution by redesigning production processes rather than relying solely on end-point technical solutions that fulfilled regulatory requirements. Their willingness to change will also accelerate as NGOs shift from taking a watchdog approach to forming partnerships with business. Emissions trading—the first "cap and trade" market for sulfur dioxide from coal-produced electricity—provided business with some flexibility: companies had an upper limit of emissions each year but also had tradable emissions credits they could sell to others if they reduced theirs (or could buy if they needed them). This program spawned new markets for new technologies, created opportunity for new consulting services in risk management and environmental practices, and for new financial instruments such as derivatives and services. It also reduced health costs by billions of dollars and reduced regulation costs as well.

CREATING CUSTOMIZED PERSONALIZED RELATIONSHIPS WITH SOCIALLY CONSCIOUS CONSUMERS. Today's better-informed workers and consumers don't want to work for companies—or buy products from companies—that are environmental violators. Conversely, companies are finding that they can use a reputation for sustainable business practices to recruit and retain the vibrant knowledge workers that they need. Corporate social responsibility is becoming perceived as a real value as people become educated and form new expectations. People also are becoming more sophisticated about the globalization of the economy and realize that there are differences in wages and working environments. Knowledge workers do not want to work for companies that pollute or take advantage of poor countries and their labor. The Internet allows coordinated watchdog NGOs to pinpoint abusers in globally visible ways.

Most big sustainability issues will be resolved by modifying the business models and standard practices of big companies. A growing cadre of activist consumers, however, are voting with their purchases of durable and consumable goods, choosing those that are environmentally sound or are made by companies with strong sustainable practices. European consumers lead the way in their willingness to pay more for environmentally sound products; surveys indicate 60–70 percent support. U.S. consumers lag far behind, with most indicators hovering around 25 percent to 30 percent, but those percentages are rising. Companies will need to engage in socially and environmentally responsible business practices or risk losing these customers over the next decade. It is still hard to measure whether action follows attitude, because real purchases are made up of millions of individual acts— consumers act alone and can't be tracked by any single registry. But anecdotal evidence, the increasing success of environmentally sound products in the marketplace, and the number of companies voluntarily making initiatives all support the conclusion that at least a tide of true support is slowly rising.

SIGNIFICANT OBSTACLES REMAIN. Despite dramatic change, a lot of confusing information is still out there, and much of it is poorly packaged. This makes consumers, policymakers, businesspeople, and other stakeholders insecure about what the real facts are, which in turn impedes action. Although more business-NGO partnerships exist, many still have legacy distrust of each other. Many in the social movement side believe that NGOs that collaborate in market approaches to solving sustainability issues are "selling out" to capitalism. Because they so passionately believe that capitalism is incompatible with sustainability and environmentalism, they often get great play in the media, which thrive on the angst they produce. Another obstacle is the lack of standards that all sides can strive to achieve, which are often socially and politically sensitive and need to win buy-in on a global basis. This means that setting any one standard will take a long time. A further stumbling block is the lack of sufficient alternative products and services. Although they have increased in number, these are far outnumbered by less sensitive choices.

LONG-TERM IMPLICATIONS. People around the world have a growing awareness that taking care of the environment and implementing sustainable business models is crucial for the well-being of all. The belief that both business goals and environmental goals can be achieved together is replacing the belief that they are incompatible. This makes it likely that response to these issues will improve dramatically going forward. Most companies will move assertively to respond appropriately to this growing consumer trend, although some will comply just to stay out of the socially negative spotlight.

SUMMARY INSIGHTS

Some of the most significant and far-reaching impacts of the Information Era will be changes in consumers. No pain is more crucial to resolve fast and completely than the Consumer Conundrum.

- The global economy is becoming more consumer-centric as the middle class grows around the world. However, this doesn't mean more homogeneity. Culture also will rise in importance. People want a global economy, not a global culture.

- The growth of the activist consumer is driving changes in purchasing and consumption. This consumer has at least some college education and enjoys doing some research before making a purchase. Consumers of this type take an active approach and will switch brands if they don't get what they want.

- Activist consumers want high-touch, high-tech relationships. They want a twenty-first-century version of the cozy relationship with the corner store, which means using technology to make purchasing convenient, full of choice, customized to them and their preferences, and highly efficient. For this customer, good relationships are not optional.

- Consumer experimentation is intense around the world, making solid forecasts difficult. This situation won't sort out for several years, so companies will need to keep their business models very adaptable and focus on the ability to target and individualize information and relationships all along the value chain.

- The changing role of women is the most far-reaching long-term social trend of this era, and it has a long way to play out. Women form a majority of activist consumers. They feel loyalty to a quality, empowered life, not to specific brands. Those businesses that catch this wave will be big winners.

- Women and young people will lead a consumer movement for more sustainable consumption. This steady trend will reach a tipping point several years into the Badlands.

- The Boomers' last stand will be the reinvention of middle age. This generation will be the first to fully experience the gift of longevity: many will live to a hundred, and few will feel old at sixty. Led by innovative American Boomers, this group will create the second stage of middle age, between age sixty and age eighty. This huge demographic will have both a big voice and a big wallet.

- Business needs to reorient its marketing toward women and older consumers. Many companies have a Competency Addiction leading them to focus on youth and those under forty. Not only does it not make economic sense, it doesn't make social sense. Activist consumers will demand to have their needs met, and in the process will redefine consumerism.

CHAPTER NINE

Learn About China

O
ver the next twenty years China will become a
major power on the global stage, coming of age in the Badlands.
Therefore everyone needs to move quickly to understand it and learn
how to engage with its people. For nearly a decade I have been forecasting and providing insights about many aspects of China's development, hoping to provide a fresh window on this perplexing giant.
There is no more uncertain future environment than China, be it
commercial, political, or social. Although a lot of information exists
about China, little of it comes together to make coherent sense. Every
day executives in both Chinese and multinational companies make
wrong turns and backslide in their quest to create China's new marketplace. Often these mistakes are costly—and sometimes they cost a
firm its very existence.

Behind the massive, ongoing changes in China are its people. Without understanding the people and culture of China, businesspeople,
politicians, and citizens of all countries will find it difficult to engage
productively in this exciting yet often opaque economy. In this chapter I present some insights about the people of China, including the

implications for generations of Chinese as consumers. In addition I provide a window on the Sandwich Generation in the workplace to provide insights into China's young knowledge workers.

CHINA'S GENERATIONS: DIVERGING LIFESTYLES

In the Badlands the largest group of activist consumers will live in China, providing a fascinating case study of an emerging consumer society. It's helpful to keep in mind that China was a production society as recently as fifteen years ago; the Chinese didn't even have a word for *consumer,* which conveys just how new the notion of consumerism is. This will create a unique Consumer Conundrum pain for companies seeking to benefit by doing business there.

The Six Shifts

Six major shifts are creating fault lines in China's social landscape, particularly in urban areas and transitional rural villages.

FROM A MASS SOCIETY TO A CLASS SOCIETY. Under communism, lifestyles were shaped and guided by the political elite and by popular media and were undifferentiated. Now, twenty years later, a growing middle class has emerged—lawyers, engineers, senior service executives, and other professionals—all exemplifying a class society in which every generation is being affected by change.

FROM A YOUNG SOCIETY TO AN AGING SOCIETY. In 1949, China's average lifespan was forty-two years, and most women gave birth to more than five children. Mao Zedong's dramatic socioeconomic reforms later in the century, however, raised the life expectancy to more than seventy years. As a result, the country's aged population, or people sixty-five and older, will double in less than thirty years, making China one of the world's most rapidly aging nations.

FROM A COMMUNIST ECONOMY TO MARKET SOCIALISM. Under China's communist economy the people had few incentives to be efficient or innovative and settled into a survival mode: "eating from the same big pot." But beginning in 1980, Deng Xiaoping's open-door policy encouraged economic production and business development. Gradually, innovation, competition, risk, efficiency, and profit are becoming part of people's lives in China. Cultural attitudes toward money are changing from scorn and disgust to pragmatism and demand.

FROM SOCIAL WELFARE TO INDIVIDUAL SOCIAL RESPONSIBILITY. China's communist government was traditionally responsible for the people's total welfare. Social reforms under the market economy—in housing, medical care, and social security—shifted the economic burden to individuals. Privatization is mistrusted in China, yet these fast-moving reforms will radically change people's expectations of future economic security, as well as their spending and saving patterns.

FROM A BIPOLAR RURAL AND URBAN SOCIETY TO AN URBAN SOCIETY. Approximately 70 percent of China's population lives in rural areas, with about half of that group living in communities that are urbanizing. Urbanization creates more social classes.

FROM LOCAL CONTEXT TO GLOBAL CONTEXT. After twenty years of development, China is poised to play a significant role in the global economy. Its coasts are no longer isolated; its imports and exports constitute the world's ninth-largest trading economy; it is increasingly attracting foreign capital; and it finds many international companies establishing a presence within its borders. Since the Chinese people find their daily lives more and more tied to international trends, they now follow current affairs more closely. They gather diverse information from around the world on television, the major source of knowledge for all generations in China, as well as an increasing amount of global news. Although members of the young Chinese elites hook into the Internet, they use it mainly for entertainment and information seeking, not news. Television is still the main source of news for younger people. Globalization is integrating China into the world, stimulating innovation, and introducing new cultural priorities.

LOOKING AHEAD. These six shifts will accelerate social change, including the rise of consumerism. The massive shifts under way in China will cause most of its generations to undergo significant changes of values and beliefs and create many divergent lifestyles. Because of the continuous wave of major events over the last half century, China's new generations will break into separate cohorts approximately every five years in contrast to ten to twenty years in more advanced economies.

In the following section I identify and describe five separate generations currently living in China (Table 9.1). These descriptions provide a snapshot of the Chinese people today and the factors that have shaped their values and behaviors.

The "Me Generation"

Most members of the "Me Generation" are still children and were raised in a starkly different social and family environment from what any of their forebears knew; this is the first generation of one-child families. The "Me's" grew up during China's most intense paroxysm of economic development; those born in the early 1980s have only vague recollections of the struggles that marked China's political and economic opening up to the outside world. They saw Hong Kong return to the People's Republic of China (PRC); they witnessed the birth of the Internet; and they saw television change from a state-controlled entity to a diverse

---

THE "ME GENERATION"

Slogans of the Times

- "Science and technology are the keys to China's productive power."
- "Go to the sea."

Data Set

- Born: 1980–2000
- Size: 410 million
- Percent of population: 33.3
- Ages: 2 to 22 (in 2002)

Five Cohorts

- Transitional Me, Teens, Tweeners, Kids, and Tots

Signal Events (1992–present)

- Return to privatization: Deng Xiaoping's socialist market economy takes hold
- Internet takes off; "networked economy" emerges

Source: Center for the Future of China, *China Five-Year Forecast*, 2002.

	The War and PRC Generation (pre-1945)	The Cultural Revolution Generation (1946–1956)	The Recovery Generation (1956–1967)	The Sandwich Generation (1968–1979)	The Me Generation (1980–2000)
Outlook	Hopful, faithful	Independent, cautious, mistrustful, struggling	Opportunity, personal security	Wary, confused	Me first
Work Ethic	Dedicated	Work hard, root out unfairness in the workplace	Workaholics	Cautious, small steps	Seize the opportunity, get ahead
Social Morality	Collective over self	From party over family to protect your friends	Social over political	Waiting to move over idealism	Self over all, with possible emerging social conscience
Values	Harmony with the collective	Survival, adaptability, nonmaterialism, socialism	Stability, humanism, corruption	Cautious commitment	Materialism
Ideology	Patriotism through communism	From the *Little Red Book* to finding a new direction	Socialism with a democratic flavor	Apolitical, flexible	Emerging

Table 9.1. China's Generations at a Glance.

Source: Center for the Future of China, China Five-Year Forecast, 2002, p. 65.

medium blossoming with foreign content. Economically privileged and optimistic, they are the first Chinese conscious of social classes and the desire to ascend within them. Their interaction with the rapidly changing world and its events, ideas, and products affords them relatively sophisticated perceptions and opinions.

The teenage years for the Me's were marked by the rise of the market economy and the advent of reform and privatization. They have some memories of the "iron rice bowl" breaking—of their families grappling with the impact of major reforms in housing, education, and social welfare. They perceive technology as critical to their future success (an increasing number of young Chinese now surf the Web). Members of this generation have no particular political ideology, although many say they identify with various social and environmental concerns. Fierce competition and a flood of new job opportunities have made them appreciate the necessity of a good education—an undying Chinese value. They also place great value on good grades and hope to attend a university overseas.

The Me's realize that their parents cannot remain their role models. Each of them must create a new and very different identity if they wish to prosper in the new China. Already individualistic (that being the natural outlook of human children), Me's cultivate open-mindedness, innovation, and creativity, and enjoy increasing exposure to Western culture. They know that China will experience radical changes and many discontinuities from its past, and—unlike earlier generations—they are optimistic about their future and are anxious to move away from home to start independent lives.

As adults, the Me's will seek a life balanced between family and work, leisure and responsibility. They are entering their working years just as China is entering the World Trade Organization, thus many expect that their country will become an important and increasingly lucrative part of the global economy.

EMERGING LIFESTYLES: INDIVIDUALITY, PRIVACY, AND LIFE BALANCE. Whereas the family was once the center for decision making, a generation of only-child households has created a class of more self-centered Chinese—individuals who exhibit new attitudes about privacy, uniqueness, and life balance. These attitudes will become more commonplace within the Me Generation over the next five years and represent a dramatic departure from young people their age a short ten years ago.

Individuality: Many factors lie behind this new individuality: one-child families, increased material prosperity, and family resources that support individual consumption are among the most prominent. Further influences include increased exposure to Western culture, parents who are no longer seen as role models, and new electronic connectedness through technology.

Privacy: Once rare in China, personal space comes on the heels of rising incomes, mobility creating dispersed extended families, and an increase in three-member nuclear families (parents and one child). Young people experience life very differently from other family members: much like their American counterparts, for example, many have their own bedrooms, decorated according to their personal taste.

Life balance: Teen life in China was once focused on studies and passing school exams, considered the key to further education and a better job. Recently, however, young people have been granted more leisure time and are encouraged to play musical instruments or indulge in hobbies. In high school, they find more focus on social responsibility and citizenship. The Me Generation is internalizing these new values and behaviors.

What's Not Changing

- Belief in caring for elders
- Memorization, not creative thinking, at school
- Parents maintain responsibility for their health
- Struggling to pass national exams
- Reading traditional readers
- Dating limited and controlled by parents

The "Sandwich Generation"

Pinned between ideologies, members of China's "Sandwich Generation" are wary and guarded. As primary school students, they saw communism fade when Mao Zedong and Zhou Enlai died, and they witnessed the questioning of the Cultural Revolution and other Mao Zedong–inspired initiatives. In 1979, they saw the rise of Deng Xiaoping, an idealistic leader who bestowed on them his pragmatism—not to mention his general openness to outsiders and market economies. Ten years of tension ensued as the two systems—communism and a fledgling market economy—wrestled to dominate. A decade of corruption, inflation, and uncertainty left the "Sandwiches" cautious—an attitude further fueled by the events of Tiananmen Square on June 4, 1989. History has thus left this generation wary about how it can achieve life's major milestones: a good job, marriage, and children, as well as adequate health insurance and saving for the education of the next generation.

The Sandwiches weren't always so distrustful of social systems. The last age group to grow up in extended families, they have happy memories of a stable home life with close sibling relations. Early Sandwiches, those over thirty years of age today, perceive their parents as

---

THE "SANDWICH GENERATION"

Slogans of the Times
- "Return the land to the household; contract for production."
- "Get across the river by touching stones."
- "No matter if the cat is black or white as long as it catches mice."

Data Set
- Born: 1968–1979
- Size: 272.16 million
- Percent of population: 22.1
- Ages: 23 to 34 (in 2002)

Two Cohorts
- Early Sandwich: 1968–1973
- Late Sandwich: 1974–1979

Signal Events (1979–1989)
- Rural reform; agriculture; from communes to households
- Economy opens to the outside; urban reform through special economic zones
- Double price system and corruption
- Heavy inflation
- June 4th event

Source: Center for the Future of China, *China Five-Year Forecast,* 2002.

role models; they are loyal to the strictures of marriage. Compared with the members of the Me and the Recovery generations, they have a good understanding of traditional Chinese culture.

Because this was the first generation to receive a modern education, where learning and knowledge were not filtered by ideology, its members are well versed in famous traditional works, including *The Dream of Red Mansion, The Warring Three States,* and *The Outlaws of the Marsh.* They appreciate modern literature and art, as well as early notions of democratic thought. Yet they are rule-followers and moderate nonextremists, embracing no specific ideology.

The members of the Sandwich Generation born in the late 1960s and early 1970s found their first jobs in state-owned enterprises (SOEs), and they now realize they must compete in the private sector—a move that fills many with dread. They are the first generation to face building a family life without the security of the "iron rice bowl." Job and career are new concepts to them: they bring few tools to the new Chinese economy. Even as they update their skills, they know their job opportunities are limited and that, for now, members of the Cultural Revolution and Recovery generations will hold the higher positions in business and government. Like so many other aspects of their lives, the career aspirations of the Sandwich Generation are being frustrated.

EMERGING LIFESTYLES: SELF-DEVELOPMENT, MOBILITY, AND FINANCIAL MANAGEMENT. Striving to create better lives for themselves and their families, members of the Sandwich Generation provide a laboratory for China's new middle class. They all understand that in today's China, income and profession will determine who makes it and who doesn't. Caught between the old and the new China, they have no choice but to change with the economic context: they face more challenges and choices than any generation before or after them. The diverse cohorts in Sandwich are changing their lifestyles in myriad ways, including the following:

Self-development: They are acutely aware of how inadequately their education prepared them for China's changing world of work. Their schooling and income is much better than that of generations that went before them, yet they must continuously develop themselves to succeed in the new society. They realize that their future income will be directly proportional to their new skills and the professional level they are able to achieve.

Mobility: Sandwichers will experience employment mobility as private-sector jobs replace SOEs, career mobility as they seek to reshape their work identity, family mobility as they move from their parents' homes toward better learning and employment opportunities, and social mobility as they strive to be part of a middle class. But the scale of change in their lives brings with it a sense of insecurity.

Financial management: As the first generation to accept individual responsibility for social welfare, the Sandwichers must budget for their housing, pay for their own educations and that of their children, pay for medical care, and support their parents. All this makes them cautious and pragmatic about money.

What's Not Changing

- Live with parents until marriage
- Traditional family roles predominate
- Education does not provide job skills
- Desire for a stable, secure job
- Strict family budgets
- Corruption hassles of daily life

The "Recovery Generation"

Born into large extended families during the years of severe turbulence and material shortages that marked the late 1950s and early 1960s, the "Recovery Generation" always has had lukewarm feelings toward communism. Its members saw several seminal political movements and events—from the Three-Year Famine that resulted from the Great Leap Forward (1958) to the events in Tiananmen Square (1989)—that deepened their disenchantment. As young adults, they became disillusioned when the Cultural Revolution was harshly criticized and the Gang of Four was tried and sentenced. As children, the "Recoveries" had few material possessions and often experienced hunger. Unlike their older siblings in the Cultural Revolution Generation, they collected few of the promises and many of the failures of major communist initiatives. Such an upbringing seeded in them strong feelings of tradition and deep cultural roots.

As parents themselves, Recoveries struggle with China's one-child policy, contrasting it with their own memories of family life and close ties to parents and grandparents. Their young leaders were iconoclasts whose ideology was—and is—socialism with a democratic flavor.

THE "RECOVERY GENERATION"

Slogans of the Times

- "Beat down Gang of Four."
- "Switch nation's and Party's focus from politics to economics."

Data Set

- Born: 1956–1967
- Size: 233.76 million
- Percent of population: 11.6
- Ages: 35 to 47 (in 2002)

Two Cohorts

- Early Recovery: 1956–1960
- Late Recovery: 1961–1967

Signal Events (1976–1979)

- The death of Mao Zedong and Zhou Enlai; the April Fifth Movement; national mourning of Premier Zhou Enlai
- The public trial and sentencing of the Gang of Four
- Deng Xiaoping comes to power; 3rd Plenum of the 11th Party Congress

Source: Center for the Future of China, *China Five-Year Forecast,* 2002.

Members of the Recovery Generation are somewhat less educated than those in younger age groups, given the poor state of primary and secondary education during their school years prior to the major reforms of the 1980s. Yet they contributed greatly to the revival of education, both as advocates and as participants. A few fortunate members born after 1960 entered universities in the late 1970s and early 1980s, just as higher education was reopening after the Cultural Revolution. A very few studied abroad, and this elite group now occupies top positions in business, government, and universities.

The Recovery Generation's older members entered the labor force during the decade following the advent of Deng Xiaoping's open-door policy, taking advantage of the opportunities provided by

China's reformed market structure. The innovators among them became the pioneers of this new economic wave—workaholics trying to seize every opportunity for upward mobility and personal security. These educated innovators of the Recovery Generation will be the economic, political, and cultural leaders of tomorrow's China. They understand and have assimilated some Western culture, and they are patient, well-educated, and watchful, hoping to build a résumé that will, in ten years, become their ticket to coveted leadership positions.

EMERGING LIFESTYLES: FAMILY RECREATION, HEALTH, AND ROMANTICISM. The Recovery Generation is in a state of flux, as its members' lifestyle shifts from a physically and psychologically stressful state over conflicts between family and career to a more balanced and multifaceted existence. With the help of mass media, which target nuclear families with children, three emerging trends will shape their lives over the next few years:

Family recreation: Prompted by television to explore China and with children now old enough to travel, the Recoveries organize activities and adopt new forms of leisure for the whole family, such as visiting an aquarium or theme park.

Health: China's workaholic generation will gradually realize the importance of a balanced lifestyle as their health gradually deteriorates and as weight gain and stress take their toll. Those with growing professional success will no longer have to devote all their energy to their work and can instead spend more time with their families.

Romanticism: Despite their workaholic tendencies, members of the Recovery generation are turning romantic, influenced by young people's acts such as giving flowers on Valentine's Day. They are ready to have more fun, to get closer to their spouses and friends, to enjoy their lives a bit more.

What's Not Changing

- Focus on children's education
- Filial piety
- Job security
- Saving for the future
- Traditional social networks

The "Cultural Revolution Generation"

Nothing if not adaptable, members of the "Cultural Revolution Generation" have been forced to adjust to a continuous stream of major changes that have disrupted their lives at almost every turn. The oldest were born three years before the founding of the PRC in 1949—at the beginning of Mao Zedong's dream—and the vast majority were mainly poor, hailing from rural families. They were strong supporters of Mao. They lived through many of the trials and tribulations of communism in China, including the collectivization of agriculture and the breakup of family farms; the drive to increase steel production by melting plows, pots, and pans; the Great Famine; and the ten years of the Cultural Revolution, from 1966 to 1976, in which schools and universities were closed and families were relocated. Many educated city dwellers, university students, and professors were sent to rural areas for years. They followed closely the prosecution and trial of the Gang of Four in 1977, as well as Deng Xiaoping's reforms that continue, even today, to reverse Mao's economic and social initiatives.

THE "CULTURAL REVOLUTION GENERATION"

Slogans of the Times

- "Country in trouble; let's unite to overcome difficult times."
- "Beat down capitalist roaders in the Party."

Data Set

- Born: 1946–1955
- Size: 141 million
- Percent of population: 11.5
- Ages: 48 to 57 (in 2002)

Signal Events (1956–1976)

- The Three-Year Famine; 30 million people perished
- The Great Cultural Revolution; rise of the Gang of Four

Source: Center for the Future of China, *China Five-Year Forecast,* 2002.

"Cultural Revolutionaries" differ from other generations in their lack of education. A decade of anti-intellectualism coincided with their teenage years, and most joined the labor force immediately thereafter, in SOEs. Most Cultural Revolutionaries continue to hold these jobs despite Deng Xiaoping's economic reforms, although the economic times are changing. These workers chose to enter the labor market rather than return to the universities and are now suffering from the unemployment caused by SOE reforms. They face daunting difficulties in retraining for a market economy, not to mention living with small or no pensions as elders in a rapidly changing social and economic environment. As a result, Cultural Revolutionaries project their unrealized dreams onto their children—although many children are themselves moving away to find better jobs.

It comes as no surprise that the Cultural Revolution Generation's outlook is cautious and at times mistrustful. Most members are painfully aware that they will have to struggle and adapt all their lives, with few resources. Those who are fortunate enough to do so are trying to consume—and do as much as possible to make up for years of deprivation.

EMERGING LIFESTYLES: ECONOMIC INDEPENDENCE, REEMPLOYMENT, AND NEW ENTERTAINMENT. Wary from many decades of being victims of China's changes, the majority of the Cultural Revolution Generation would prefer to resist the next wave of change. However, they will be forced to adapt again early in this new decade to shockwaves from the major reform movements driving China forward. Over the next five years they will change their lifestyles dramatically in the following ways:

Economic independence: They began their adult work lives eating from the iron rice bowl and have little experience managing their daily lives. Now, besides providing for their own medical care, food, supplies, and education, they also must face the responsibility for health care and for social security. This will be the first generation to live independently from their adult children.

Reemployment: The vast majority work for SOEs, which means they will soon be out of work. They have neither savings nor retirement funds to enable them to stop working, so they will need to find new jobs. Many will work part time in the state sector where they feel comfortable; others will start small businesses. The most motivated will take advantage of China's many "elder universities," which have been developed to ease this transition.

More entertainment: After the hardship and frugality of their youth, this generation deeply desires more fun. They will explore new leisure activities, including neighborhood dancing and singing clubs, domestic travel, and light gift-giving. Those with more education are diversifying their entertainment choices.

What's Not Changing
- Desire for a stable working environment
- Learning to improve their employability
- Utilitarian consumers
- Concern for children's well-being and success
- Worry about future finances
- Maintaining health

The "War and PRC Generation"

The "War and PRC Generation," China's eldest, experienced much hardship. Its members value social prosperity and stability above all else and espouse strong nationalistic sentiments, having witnessed China's sovereignty after the founding of the PRC, its increased domestic wealth, and the rise of its international status following adoption of the open-door policy. History through eyes of this generation is attached to great figures like Mao Zedong and Deng Xiaoping. Being the last generation whose ideology is "patriotism through communism," this group possesses an outlook of hope and faith.

This generation consists of two distinctly different cohorts: "Nation Builders" and "True Believers." Nation Builders experienced decades of turbulence: the May Fourth Movement of 1919, the Japanese War (1937–1945), and the civil war between the Communist Party and the Kuomintang (1945–1949). The founding of the PRC finally restored social order and peace to China, and those alive today witnessed all the changes that attended twentieth-century China. Now seventy and older, they are fatalistic and believe in cycles; understandably, they long for the past.

At birth, Nation Builders had a life expectancy of about forty-seven years. They were predominantly poor, uneducated, and rural; they are the parents of the Cultural Revolution Generation and grandparents of the Recovery Generation. While they are the most informed about

---

THE "WAR AND PRC GENERATION"

Slogans of the Times

- "Beat down Chiang Kai Shek; liberate the whole country."
- "Chinese people finally stand up."

Data Set

- Born: Before 1945
- Size: 174.29 million
- Percent of population: 14.5
- Ages: 58 to 80+ (in 2002)

Two Cohorts

- Nation Builders: Up to 1935
- True Believers: 1936–1945

Signal Events (1931–1955)

- Japanese invasion and occupation
- Civil war: Chinese Communist Party against Kuomintang
- Founding of People's Republic of China
- Socialist transformation: diffusion of communism into society

Source: Center for the Future of China, *China Five-Year Forecast,* 2002.

---

traditional values and cultural ceremonies, they have met great obstacles in passing this knowledge down to younger generations. The long-established lifestyle embodied by this generation will gradually disappear, just as modern high-rises have replaced the old neighborhood communities.

The younger True Believers were born during the Japanese War and were teenagers at the founding of the PRC. They strongly supported the rise of communism and participated in Mao's initiatives. They believe in a strong family value system, the primacy of stability, and the importance of the group over the individual. True Believers are the first Chinese generation to enjoy a long lifespan in large numbers. Now fifty-five to seventy years old, they provide China's leaders, its government officials and managers, and the leadership of the Communist Party itself. They are better educated than Nation Builders and exhibit greater self-confidence and a more positive sense of history than that of their elders. They embraced Deng's open-door policy reform after having suffered during the Cultural Revolution; most were willing to participate in rebuilding China, and the elite of this generation now enjoy a prosperous life.

EMERGING LIFESTYLE CHARACTERISTICS: NEW FAMILY ROLES, HEALTHY PRACTICES, AND ELDER TOURISM. Even though China's social welfare reforms will hit them hard, most of the War and PRC Generation are happier and more hopeful than ever. Among them, especially in the True Believer cohort, a new desire is forming to enjoy their last years by living a whole new kind of life. With increasing social mobility, more elders are living apart from their children, strengthening the power they have to choose their own lifestyle—one with many new attitudes and behaviors:

New family roles: Members of this generation will be the first to negotiate new family relationships with their children. In the past, work and family left them no time or energy to develop their own interests; now they finally have time to live for themselves. Besides many years' savings and their pensions, they will still receive some economic support from their children as a part of filial duty. This gives them extra purchasing power.

Healthy living: Longer life spans mean more elders, and people in the War and PRC Generation know they will live many more years. They intend to spend them in good health, experimenting with new wellness techniques.

Elder tourism and entertainment: The generation that built the new China is intensely patriotic, and its appetite for travel is stimulated by television travelogues and advertisements. Travel complements other leisure activities such as recreation groups, dancing groups, choruses, teams, or volunteering for environmental or children's programs. After a hard life of work, people in the War and PRC Generation are very enthusiastic about entertainment.

What's Not Changing

- Saving money
- Worries about long-term social welfare
- Desire for respect and acknowledgment from society

- Unacceptability of divorce
- Job loyalty
- Family priority

GUIDEPOSTS FOR UNDERSTANDING THE CHINESE CONSUMER

Despite the slow diffusion of lifestyle innovations into the larger Chinese population, a number of guideposts are worth watching over the next five years:

Young Chinese identities and lifestyles will be shaped by a rapid succession of powerful external drivers. The massive social and economic changes under way will come in successive waves—each of which will be different in both type and scale.

The classic S-curve of diffusion of innovation will play out differently in China, affecting the adoption of new ideas, services, and products, including information and communications tools. Because China is relatively poor and not a cosmopolitan society, new ideas will initially be adopted and diffused slowly. But because it is a mass society, once new ideas catch on they will spread rapidly. It is a mistake, however, to believe that once new concepts and products start to diffuse, they will reach mass-market proportions. In China, as discussed earlier in the context of Coca-Cola's misfortune, there are huge differences between purchase and use of products and services for "face value" and use in daily life. Additionally, there will be unsustained mass diffusion; people will adopt certain goods and services at first but give them up quickly.

Circles of influence will differ among generations. Each generation has a different set of important influences. The role of family, friends, and media vary among the generations. Chinese are extremely ambivalent about adopting other cultures' values and norms; fundamentally, they are not highly "other-oriented."

China will remain a utilitarian consumer society. Most purchases and decisions are affected more by pragmatic considerations of value, price, and function than by brand, fashion, or image. Utilitarianism is deeply rooted, both culturally and economically.

Work will be the prime driver of change in Chinese lifestyles. The workplace will be a major source of new concepts and innovations in identity, social relationships, and technology. Innovation will spread from the workplace out to the household.

Technology will be the key to new identity and success. The impacts of using technology will be profound in legitimizing a knowledge-based society (versus an ideological society), and in interconnecting people in new ways.

Over the next ten years China will become a unique information society with specialized niches. A key driver of new consumer groups will be access to diverse information. Most age groups place a higher value on the adoption of new concepts and ideas and on distinct new lifestyles rather than on new products, an emphasis that will only accelerate the already tremendous pace of change. Table 9.2 lays this point out generation by generation.

CHINA'S CHANGING WORLD OF WORK

An important part of China's future success will be creating its own new breed of knowledge workers, who will provide the innovation needed for sustained socioeconomic development.

Just as China's people are challenging consumers, so are they complicated workers to understand as well. A good place to start is by understanding the legacies from the old work units in SOEs. All generations except for the up-and-coming Me Generation entered the workforce through assigned jobs from the government. Even today's knowledge workers have deeply ingrained memories of state control of their work lives.

Legacies from the Old Work Units:
The Generations' Similarities at Work

Despite movement recently toward an open economy with private-sector jobs, many Chinese carry legacy mind-sets and behaviors from the now declining state work system—a central tenet of life for most—and the adoption of new attitudes and behaviors will be slow. History is responsible for this. People lived in communities developed around the SOEs in which they worked and were assigned to jobs they kept for life; children went to work in the same SOE or another factory in the same complex; and there was little variation in corporate culture among work units and little job mobility. Entrepreneurship and

Generation	Core Values	Desires	Implications for Consumer Behavior
Me • Born 1980–2000 • Size: 410 million • Percent of population: 33.3%	• Individuality and uniqueness • Materialism • Independence • Open-mindedness • Innovation and creativity • Balanced life • Broad experience	• Study and live abroad • Find the ideal job • Be a unique person	• Packaging important • Loyal to innovative and creative products • Seek latest technology devices • Price first, brand second determine purchases • Comparison shoppers • Influence parents' purchasing decisions
Sandwich • Born 1968–1972 • Size: 272 million • Percent of population: 22.1%	• Loyalty in marriage • Generational harmony • Energetic and vivid • Successful career through learning and hard work • Honesty • Pragmatic idealists • Follow the rules	• Car and house • Private sector job or own business • Travel	• Forego immediate consumer needs to save money for future purchases • Consider technology essential • Create strict family budgets • Buy gifts for parents • Don't care much about brands
Recovery • Born 1956–1967 • Size: 233 million • Percent of population: 11.6%	• Adaptation • Attention to reforms • Valuing old friends • Family unit • Security • Upward mobility • Having fun	• Leadership positions • Make more money • Enjoy life more	• Seek to compensate for nonmaterial past • Utilitarian consumers • Collect status by buying designer items • Many gifts in place of time in relationships • Latest technology toys for boys • Buy health tonics for parents

Cultural Revolution • Born 1946–1955 • Size: 141 million • Percent of population: 11.5%	• Family harmony • Frugality • Hard work no matter the conditions • Social responsibility • Adaptability • Fairness • Survival	• Learn to drive • Travel abroad • Make money on stock exchange	• Brand purchase of big items to ensure quality • Health products • Buy so as to compensate for years of deprivation • Seek entertainment • Home decoration • Utilitarian
War and PRC • Born 1900–1945 • Size: 174 million • Percent of population: 14.5%	• Stability, social prosperity • Job loyalty • Good interpersonal relations • Contribution to society • Good manners • Generosity • Patriotism	• Prosperous old age • Experiment with new wellness products • Travel around China	• Utilitarian consumers • Save for emergencies • Seek comfort and fun through purchases • Experiment with new wellness techniques • Domestic travel as a priority

Table 9.2.   Generations as Consumers.

Source: Center for the Future of China, *China Five-Year Forecast,* 2002.

innovation were nonexistent. Because innovation, creativity, and individuality were not valued, people lost their sense of self at work. The culture supported obedience to authority; workers who had lower positions had to accept them. The old work units were rife with interpersonal tension, and in the worst cases, passive adaptation to an oppressive environment led to low morale and cynicism toward work. These attitudes are changing: Many Chinese now view the workplace in a progressively positive light.

Today, about 60 percent of the Sandwiches' jobs are still in SOEs, and they possess legacy attitudes. For example, they believe being your own boss is risky and prefer being an employee so they are less visible. The concept of career and job mobility is still new to them. Prior to the late 1990s they had little hope of changing jobs; mobility was controlled by the system, not the individual, and they could not move without permission. Most Chinese workers feel satisfied that they possess adequate skills for their work. They are still building awareness that they will have to move on and have yet to reject the old work unit system. They have not yet internalized the need to seriously upgrade their skills or to embrace lifelong learning—both of which are necessary if they are to truly succeed in China's next development phase. Under the old work system, time off and leisure were not valued. People worked six and seven days a week, and entertainment practices were discouraged.

SOE Work Unit Characteristics

- Hierarchical
- Assigned jobs and tasks
- Underemployment
- Innovation not encouraged
- Political promotions—*guanxi* over performance
- Crude egalitarianism
- Group needs over individual needs
- Limited, slow flow of information from top down
- Authoritarian
- Parents key to getting first job

Recently mass media and government policy have made a sudden and massive shift to support the five-day workweek, equating it with a modern way to live and work. This is an explicit government strategy designed to support mass consumption. In a dramatic shift of attitude that shows the continuing power of the media and existence of a more mass than class society, all generations report that they maintain strict boundaries between their work and personal life and feel they don't need to work weekends to make an adequate living.

The Sandwich Generation: Knowledge-Worker Pioneers of China's Changing Workplace

The Sandwich Generation will be the first where people spend most of their careers in the private sector and will be forced to adapt to new work structures and expectations. They will experiment with new work identities and explore the new concepts of free job mobility and career.

THE NEW KNOWLEDGE WORKER AT A GLANCE: YOUNG MALE SWITCHES TO THE PRIVATE SECTOR

His Dream: To Earn an Architectural Certificate and Start His Own Business

Ren Zhi Hao lives with his parents in a three-bedroom apartment that used to belong to the hospital work unit. His parents, both doctors, purchased the flat for a low price during the housing reforms. His mother takes care of his daily diet and health and cooks his meals. After quitting his job at a state-run construction company, Ren Zhi Hao attended vocational school to study architecture and interior decoration. He now makes more than 5,000 RMB per month at a privately owned decorating firm where, through his hard work, he now has a company car, an enviable salary, and—most recently—a promotion to the position of Quality Monitor. Optimistic and highly motivated, Ren Zhi Hao sees a bright future in working for private enterprise. He believes that if he continues to gain experience and knowledge in the professional world, he will be well equipped to start his own business when he is older—that is, he doesn't feel he needs additional academic certification to learn what he needs to be successful. He is irked by the corruption and speculative behavior he has witnessed, and strives to avoid any such practices in his own career. Ren Zhi Hao is very conscious of his need to build a stable financial future, and occasionally works overtime on weekends to earn extra money. He divides his paychecks into three, giving one-third each to his mother and his girlfriend, to whom he turns over most of his personal purchasing decisions since he does not consider himself an experienced consumer. He keeps the remaining third of his paycheck for himself, and spends it mostly on nights out at cafés or restaurants or on gifts for his girlfriend. The two of them plan to get married soon, and Ren Zhi Hao feels great pressure to ensure that he can provide for his future family. His two greatest challenges, he says, are to develop his career and to prepare separate housing for his future family. When he has time, Ren Zhi Hao loves to socialize, and particularly enjoys playing card games or chess at cafés.

He is also a soccer enthusiast and plays with a group of regular soccer friends. For Ren Zhi Hao, playing soccer is a social forum and a way to relieve stress.

Like all knowledge workers of this generation, he has begun to imagine new work roles and find ways to build his skills to fill them.

Work Characteristics

- Made the shift from SOE to the private sector early
- Believes more opportunity exists in the private sector
- Doesn't take training courses; feels he learns enough on the job
- Expects rewards for hard work, not time
- Expects to change his job
- Likes weekends off but sometimes works overtime for more pay
- Adjusting to contract work instead of full-time work

Sandwiches are the beneficiaries of the first widespread educational reform that followed the devastating years of the Cultural Revolution. When they entered high school in the early 1980s, they found the curriculum reflected a return to the value of a broad education that was not totally filtered through communist ideology. English was taught once again, and the university entrance examination system was restored.

On the other hand, the Sandwiches have a unique profile determined by passing through their formative years as China struggled between returning to the old state-run economy or staying with the market. That has left them wary, cautious, and with conflicted attitudes toward authority, collaboration, rewards, and the role of *guanxi*, the powerful social networks that are critical to getting anything done in China.

Upgrading Skills Is a Major Concern

Improved curricula since "opening up" have increased workers' general capability for analytical problem solving and broad thinking, yet the gap between workplace skills and what is taught in school remains wide. While the Sandwich and Me Generations have an education, most of their members will lack the skills and mind-sets necessary in the new private work environment. Many Chinese workers slowly are becoming aware of the need to develop new skills to enable them to find new jobs: the Sandwich Generation is the first to be composed of lifelong learners. Most Sandwiches are taking courses after work for a wide variety of reasons, but primarily for personal development, motivated by the long-held value of education in Chinese society. But their motivation for taking courses is changing, reflecting their awareness that the majority will need to leave their first jobs in SOEs and find new ones in the private sector.

Workforce Pioneers: Sandwich Knowledge Workers

China needs to develop its own knowledge workers. As the economy diversifies and develops, it will create a full complement of professional service jobs that will need to be filled. For these new knowledge workers, career is a new concept. The most adventuresome and skilled among them will have several careers during their work lives, adding competencies to take advantage of growing opportunities.

When they first entered the workforce, most Sandwich Generation members with some college education or advanced vocational training went to work as professionals or highly skilled workers in the formal state sector, in government positions, academia, or state-owned research institutes. As increasing numbers of multinational corporations moved into China, the best and brightest were recruited away. Now, as the private sector grows and SOEs reform, the most educated workers are being sought to fill the many new professional jobs, technical and management positions alike. These highly skilled workers will have many opportunities as the economy diversifies.

NEW ATTITUDES AND POTENTIAL. A new prototype for China's knowledge workers will evolve from the Sandwich Generation. Although their numbers will be few, their impact on the workplace will be noticeable. Their more integrated education will give them self-confidence, adaptability, and a greater set of practical and analytical skills. They will have backgrounds in both science and liberal arts and will understand the rules of social discourse, allowing them to take advantage of their preference for teamwork and consensus-based leadership. They are the first generation to hope for meritocracy and reject the old authoritarian style. They are wary of bosses and have little loyalty. As the old constraints of the workplace and culture melt away, they will develop their potential more fully. Currently they possess a strong humanistic spirit that includes a new morality with an emphasis on justice and independent thinking, and they aspire to take on greater social responsibility. Their exposure to English and to Western thought gives them an advantage for cross-cultural communication. They have lived much more diverse lives despite their young age, making them more adept at adopting new tools and ideas.

ASSETS AND LIABILITIES. The Sandwich Generation displays a cautious optimism toward work. They realize they must focus on personal development to have a successful work life, yet they lack the tools and sophistication to plan a sustainable career path (Table 9.3). They also can be overconfident at times, and fail to understand how their skills and ideas fit into the new work context. Well educated, they possess analytical skills, discipline, and flexibility, but lack the street smarts of earlier generations. They have a stronger sense of teamwork and want to adopt more consensus than authoritarian leadership styles. Their

Assets	• Good analytics • Some English proficiency • Cross-cultural brokers • Adaptable • Reliable workers • Independent thinkers • Learners
Liabilities	• Intentionally not competitive • Cautious about new things • Overly worried about fairness; cynical • Limited loyalty • Passive adapters • Lack market savvy

Table 9.3.   Sandwich Assets and Liabilities at Work.

Source: Global Foresight, Center for the Future of China, *Lifestyle Ethnographic Research Study.*

exposure to Western thinking and literature in college makes them able to broker cross-cultural understanding and adapt to the work processes needed for the new Chinese workplace. They are anxious to see the old system of political and *guanxi* promotions die along with the SOEs, and they see mastery of technology and computers in particular as the key to their future success.

Members of the Sandwich Generation prefer collaboration to competition. They consider the more aggressive and sophisticated Me Generation to be socially inexperienced, with weak work ethics. Their early learning and work experiences make the Sandwiches overly worried—even occasionally cynical—about being treated fairly, so this fear is not out of the ordinary. Sandwiches adapt by remaining passive rather than by being proactive; they are only partially loyal to the job and their employers, ready to move on if they feel undervalued.

These new knowledge workers include many different types of people and there is much regional variation. The case study of Ren Zhi Hao from Guangdong Province provides insights into one common category of knowledge worker—those who move from an SOE to the private sector in their late twenties.

The Forecast: Sandwiches
Adapt to a Churning Workplace

The period that lies immediately ahead is likely to be painful for both employers and employees, as they create a new workplace and culture that will be uniquely Chinese. The Sandwiches will be the pioneers that map this new territory.

Legacy attitudes, behaviors, and work environments from the SOEs will have a long tail. The transformation of the Chinese work environment and workers—even at the knowledge worker level—will have to overcome rigidity, structure, culture, roles, and reward systems that have been embodied in Chinese organizations and people for many decades. Like any social evolutionary process, it has many stages and will take time. Change will come as young workers learn new ways of working. Employers in multinational corporations need patience, practical strategies, and good teaching tools to aid in the development of productive workplaces.

New work identities are in the making. All workers, but especially knowledge workers, professionals, managers, and skilled technicians, will have to experiment and build identities in China's transitional economy. Although a few Chinese role models will be extrapolated from other cultures, the depth and power of the underlying Chinese culture and unique socioeconomic context ensures there will be an evolution unique to China.

SUMMARY INSIGHTS

- Sense of structural and historic disadvantage. The educated workers and professionals of the Sandwich Generation find themselves caught between the Recovery professionals—still young but already holding many of the best jobs—and the better educated, more sophisticated and techno-literate Me's. This leaves Sandwiches, as a group, feeling vulnerable to a "glass ceiling" on one side and a highly competitive group with many comparative advantages on the other side. They will be passive adaptors who are always wary of their future.

- Limited loyalty. Given they are not sure whom to trust or how best they can survive in the future, they will give only limited loyalty and will be ready to switch jobs or careers if there are real or perceived signs of insecurity.

- Job mobility high. They want to take advantage of the many opportunities they believe will emerge during their prime career years. Their expectations will exceed the reality of the fit between their skills and the new jobs.

- Learning oriented. Sandwiches place an unusually high value on learning, and their desire to learn usually outweighs their desire for money. They need to feel they are learning on the job and even after work. Employers need to have attractive education programs.

- Desire social recognition. They suffered in their early years with the old *guanxi* system, and now they feel caught between two more advantaged generations; what they really want is recognition for their knowledge and skills. The Sandwich Generation was the first to develop a middle-class consciousness, an important part of which is status. They will respond very well to personnel policies that publicly recognize accomplishments.

- A tense group. This is a group with many inner tensions, an inevitable result of being caught between two systems. These inner tensions are also part of the legacy of the old work system, where individuality was subordinated to the will of the group. Resolving these tensions constructively will be a challenge.

PARTING THOUGHT

What an opportunity the rapid development of China brings the world! How much better off we would all be if 1.2 billion more people avoided getting stuck in the black hole of marginalization the Information Era creates with its demanding knowledge economy. China is poised to make this transformation and deserves a strong partnership of the rest of world. China's economy, despite many structural and institutional barriers, has rich opportunities for strong growth. For at least the next five years, China will continue to benefit from the advantages of backwardness—the ability to maintain economic growth by successively eliminating structural and institutional barriers. At some point the low-hanging fruit will become more scarce and government policies less effective. This will be the time of greatest uncertainties and danger, but I believe the government and people are committed to making the full transformation. It will certainly be a wild ride.

CHAPTER TEN

Embrace Global Interdependence

─∾∾─ How do we *Act with Integrity* on a global scale? As we trek through the Badlands we are living in a new age where the morphology of society is being transformed into networks, and both opportunities and threats come from our connections. All around us we experience the mismatch in scale between our organizations and our issues. Most leaders limit their efforts to special issues in their own domains, yet a new global story is unfolding and we all have lead parts to play. Of paramount importance is the creation of new values that are congruent with what we know to be true—that globalization must include more people in its promise of prosperity or it will devolve into a more unstable and dangerous world.

One aspect of the future is certain: technological change and economic shifts will continue to outpace society's ability to adapt, eroding both old and new social bargains. Everyone's way of life will be affected, leaving each of us with the huge challenge of rebuilding our personal lives, communities, and societies—as our efforts are undermined again and again. How many communities and nations will be resilient enough to sustain this relentless process and prosper? Historically, no clear pattern indicates that social order inevitably follows technological and economic change; these disruptions provide society with choices and challenges that it is free to address or to ignore.

In the creative foundry of capitalism, remarkable technological and economic innovations come at a price. Our stock of shared values, norms, experiences, and commitments to each other as part of a local and global community—our social capital—gets depleted. This social

---

PAIN #7: VALUE VEXATION— DISCOMBOBULATION AND LOSS OF IDENTITY

At this point in the development of globalization most of us feel vulnerable to forces and people we can't see and don't understand. The edges of our secure world are frayed and pieces of it are being pulled apart through offshoring of jobs and flows of capital and technology to far-flung places. Our lives feel more discombobulated each day and our very sense of identity seems fluid.

Further, we see extremely disturbing situations through our vast networks of interconnection. Television brings us images and stories of wars, ethnic cleansing, disease, and poverty. The Internet provides continuous access to vastly different views of global events and interconnectivity with people around the world challenging our beliefs. Our deep human values call us to extend support to global people struggling to move up, but we feel frustrated—even angry—about having to give up a comfortable way of life. The pain of value vexation at the global level is extreme.

New Capability: Sustainable Globalization

The competencies to support global interdependence of the economy, society, and political systems are new to everyone. They are underpinned by new values that allow us to make trade-offs that result in giving everyone the opportunity to be included. The innovation imperative casts a wide net, particularly in stimulating a global education renaissance that can support the development of workers able to plug and play in a networked economy. The current system is mismatched to the new issues and needs and must be transformed. It demands skills at cross-cultural trust building. It demands the invention of a new safety net paradigm that doesn't simply soften the blow of being marginalized but gives people a way to engage and become self-sufficient.

capital undergirds how all groups function as well as the social programs and institutions that arise in support of shared goals. In turn it is made possible by a trade-off between individual freedom and community needs, held together by specific rules of engagement and values that include honesty, reciprocity, and living up to agreements; ethics are not optional in the creation of social capital.

Social organizations and social order are less resilient than technology and business in the face of structural shifts. Social systems require time to adapt to new conditions. Where civil societies are inflexible and intolerant of change, people depend on centralized authority and homogeneous cultures to hold them together. China, Mexico, Saudi Arabia, Japan, France, and Brazil, for example, have strong cultures where bonds of trust do not extend far beyond the family, compromising people's ability to create the kind of social capital that allows them to participate fully in globalization and the networked economy.

By contrast, like a handful of other countries including Sweden, the United States has a culture that makes it easy for groups of people to self-organize in the pursuit of shared goals. It develops social capital easily, and that cultural characteristic is in large part responsible for its leadership in economic and technological innovation. America's challenge will be to keep up with the pace of change, innovate the new industries, and be more generous in helping others less fortunate. We are a culture that reluctantly provides a safety net to our own poor—we tolerate the largest wealth gap of any nation and we show little empathy for our global fellow citizens in terms of sufficient aid. We benefit most from globalization, yet do not feel we should contribute most to make it work for others. Our leaders need to tell the truth to Americans: their way of life is threatened not by globalization but by an unwillingness to share its benefits. Over the long run this is the only approach that will allow us to continue our prosperity. The United States must take on a key leadership role toward sustainable globalization.

Culture is much more important in determining the ultimate development of a global society than many believe. Global economic development does not obliterate underlying cultures to create a homogeneous global culture. Global peoples do not want this, and will resist it forcefully. Since cultural differences will persist, merely tolerating them won't be enough in the future. We must embrace and value them, learning how to collaborate in their presence. Globalization demands that cultures retain their integrity yet learn to be interdependent. We must achieve this transformation as each culture struggles to rebuild its social capital in its own context. The hurdle of maintaining economic and technological innovations pales in comparison to this ultimate challenge. There is no viable alternative, only the illusion of escape from this inevitable goal we must achieve. This is all part and parcel of the global pain of Value Vexation with its inherently dichotomous opportunity and threat.

The greatest challenge facing global peoples today is how to create a vibrant interdependent global society that balances individual freedoms and the global good. History offers no precedent for change on such a grand scale. We need to apply *Radical Innovation* to the creation of social capital in all sorts of societies to meet this global challenge.

MAKING SUSTAINABLE GLOBALIZATION A REALITY

At present we have an imbalanced system of globalization that is unsustainable. We have an overdeveloped global economic system and an underdeveloped social and political system. Looking into the future we see not one end result that is guaranteed but several divergent scenarios; where we end up depends on what choices we make. So how do we achieve sustainable globalization? First of all, we need to understand what globalization is, and believe that making it sustainable is achievable. This is a responsibility that falls to business, political, social, and media leaders. Tragically, we have failed to educate people well enough thus far. Few people understand the interdependence among nations wrought by globalization and the new technologies of connection. Yet it is critical that people understand that the well-being of developed economies cannot be sustained without improving the economies and social systems of developing nations.

Trade, free markets, and transparent financial systems are essential to economic development. Cynicism and skepticism about globalization from those who are deeply concerned about poverty offers no compelling alternative. Yes, we need better policies to support more equitable development. But globalization, with its vibrant trading system that exchanges far more value than just goods, can contribute greatly to improving the quality of people's lives. We have already seen its positive impact on millions of people in China, India, Brazil, and Mexico. Globalization certainly has a shadow side, but we can learn to do it better. It is very, very difficult to create conditions that support

FOUR SCENARIOS FOR THE GLOBAL FUTURE

A *scenario* is a logical, internally consistent story about the future. I don't think it is possible to forecast the long-term future of globalization; there is too much uncertainty about the ultimate outcome. In situations like this, scenarios can be useful, providing strategic windows that bracket the best and the worst cases.

Here are four scenarios for the year 2020, each of which seems quite plausible depending on the choices we make. (Figure 10.1 summarizes the four possibilities.)

Extended Badlands: Prolonged Volatility

The Badlands continues to present fast cycles of boom and bust. The United States remains the sole superpower and uses the threat of military intervention to keep some semblance of world order. The United Nations continues to decline as a global arbitrator. Business is cautious and risk averse, but is able to sustain itself by picking and choosing how and where it operates. The social safety net continues to fray—insecurity is pandemic and the appetite for globalization remains anemic.

Global Village: Integration

Social values dominate, and leadership comes most strongly from the social sector. Business is a strong contributing partner but not the main driving force. New global institutions are created to address issues and investment is sufficient for the long term to initiate the move toward the proverbial rising tide that will lift all boats. Social innovation abounds.

Market Mania: Business Rules

The only robust leadership comes from business, which continues to network globally, successfully creating new markets. An increasing number of people who are already part of the Global Silicon Network make gains, enough to allow the rest to hope that they may be included somehow, some day. Governments are weak. There is social unrest, but economic success keeps the lid on it, at least for the short term, because social concerns are slowly being addressed.

Global Blade Runner: Extreme Fragmentation

Globalization fails. Terrorism expands dramatically and global criminal networks proliferate. People withdraw to their own communities and try to build firewalls between themselves and the rest of the world. Trade slows, and there is a global economic depression.

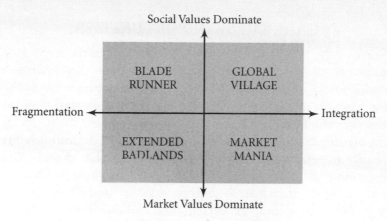

Figure 10.1. Four Futures for 2020.
Source: Global Foresight, 2004.

development in the most impoverished countries, but it is not impossible, and the consequences for all of us will be very grave in the long term if we don't succeed.

We have the human and financial resources, but we need to make the choice to use them in service of sustainable globalization. We can't do it by focusing solely on economic and political issues in support of national interests—those are the low-hanging fruit. We need to step up to the bigger global plate and make the right social choices, and begin to include people from every region of the planet. If we do not take this step, the promise of globalization, greater prosperity, will not be achieved, yet we will still experience globalization's downside: an increasing amount of ugly dislocation, with all its unintended consequences.

This is not to say that no adjustments and innovations are needed in the economics of globalization, but these will evolve more readily than social changes, and ultimately will not succeed unless the social innovations take place. We need new forms of organizations and alliances that match the networked economy. Business leaders have a special role to play in shepherding this metamorphosis as well as partnering wholeheartedly in the critical social innovations. Smarter geopolitics and policies will also be necessary. In short, it takes focusing and innovating on all three fronts—social, economic, and political—with the strong awareness that inventing a global society is the most demanding task that lies ahead. We must put as much effort into social innovation as we have put into economic and technological innovation.

ENGAGE THESE OPPORTUNITIES: INNOVATE AND LEVERAGE HERE

The emergence of a dominant social form—a networked society—provides a fresh opportunity to invent a new, more inclusive social order. A networked society has a better chance of supporting sustainable globalization than one based on hierarchy because groups of people informally connected through shared values and commitments can easily and efficiently work together to achieve shared goals. The transaction costs of networks are much lower than those in a hierarchy. Yet networks are harder to understand than hierarchies because they are much more complex and dynamic, and much less visible; influencing them is a more subtle process.

Not all social networks are good. The Mafia and networks like Al Qaeda remind us that societies create the climates in which social networks flourish—for better and for worse. Influencing this process for the benefit of all is critical to sustainable globalization. The cross-cultural human engagement inherent in economic globalization can encourage social innovation in cultures that operate mainly under centralized governments where trust is limited to families, tribes, villages, or ethnic groups. As increasing numbers of people around the planet become better educated and more sophisticated, they become more open. Networked leadership in pursuit of social innovation also can be a very powerful force for the good. Although we have no guarantee that a new global social order can be established or a global commons can be constructed, it is certainly within the realm of possibility.

Despite the current momentum for creating a sustainable global society, we need to add to it by promoting certain global trends.

Globally Interconnected Youth

Young people growing up today have far more power to create positive change than any previous generation, and they have a huge stake in the outcome. There are more than one billion young people between the ages of fifteen and twenty-four. About 15 percent of them will have college educations, and another 40 percent will have secondary educations; most of these educated young people will be connected to the Internet.

In a networked society not all sources of influence come from the top. Young people are growing up in an environment where their formative leadership experiences include participation in effective networks of collaboration and knowledge sharing spanning the globe. Their attitudes toward decision making and effective problem solving derive from their experiences in the virtual world, where interaction and inclusion of multiple perspectives is essential to achieving common goals. Most heartening, they are applying this capability to projects of great significance in their communities. Young people, like *all* people, rich and poor, want to be included and valued; they desire opportunities to contribute.

The growth of youth-focused organizations is accelerating, particularly given the support of the Internet. These range from U.N. organizations to regional and national organizations like the European Union Youth Forum to informal groups focused on special projects. TakingITGlobal (introduced in Chapter Seven) exemplifies the way youth organizations can build on one another's work for the common good. Jennifer Corriero, one of its founders, was named among the top young global leaders by the Davos Economic Forum in 2003. This dynamic organization extends itself to all youth organizations around the globe, providing online support at a reasonable cost. Jennifer and her huge network of young leaders are tireless in their efforts to lobby global organizations to include young people as advisers and decision makers. No wonder TakingITGlobal is so successful and inspiring.

Young people like Jennifer are optimistic about the future. Quickly and globally we must engage young people as key participants and decision makers at all levels of society. With their help sustainable globalization can happen at a much faster pace.

Rising Power of Women

The most powerful social trend in this cycle of innovation that began in the 1950s is the changing role of women. Now this social movement, which is more than fifty years old, is gaining momentum because enough women around the world have become better educated, have joined the workforce, and have become business, government, and social leaders. It has taken women time to learn to trust one another and to form global networks. One catalyst was that the number of women in business management traveling globally and meeting other powerful, committed women reached critical mass. Women have taken advantage of these encounters to build an informal system of overlapping networks focused on critical social issues and economic development.

They have formed organizations such as the International Women's Forum to support their efforts.

The Badlands will be a crucible for women's leadership that will push this movement to its tipping point. Women will gain power as major decision makers, another critical step toward making globalization sustainable. Men do not have an entitlement to leadership, and women do not want to live in an alienated, disconnected world. Women have learned how to create social change in small and large ways, applying their knowledge of interdependence, their respect for multiple points of view, and their understanding of empathy. Women have an enormous competency for the very thing we need to do most as a global society. Women will unleash their power to provide the networked leadership we need to build the global commons, increasingly filling key leadership positions in business and government, and forming social organizations with the ethics and skills to accelerate sustainable globalization.

The Emergence of a Second Middle Age

What would you do if suddenly you were handed an extra quarter century of life? America's 80 million Baby Boomers and millions more of their global cohort are about to come up with an answer. The greatest success story of the twentieth century is the extension of life, not just in advanced economies but around the world. Globally, people eighty years of age and older are the fastest-growing demographic, the consequences of which are often viewed with concern. That is not unjustified, but far more important is the fact that these additional years of life will primarily be tacked on to a vigorous middle age that will now extend to eighty. In the United States, the majority of Baby Boomers are slowly realizing that they will live long and healthy lives well into their nineties, and many will live to a hundred and beyond. It is unlikely that the Boomers who have reinvented and transformed almost everything they encounter will respond to this amazing gift passively.

At the end of the nineteenth century the average lifespan was less than fifty years, so this gift of long life is an extension of a gift we have already received and considered. In her groundbreaking book *Passages: The Predictable Crises of Adult Life,* Gail Sheehy explored the notion that human development is determined not by external events rather by changes that come from within. The impulse to change is driven by the need to find new meaning in life. A still timely passage from Sheehy's book provides a glimpse into this process:

We are not unlike a particularly hardy crustacean. The lobster grows by developing and shedding a series of hard, protective shells. Each time it expands from within, the confining shell must be sloughed off. It is left exposed and vulnerable until, in time, a new covering grows to replace the old. . . . We are left exposed and vulnerable—but also yeasty and embryonic again, capable of stretching in ways we hadn't known before.

Today we look to this as-yet-unknown new stage of adult life with great hope. This new middle age will be accompanied by a deep renewal process resulting in the innovators stretching in new ways to create the models for this new, promising stage of adult development. There are some things we know it won't be—it won't be merely a form of extended retirement or a lengthy period of preparing to die, and it won't be simply an extension of middle age as we now know it. Will this new stage serve as additional incubation to fulfill the pressing need for new leaders in a global society? Perhaps those of us now passing through or entering the decades between sixty and eighty will create the great good global commons, the shared territory that feeds the global village. Can we take heart from the fact that our compelling need to reinvent social institutions and civil society coincides with the first generation of people in their sixties, seventies, and eighties who have the education, wisdom, time, and money to provide the leadership to leave the world as a better place?

Here, too, I see a powerful convergence between the now maturing women's movement and the aging of our global society. Never have so many middle-aged women had so much education and work experience. The trend of older women's leaving successful high-end jobs in corporations to start their own companies or join organizations with more social purpose provides a window into the choices women between the ages of sixty and eighty could make—leading the way with innovations our societies so desperately need. These women will become modern-day elders, much like those who were respected and followed by communities of hunter-gatherers and simple agrarian societies.

THE SOCIAL SAFETY NET CONUNDRUM

Left to its own trajectory the Information Revolution will further marginalize those already suffering in poverty. The safety net that developed in response to the Industrial Revolution is in tatters, along with other basic social bargains. This presents a huge opportunity to invent a new paradigm that better suits a globalized society and a networked knowledge economy. If globalization is to succeed it must include more people.

The best safety net is a strong economy, a good job. In both the advanced and developing world we have learned a lot about how to create good economic conditions. We know the constellation of factors needed for an economy to grow sufficiently. We must move quickly in putting that knowledge to work. Microloan projects have had huge success, and should be expanded much more quickly. We must become intolerant of the corruption that plagues far too many poor countries, resulting in the squandering of the few resources they receive. We must collaborate in new ways with social systems and cultures that provide insufficient trust to create informal networks to support entrepreneurs and innovation.

One of our biggest challenges is resolving the safety net conundrum. We cannot expect poor and poorly educated people in developing as well as advanced economies to somehow close the widening gap between their skills, knowledge, and sophistication and the demands of the knowledge economy. We will have to provide some traditional safety nets—access to resources addressing basic needs, including health care. Cushioning those who are less fortunate is important but not sufficient. We need innovation in tools and partnerships that will extend the opportunity to participate in globalization to more people. This effort must be sufficiently funded and executed to make it effective in the long run. This will require a massive long-term investment, but it pales in comparison to the cost of not providing it. A critical investment is needed in educational innovation and capacity around the world. This is foundational to a new type of safety net.

The wealth and opportunity gap will not be closed overnight or even in a decade. We have the human and fiscal resources to do it—but thus far not the will. We need to apply the competencies of women and the global concerns and energy of the Net Generation to help accelerate the development of an economy that can bake a pie big enough to feed everyone well.

PARTING THOUGHTS

We must seek out the best ways to sustain globalization, apply them quickly, and continue the quest for more. The solution will come through a process of learning and successive approximation. Engaging in this process is an essential part of the hero's journey. We need to step up to the big global plate. We must be more than optimists. We must be activists, radical social activists. We must apply all the principles of transformation to our global society—all are important but none so much as *Act with Integrity* and *Radical Innovation*. This will take courage, guts, and soul. We *are* interdependent, for good or for ill. If we do not invest consciously and substantially in creating positive global interdependence, the Information Revolution will continue to marginalize those who can't engage. I believe all of us share this leadership responsibility, and I urge everyone to take the journey of our lifetime—networked together in pursuit of sustainable globalization.

⟨ Notes and Resources

This book is primarily based on global primary research I have conducted over the last six years. In these notes I provide references to quotes and also list some of the research and ideas of other people that have most influenced my thinking. More people than I can possibly acknowledge have influenced my thinking over the past several years. I thank all of them and list a selected few who most influenced this book.

This book could include only the highlights of the mass of data developed in the course of my research. To see more of the detail, visit the online store at http://www.global-foresight.org, which also has other tools that support the recommendations made in *Navigating the Badlands.*

Chapter One

Peter F. Drucker, *Post-Capitalist Society* (New York: Harper Business, 1993).

Thomas L. Friedman, *The Lexus and the Olive Tree: Understanding Globalization* (New York: Anchor Books, 2000).

Daniel Bell, "The Third Technological Revolution," *Dissent* 36, no. 2 (Spring 1989): 164–176.

Charles Weiner and Alice K. Smith (eds.), *Robert Oppenheimer: Letters and Recollections* (Stanford, Calif.: Stanford University Press, 1980).

Richard Rhodes, *The Making of the Atomic Bomb* (New York: Simon & Schuster, 1986).

Chandra Mukerji, science studies director and professor of communication at UC San Diego, from a lecture for "Introduction to Communication" course, 2000.

Chapter Two

Joseph A. Schumpeter. *Capitalism, Socialism, and Democracy* (New York: HarperCollins, 1975), pp. 82–85. (Originally published 1942.)

Mary O'Hara-Devereaux, Robert Mittman, and Ma Rong. *China Five-Year Forecast: Creating the New Marketplace* (San Francisco: Tibuscio Press, 2002).

Manuel Castells, *The Information Age: Economy, Society and Culture* (3 Vol.), (Malden, Mass.: Blackwell, 1997).

Views of a Changing World 2003: War with Iraq Further Divides Global Publics, The Pew Research Center for the People and the Press, June 2003. Available online: http://people-press.org/reports/. Access date: May 10, 2004.

United Nations Conference on Trade and Development, *World Investment Report 2002: Transnational Corporations and Export Competitiveness,* 2002.

United Nations Conference on Trade and Development, *World Investment Report 2003: FDI Policies for Development: National and International Perspectives,* April 2003.

International Monetary Fund, Economic Statistics.

World Bank Development Indicators, *World Development Indicators Online,* 2003. Available online: http://www.worldbank.org/data/. Access date: May 10, 2004.

World Bank, *Globalization, Growth and Poverty: A World Bank Policy Research Report,* 2002.

"Wielding the Axe," *The Economist,* October 25, 2003, p. 72.

Thomas L. Friedman, *The Lexus and the Olive Tree: Understanding Globalization* (New York: Anchor Books, 2000).

Robert Rubin, *In an Uncertain World: Tough Choices from Wall Street to Washington* (New York: Random House, 2003).

Organization for Economic Co-operation and Development (OECD), *Trends in International Migration: Annual Report* (2001).

Chapter Three

Warren Bennis and Robert J. Thomas, *Geeks and Geezers: How Era, Values, and Defining Moments Shape Leaders* (Boston: Harvard Business School Press, 2002).

Chapter Four

Jeffrey Pfeffer and Robert I. Sutton, *The Knowing-Doing Gap: How Smart Companies Turn Knowledge into Action* (Boston: Harvard Business School Press, 2000).

Robert I. Sutton, *Weird Ideas That Work* (New York: Free Press, 2002).
I invited Robert Sutton to speak to the Emerging Technologies Outlook Clients of IFTF during the early phases of our research on the Badlands.

The ideas in his presentation as well as published and unpublished accounts of his research contributed to the research I did on Competency Addiction and creating climates for systemic innovation. He is an innovative researcher and his candor is refreshing. I appreciated his generosity in sharing his ideas.

Malcolm Gladwell, *The Tipping Point: How Little Things Can Make a Big Difference* (New York: Little, Brown, 2000).

Gary Hamel, *Leading the Revolution* (Boston: Harvard Business School Press, 2000).

Chapter Five

Karen Stephenson, a Harvard University professor and president and CEO of Netform (www.netform.com), has contributed greatly to my thinking about social networks. Karen and I both have been frequent speakers and resources for Leadership California. The ideas I reference in this chapter come from listening to her presentations in that forum and personal conversations 2001–2003.

Chapter Six

Gary Hamel and Liisa Valikangas, "The Quest for Resilience," *Harvard Business Review*, September 2003.

Gary Hamel, *Leading the Revolution* (New York: Plume, 2002).

Tom Chin, CEO, Sino American Industries, personal conversations about global strategy and strategy for the China Market throughout 2002–2004.

Chapter Seven

Jennifer Corriero, *Global Youth Survey: Taking IT Global, 2003;* personal conversations in 2003 and 2004. See also http://www.takingitglobal.org.

Chapter Eight

Martha Barletta, *Marketing to Women: How to Understand, Reach, and Increase Your Share of the World's Largest Market Segment* (Chicago: Dearborn Trade Publishing, 2003).

Ranny Riley, personal conversations about the new middle age.

D. M. Eisenberg and others, "Trends in Alternative Medicine Use in the United States, 1990–1997." *Journal of the American Medical Association* 280 (1997): 1569–1575.

Chapter Nine

Mary O'Hara-Devereaux, Robert Mittman, and Ma Rong. *China Five-Year Forecast: Creating the New Marketplace.* (San Francisco: Tibuscio Press, 2002).

Liu Neng, Mary O'Hara-Devereaux, and Robert Mittman, *China's Generations: The Transformation of Daily Life* (San Francisco: Tibuscio Press, 2002).

Chapter Ten

Francis Fukuyama, *The Great Disruption: Human Nature and the Reconstitution of Social Order* (New York: Free Press, 1999).

Paul Ray and Sherry Ruth Anderson, *The Cultural Creatives* (New York: Three Rivers Press, 2000).

Lynne Twist, *The Soul of Money: Transforming Your Relationship with Money and Life* (New York: Norton, 2003).

Thomas L. Friedman, *The Lexus and the Olive Tree: Understanding Globalization* (New York: Anchor Books, 2000).

Robert Rubin, *In an Uncertain World: Tough Choices from Wall Street to Washington* (New York: Random House, 2003).

~~~ Acknowledgments

Navigating the Badlands is based on more than six years of research and strategic consulting on long-term structural change and how it affects business, organizations, nonprofits, and government, as well as the legions of knowledge workers in this fast-globalizing environment. I founded two action-oriented think tanks to focus on this work: Global Foresight in San Francisco and the Center for the Future of China at Peking University in Beijing and San Francisco. Prior to founding my own organizations, I was fortunate to be a director at the Institute for the Future (IFTF), a spin-off from the RAND Corporation based in California's Silicon Valley, for more than eight years.

Like any book, *Navigating the Badlands* reflects the work of many people and would not have been possible without each and every one of them. Many people—family, friends, colleagues, and clients—joined me on this adventurous trek in the global Badlands, giving generously of their ideas, time, and support to bring this book to life. I thank them all and cherish the challenging and hilarious moments we spent together in service of sharing this story of the future. I am deeply grateful for all the collaboration.

My deepest thanks go to Joelle Delburgo of Delburgo and Associates in New York, my literary agent, who believed in me and the book and encouraged me to write it. She was a wonderful guide through the process of writing the proposal and world-class in shepherding it through to the perfect publisher. A very special thanks to Peter Guzzardi for the expert developmental guidance and exemplary line editing of the book. It was amazing how he turned my rambling sentences into good prose. Peter was the perfect collaborator—as a critic, an encourager, and a great friend, he offered many insights and pushed me to work hard to bring the complexity and ambiguity of Badlands to life.

Jossey-Bass was that perfect publisher, in large part due to its incredible team. Susan Williams, executive editor, was immensely supportive and accurate in her editorial comments, as was Byron Schneider, senior development editor. Byron was a great guide and kept his sense of humor as we pushed hard to meet our deadline and then oversaw the publishing process. Rob Brandt, assistant editor, worked closely with Byron and me to make sure all the pieces of it fit together. Carolyn Miller, senior marketing manager, and Akemi Yamaguchi, senior marketing assistant, always showed great enthusiasm and energetically supported the book as did Bernadette Walters. The final book production team, led by Mary Garrett, was a joy to work with. Hilary Powers completed an exemplary final copy edit with amazing perfection and great humor.

The Global Foresight team were the ultimate midwives. Amy Hanson has been a wonderful research colleague over the last two years as well as taking a major role in the assembly of the book. She was steadfast in hunting down the data, checking on stories and facts, and never lost her sense of humor. Maureen Gill took on the project management of the book and kept me on track as well as reading and rereading every draft of every chapter, giving insightful comments and keeping the whole book moving along. A big thank you to Mark Woodworth, who worked with me to edit the early drafts; it was not just his great editing but his constant up-beat encouragement that made a big difference. Thanks also to Kristen Spence, who edited the book proposal, bringing it to life in words for the first time.

Ranny Riley, lead partner in Global Foresight and thought leader in the coming second middle age contributed many of the ideas about what the Boomers will invent with the additional twenty-five years of life we now have. She also provided continuous support and feedback on different chapters. Jennifer Corriero, founder and executive director of TakingITGlobal in Toronto, along with Michael Furdyk and Huss Banai, collaborated with Global Foresight to do a survey of global youth and work. They were great colleagues and provided much wisdom about how young people around the world look at the future. They were generous in sharing other major research they completed in support of the book. Robert Mittman has been a coconspirator in all of the Badlands research since the beginning as well as a co-founder of the Center for the Future of China. He is a wonderful colleague and dear friend who made major contributions to all the critical components of the Badlands thinking. I wouldn't do a forecast without him. Ellen Friedman, vice president of the Tides Foundation, supported me to complete a customized version of the Badlands forecast for health care. She and her colleagues, Kathy Ko, Jane Stafford, and Kendall

Guthrie of Blueprint Services, were unstinting in their encouragement and critical review of that work. Jeremy Nobel from Harvard joined the health care effort, contributing major ideas to all the Badlands thinking. He was a key thinking partner and support throughout the process. Cynthia Scott and Dennis Jaffe of Changeworks Global were major supporters and helped shape the ideas around the impact of the Badlands on organizational change. Cynthia worked with me on some of the early generational research at IFTF, as well. Pam Heman, executive director of Leadership California, provided me with steady support for many years as well as many contacts with key women leaders to test out the Badlands ideas as they developed. She and all the Leadership California members provided ongoing feedback and support which was critical to its development. Thanks to Tomi Nagai-Rothe of the Grove Consultants International for her intellectual and visual thinking partnership. She helped more than anyone in creating the Badlands Map and identifying tools to help people use the framework and ideas. Thanks to both Janet Schatzman and Anthony Weeks, who designed early versions of the Badlands Map.

A heartfelt thanks to the team at Institute for the Future who worked together in the foundational research: Shelley Hamilton, Lonny Brooks, Robert Mittman, Chuck Sielof, Patti Zablock, Jim Herriot, and Kevin Wheeler were critical to creating the framework, analysis, and foresight of the Badlands. Shelley's research about the future of organizations was incredible, and Lonny Brooks led the deep dive into the historical cycles of disruptive innovation that underpins the understanding of the cycle we are in today. Jim Herriot, formerly of Sun Microsystems, of the Santa Fe Institute and the Bios Group in Santa Fe, was central to sorting out the complexity of the Badlands as well as thinking through the pains organizations have to experience to change. IFTF's health care team, Katherine Sansted, Mary Cain, and Wendy Everett worked with Robert Mittman and me to do the first customization of the Badlands for health care for their clients.

No country is more important to the long-term success of globalization than China. I have been extraordinarily fortunate to have had a deep and rich experience of that complex country thanks to my wonderful colleagues at Peking University. Professor Chen Zhangliang, vice president of Peking University (now president of the China Agricultural University), leading biotechnologist and member of the National People's Congress, is one of China's outstanding young leaders and has been a mentor and friend par excellence for more than ten years. He helped me found the Center for the Future of China at Peking University along with professors Ma Rong, Pan Naigu, and Liu Shiding of the Department of Sociology and the Institute of Sociology and Anthropology, who are my research partners. A special note of recognition to professor Fei Xiao Tung, founder of PKU's social sciences: a visionary leader in China and still lecturing at ninety-three, he is an inspiration for all of us. Other close colleagues include professor Qui Zegi, who offered great insights into China's future. No one at Peking University was more important than assistant professor Liu Neng, who was a great young researcher and friend throughout all our many projects. His insights and research rigor contributed immensely to my understanding of China and led to valuable results for our many clients. Jeanne Marie Gescher, O.B.E., Claydon-Gescher Associates in Beijing, and Tom Chin, CEO of Sino-American Investments, were both critical to my thinking about how Chinese businesses would grow in this new global environment and key insights into success in the China Market. Thanks to Nisa Leung and Sophie Leung of Hong Kong who have been steadfast supporters and good thinking partners over the last ten years. A very special thanks to Ian Morrison, who was President at IFTF when I first went to China. He was an invaluable support in developing the China Initiative and has continued to be a great friend and generous mentor in my current adventures.

Hughes, my husband, listened attentively to all my early and late ideas—adding great insights and suggestions. Jim, my brother, and Anne, my sister, and my two great dogs—Jake and Zeus—all put up with a lot and were great supports—thanks to each of you—you are all great!!

To all the great clients who worked with me and the Global Foresight, Center for the Future of China and IFTF teams and generously shared their stories of Navigating the Badlands, thanks for the privilege of working with you and sharing your challenges, which are the underpinnings of this book.

San Francisco, California   Mary O'Hara-Devereaux
May 2004

━∾∾━ About the Author

Mary O'Hara-Devereaux is an internationally known futurist and the author of several influential books, including *Global Work: Bridging Distance, Culture and Time* and *China Five-Year Forecast: Creating the New Marketplace.* Drawing on a wealth of twenty years of experiences on the cutting edge of globalization in more than fifty countries on seven continents, she is an innovative thinker and strategy partner who advises leading companies and organizations on emerging issues, helping them make sense of the structural economic and social changes under way in this transformational decade. Known as a steady-eyed futurist, she paints a vivid, accurate picture of the implications for each organization, helping them make better choices today for the long term. She works closely with clients to build capacity for radical innovation and focus strategy on their best opportunities. After several years at the Institute for the Future in Silicon Valley, she founded Global Foresight, in San Francisco (http://www.global-foresight.org), and the Center for the Future of China (http://www.china-future.org) at Peking University and San Francisco, where she is a professor. Other faculty positions have included the University of California, the University of Hawaii, and the Fielding Graduate Institute.

~~~ Index